A thousand miles from anywhere

BY THE SAME AUTHOR

Dolphins Under My Bed
ISBN 978-1-4081-3288-3
ISBN 978-1-4081-5523-3 (ePub)
ISBN 978-1-4081-5524-0 (ePDF)

Turtles In Our Wake
ISBN 978-1-4081-5282-9
ISBN 978-1-4081-5936-1 (ePub)
ISBN 978-1-4081-5585-1 (ePDF)

At a time when their contemporaries already had one eye focused on their pension, and conscious that age and ill health could prevent them sailing away to warmer climes, Sandra and David Clayton left the world of work behind to grasp their dream. The *Voyager* books are Sandra's charming account of the journey that became their adventure of a lifetime.

'A "sticky book". I couldn't put it down'
Cruising Magazine

'I can't emphasise enough how well Clayton writes… her prose is so vivid that the reader is left with indelible images'
Living Aboard

'A most charming read'
The Lifeboat

Sandra Clayton

A thousand miles from anywhere

ADLARD COLES NAUTICAL
LONDON

Published by Adlard Coles Nautical
an imprint of Bloomsbury Publishing Plc
50 Bedford Square, London WC1B 3DP
www.adlardcoles.com

First edition published 2013

ISBN 978-1-4081-8768-5

A CIP catalogue record for this book is available from the British Library.

This book is produced using paper that is made from wood grown in managed,
sustainable forests. It is natural, renewable and recyclable. The logging and
manufacturing processes conform to the environmental regulations of the
country of origin.

Typeset in 10.5 pt Baskerville MT

Printed and bound in Great Britain by CPI Group (UK) Ltd, Croydon CR0 4YY

Note: while all reasonable care has been taken in the publication of this book,
the publisher takes no responsibility for the use of the methods or products
described in the book.

Contents

The Journey

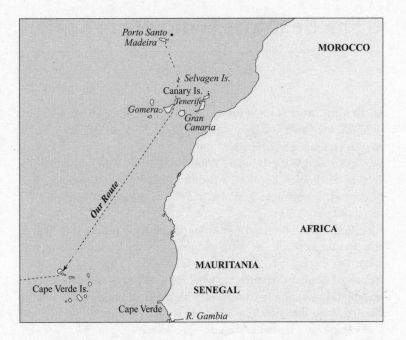

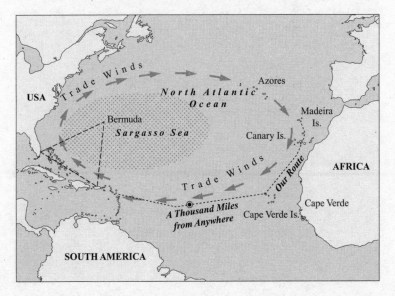

The Beaufort Wind Force Scale

In Britain, and much of Europe, wind and vessel speeds are described in knots. One knot equals a nautical mile covered in one hour and is roughly equivalent to 1.15mph.

Also used is the Beaufort Wind Force Scale. This was created in 1805 by Sir Francis Beaufort, a British naval officer and hydrographer, before instruments were available and it was subsequently adapted for non-naval use.

When accurate wind measuring instruments became available it was decided to retain the scale and this accounts for the idiosyncratic speeds, eg Force 5 is 17–21 knots, not 15–20 as one might expect. Under numbered headings representing wind force, this scale also provides the sea conditions typically associated with them, although these can be affected by the direction from which the wind is coming.

The scale is reproduced on the opposite page.

Force	Knots	mph	Sea Condition
1 Light Airs	1–3	1–3	Ripples.
2 Light Breeze	4–6	4–7	Small wavelets.
3 Gentle Breeze	7–10	8–12	Large wavelets with scattered white caps (also known as white horses).
4 Moderate Breeze	11–16	13–18	Small waves with frequent white caps.
5 Fresh Breeze	17–21	19–24	Moderate waves with many white caps.
6 Strong Breeze	22–27	25–31	Large waves with foam crests and some spray.
7 Near Gale	28–33	32–38	Sea heaps up and foam begins to streak.
8 Gale	34–40	39–46	Moderately high waves with breaking crests forming spindrift (spray blown along the sea's surface).
9 Strong Gale	41–47	47–54	High waves with dense foam. Waves start to roll over. Considerable spray.
10 Storm	48–55	55–63	Very high waves with long overhanging crests. The sea surface white with considerable tumbling. Visibility reduced.
11 Violent Storm	56–63	64–72	Exceptionally high waves.
12 Hurricane	64+	73+	Huge waves. Air filled with foam and spray.

Acknowledgements

Voyager's crew would like to express its gratitude for the following:

Admiralty Charts
Cruising Association
Herb Hilgenberg
Imray Cruising Guides and Charts
The late David Jones
Radio France Internationale
Reeds Nautical Almanac: North American East Coast
Royal Yachting Association
The Atlantic Crossing Guide published by Adlard Coles
Nautical, its 4th edition revised and updated by Anne
Hammick and Gavin McLaren
The Big Fish Net
World Cruising Routes by Jimmy Cornell, published
by Adlard Coles Nautical

We should also like to thank the publisher Orion for permission to use the extract from *Under Milk Wood* by Dylan Thomas in the English language throughout the world, excluding the US, in our print and eBook editions. And for US permission to use the excerpt from *Under Milk Wood*, copyright © 1952 by Dylan Thomas. Reprinted by permission of New Directions Publishing Corp.

About *Voyager*

Voyager is a heavy cruising catamaran that was built by Solaris Yachts at Southampton. They built strong, comfortable boats but ceased trading after a disastrous fire spread from a neighbouring yard. *Voyager* is their Sunstream model, 40ft long x 16ft wide with twin 27hp diesel engines.

She is a typical British catamaran in that she has a small mainsail and a large genoa which is her main source of power. She is cutter rigged and therefore has a small staysail as well as the other two sails.

Her two hulls are connected by a bridge deck with a cabin on it which provides the main living area, or saloon. It contains a large sofa, a coffee table, a dining table and a chart table. Opposite the chart table, and over-looking the galley, the starboard dining seating quickly converts to a breakfast bar which also makes an ideal dining area for any meal on a bouncy sea as there is less potential for loose objects to move about.

From the saloon, you enter the starboard or right-hand hull down three steps. Immediately in front of you is the galley. Turn right and there is an additional food preparation area, storage for cutlery and crockery and a large chest freezer. In the stern is a double bunk, a wardrobe, dressing table and clothing cupboards. Underneath the bunk is one of *Voyager*'s engines. At the bow end of this hull there is a head containing a toilet, wash basin and a bath.

The port hull contains in its stern an identical suite to the one in the starboard hull plus a shower, toilet and vanity. There is a further cabin in the bow of this hull but for the voyage we converted it into a storage space with a small workbench and vice.

Out on deck *Voyager* has a deep, well-protected cockpit and all her sails can be handled from within it.

Prelude

Looking back on my life, there was never a time when I envisaged crossing the Atlantic two-handed on a forty-foot boat. Yet here I am. Testimony to the sublime unpredictability of human existence and the dangers inherent in uttering those immortal words, 'Oh, alright then.'

David and I had wanted to make a fundamental change to our lives. Overworked, unfit and living in a cold damp climate, we had already reached that age where you see one of your parents looking back at you when you inadvertently catch sight of yourself in a mirror. We wanted a little warmth and to be physically active before we got too old.

The answer – although not without some initial resistance on my part – was to exchange our house in the north of England for a catamaran called *Voyager* and set sail for the Mediterranean. It was not only a time for putting our seamanship to the test but also for revelling in small coastal towns and villages and the joy of dolphins swimming with our boat. This was how *Dolphins Under My Bed*, the first of the *Voyager* books, came into being.

The second stage of our odyssey was a summer spent dawdling around the Mediterranean as we finally shed our house and possessions, not to mention quite a few pounds in weight. We were getting fitter from the daily exercise required by sailing, and healthier from outdoor living and a simpler diet. And it would become something of a personal journey as well as a physical one, with a developing sense of what was really important in our lives.

My second book, *Turtles in Our Wake*, reflects a growing confidence in our abilities as yachtsmen. We had come late to sailing and felt we lacked experience. We'd had our sights on the Caribbean, but only if we felt up to it. After a summer around Spain's Balearic Islands and the Italian island of Sardinia, we decided we were. Accordingly, we left our comfort zone of coastal waters and headed out into the Atlantic.

As this third book begins, David and I have just completed the first leg of a voyage to the Caribbean – that Northern European's daydream of coral sand, warm sea, waving palm trees and friendly, happy people.

We are currently anchored at Porto Santo, a very small island 500 miles off the north-west coast of Africa. Only seven miles by four, it is one of the Madeira Group of Atlantic islands and a convenient stopping off place for yachtsmen on their way from Europe to the Caribbean.

What lies between us and that mecca of laid-back living and coral sand – apart from several thousand miles of open sea – is the North Atlantic hurricane season. So while we wait for that to blow over we plan to spend the time exploring some captivating Atlantic islands which, along with Madeira, include the Canary and Cape Verde Islands.

After four months soaking up the charms of the Caribbean there will come the crucial question: where do we go from here to escape the Hurricane Zone? There are a number of options, the most alluring being the United States of America and an entirely different kind of sailing from anything we have done so far. As a result, *A Thousand Miles from Anywhere* ends with us bobbing on the Gulf Stream and gazing through the darkness at the flickering lights of the Florida shore.

For now, however, we are about to embark on the delights of the Madeiras.

THE MADEIRA ISLANDS

PORTO SANTO

I

A Friendly Little Island

Graffiti, as everybody knows, is the domain of adolescent males in hoodies. It is usually perpetrated under cover of darkness and it is a prosecutable offence. So as we disembark from our dinghy on this bright afternoon, it comes as a surprise to see a middle-aged couple hard at work on the harbour wall under the noses of the authorities.

This is the first place we have ever visited that welcomes, or at least tolerates, graffiti. As a result the long quay wall, which protects Porto Santo's harbour from the sea, is bright with tributes from visiting yachts. Not the casually-scrawled *Joe Bloggs was here* sort of thing that has traditionally sidled onto walls. Nor the enormous tagging in spray paint that nowadays defaces so many public buildings, trains and bridges.

Restricted to the sea wall, these take the form of a modestly-sized circle, square or triangle and range from the simple to the elaborate. Anything from just the name of the boat and crew and the year they came here, to composed pictures of the boat itself complete with sunset and seagull, to abstracts, variations on a national flag or caricatures of the crew. They are as varied as the people who paint them.

Some are faded survivors of the Atlantic weather. Some have lost corners thanks to the over-zealous efforts of later arrivals. But all have been done with care and pride, because each picture is a celebration of a challenge accepted, a voyage undertaken and a safe arrival. Especially the safe arrival. And, subconsciously at least, they represent an offering for the much greater journey still to come. Just as ancient Greek mariners poured libations of wine from the decks of their ships before sailing into the unknown.

And so it is that halfway along the sea wall a middle-aged couple from Dublin, newly arrived, are hard at work with an artist's brush and a small pot of paint apiece; one spouse to the left of their picture, the other spouse to the right.

David and I arrived at this little island this afternoon, on our catamaran *Voyager*, following a six-day passage from Gibraltar. And after setting our anchor we had hoisted a courtesy flag. This, as anyone who sails to a foreign country knows, is a miniature version of the national flag of the country currently being visited. It says that the crew of this vessel recognises that they are in that country's waters and subject to its laws. Despite being hundreds of miles out into the Atlantic and off the coast of Africa, the Madeira Islands are an autonomous region of Portugal. Accordingly the little courtesy flag now fluttering in our rigging is Portuguese.

Our next task is to register our presence with the local authorities here, or *clear in* as it is universally known. So we have unstrapped our dinghy from the foredeck, attached the outboard, and chugged into the harbour to present ourselves, our passports and our ship's papers to the scrutiny of Porto Santo's Customs & Excise, Immigration and the Maritime Police.

The Customs officer and the policeman ask almost identical questions and you wonder why they don't pool information. They are the same questions that their counterparts in their mother country asked, and you wonder all over again why the Portuguese want to record your engine number and the colour of your sails when nobody else is interested. But it is the price of entry to their country, so you dutifully fill in the forms.

The Immigration Officer, by contrast, observes our wine-red passports, says, 'Oh, EU! Great!' and simply shoves them, and our ship's papers, through his photocopier. We are asked how long we'd like to stay, but it is 'only a formality, you are welcome to stay as long as you like.' Porto Santo is developing its tourist industry and is pleased to have you there.

It rains before dinner. We are rather disappointed. If we had wanted rain we could have stayed in Manchester. But at least it washes the boat free of salt after our passage here. Every cloud, as my mother used to say, has a silver lining.

After six nights of sleep broken up into three-hour watches we have little energy for anything beyond dinner and observing the variety of nationalities at anchor around us: German, American, French, Swedish, Dutch and a little British boat called *Antares* that I recognise from somewhere, but can't remember where.

We are semi-comatose by early evening and asleep in our bunk by 8.30.

Next morning we get up feeling surprisingly energetic and buoyant. It is as if there are positive ions in the air – or whatever those things are that make you feel lively – and we set off for a trip into Vila Baleira, Porto Santo's little capital. We dinghy into the harbour again, through surprisingly choppy water for such an otherwise gentle day, tie up and begin the two-mile walk into town.

In this kind of life you quickly learn to expect the unexpected. Indeed, almost to take it for granted. Even so a surprise awaits us, because one of the last places we might have expected to find a rally of classic English cars would be a tiny island out in the Atlantic Ocean with very little in the way of roads. Yet here we are, walking down the beach road, along the edge of which is parked a selection of English motoring history, most of them dating from the 1950s but a few from the '30s and '40s. A Triumph Herald, Morris Minor, MGB, Sunbeam Talbot, an Austin A55 and A90, an Austin 10 and a Triumph TR4. Also being celebrated are classic American Chevrolets, Pontiacs and Fords and several French Citroëns.

This is a brown, barren island. It was once covered in giant spiky dragon trees, but they were cut down long ago. Some sources say to grow food, others to build boats. Reforestation is now underway at its centre, while down here on the margins it is lush with palm trees and oleander. We have gone some way towards the town when we see a man beside a garden wall preparing a small cart. Before he has finished, there is a commotion among the palms and oleanders and something resembling a large dog jumps over the wall to join him. It is in fact a very small donkey, which positions itself in front of the cart and waits patiently to be put into the shafts.

The only other traffic on the road illustrates the contrast between a gentler past and the economic imperatives of the present. The drive to bring tourism to the island means that a large inter-island ferry berths regularly in Porto Santo harbour. Its latest batch of passengers now sweeps past us, down the road towards the town, sealed inside large tourist buses complete with tinted windows and doors that hiss compressed air.

Following some distance behind is a rather disconsolate middle-aged man in the driving seat of a small white trap pulled by a brown and white horse. We had noticed him at the harbour, waiting for customers, dwarfed by the fleet of luxury buses. Now his horse is clip-clopping along pulling an empty trap. All the ferry passengers have boarded the coaches and the little white trap has no takers. It has blue and white curtains and seat covers under a blue awning. As we approach the town we see it parked on the cobblestones beside the road. The brown and white horse is standing on two wooden duckboards; only small ones, but so much kinder to the feet than cobblestones.

At Vila Baleira we have coffee at a street café with a favourite from our time in Portugal, *pasties de nata*, little egg-custard tarts with a thick, soft pastry case and a scattering of nutmeg on the top. After that we do a little sightseeing: Christopher Columbus's house, the 15th century church opposite and possibly the world's smallest town hall.

Porto Santo was discovered by accident in 1418 by two explorers called Zarco and Teixeira, heading for Africa but blown off course by a gale. They had been sent out by Portugal's Prince Henry, better known as Henry the Navigator from the expeditions he sponsored.

These were initially down the African coast and for the purpose of exploration, but later their aim was to discover the world's riches and bring them back to Portugal. To this end, the caravel was developed – a light, manoeuvrable ship able to carry cargo – in which many of Henry's navigators sailed, although he never went on any of their voyages himself.

After the discovery of this small island, Henry quickly colonised it. Its first governor was a Genoese nobleman whose daughter Filipa would become the wife of Christopher Columbus.

Vila Baleira is a neat and tidy little town with clean streets, flowers everywhere and friendly people. After sight-seeing, and a wander through a pretty little park, we seek out our evening meal. We are late for the fish market. It has no refrigeration, only concrete slabs. The day's main business was concluded long ago and the only fish remaining on sale lie curling in the heat before a single, resigned vendor with a cloud of large black flies buzzing overhead.

We leave the fish market and go in search of a supermarket. Outside *Pingo Doce* our 100-escudo coin gets jammed in the shopping trolley's mechanism, but not far enough in to free it from its fellows. A nice young manager I lure out from inside the store prises our coin free with a pair of scissors. By this time it is a little the worse for wear, so he substitutes it for a new one from inside the store and then has to prise that one out with his scissors as well. But he perseveres cheerfully until he is finally able to release a trolley from its chains and present it to us.

We buy bread, fruit, vegetables, fresh sardines and a speciality of Madeira, honey cake. Also, for a paltry sum, a bottle of five-year-old

Madeira wine. A small white label on the back says helpfully in English, 'It is likely to throw a deposit. Serve gently without shake the bottle.' We wedge it into one of our rucksacks along with everything else and then begin the two-mile journey home, but along the beach this time.

It is golden, deserted and beautiful with its backdrop of dunes and occasional clusters of large rocks. The tide is coming in. We take off our shoes, tie them to our rucksacks and roll our trousers up to mid-calf. The waves rush in with surprising speed, scattering sandpipers in all directions, heads bobbing, little legs pounding like pistons, tripping into sand holes.

There are a few ramshackle wooden beach houses in the dunes, with a barbecue made from an old oil drum wedged into the sand beside them. Pausing to gaze at one of these huts, more picturesque than the rest with its roof shingles and tiny porch, a particularly large wave overtakes us and our trousers are soaked to the knees.

When we reach the quay we find that two of our German neighbours from the anchorage, tired of their yachts' rolling, are now anchored in the harbour. At the sea wall, the Irish couple are busy stencilling a frame of shamrocks in emerald green around the painting of their boat.

The strength of the wind is increasing and the growing turbulence in the anchorage means the harbour is becoming more crowded with boats. Its berthing capacity is limited. On the dock a group of yachtsmen grumble about the anti-social behaviour of an Australian yacht-owner who is taking up a large stretch of it but who refuses to allow any other yachts to raft up to him. To reinforce his message he has fastened a couple of large NO RAFTING UP! signs to his side rails which are attracting particular resentment.

We dinghy back to *Voyager*. It is an even bumpier ride than the one going ashore this morning and at one stage the backpack with the bottle of Madeira wine in it topples off the seat. It has already bumped along for a couple of miles during our wave-dodging progress along the beach, and been roughly handled when we rescued it from the surf while hopping about trying to get damp, gritty feet into our shoes. Now it is heaved unceremoniously aboard during our scramble up out of the dinghy, currently tied to *Voyager*'s stern, and which thanks to the pounding of the sea swell is snatching violently at her transom.

Despite its rough treatment, and notwithstanding the warning notice on the back of the bottle, after a period of quiet in a cool place the wine is delightful and not at all lumpy until we reach the very bottom some days later. It is something you never think about, when you buy imported, quality-controlled, factory-bottled wines from a supermarket or wine store. But where wines are produced and bottled locally, in small family vineyards, there is often a deposit of grape skins; and with fortified wines such as sherry, port and madeira, as well as some of the heavier reds, it is automatically assumed that you will decant them before serving.

We dine on fresh sardines cooked in olive oil with garlic, a little coarse mustard and a dash of brandy, served with steamed leek and carrot and Gibraltar's delicious yellow potatoes topped with a little butter and black pepper. The sea swell continues. We rock gently, as in a cradle, our mouths filled with the warm sweetness of coffee and honey cake.

The wind changes direction during the night. It has been coming from the north since our arrival and we have been sheltered by the island, but by morning it is from the south and the anchorage is now untenable in the resulting heavy swell. So we lift our anchor, motor into the harbour and drop it there.

We are the last but one boat to leave the anchorage and with all our former neighbours already ensconced, plus some newly-arrived boats, it is difficult to find a large enough space. Not least because, with our arrival, there are now ten catamarans and three trimarans forming something of a multi-hull ghetto in the midst of all the monohulls. One of the latter is a little single-handed yacht called *Antares*.

Antares is the name of an enormous red star in the constellation of Scorpio, which astronomers call a supergiant because it has a diameter more than 700 times that of the Sun. It takes audacity to call a 27-foot boat after a star that big. But then, it takes nerve to cross the Atlantic Ocean single-handed on a boat that small.

After a lot of mental struggle, I finally remember where we saw her last. It was off the island of Alderney, in the Channel Islands, shortly after we first set out from England. We were still rather green at anchoring then, and ended up a bit too close for politeness although her young skipper hadn't seemed to notice. Or if he had, he hadn't seemed to mind.

We shall be a bit close again, when we turn, but our anchor is well dug in and there is not enough room to mess about trying to get a few feet further away. We shall simply have to be alert to anchor-chain lengths when the wind or the tide begins to turn us all.

As well as intrepid solo sailors, yachting also produces a breed of mariner that eschews engines, electrics and all modern instrumentation, using only wind power, a compass, a sextant and sheer muscle. Two such people are the last to seek the protection of the harbour for the night and they have only a small space in which to anchor without nudging either the sea wall or other boats.

Firstly, in lieu of an echo sounder, they establish the water's depth by using a lead line – a lead weight on the end of a length of thin rope with depths marked on it. Then with consummate and shaming skill they proceed to position themselves in their confined space, and set their anchor, using a long oar off their stern as their only means of propulsion.

During our second night in the harbour the wind returns to the north. By the following morning it has lost most of its power and the sea swell has diminished. So we dinghy to the quay, pay for our two nights' stay in the harbour and then set off on the 42-mile journey to Madeira's capital, Funchal. After such a rough forty-eight hours the Atlantic is now unexpectedly flat. It is also surprisingly blue.

Five islands make up this part of the Madeira archipelago. The one from which it takes its name, and to which we are now heading, is the largest at 286 square miles compared with Porto Santo's sixteen. There are also three tiny uninhabited islands called Ilhas Desertas (one little more than a large rock) off the shores of which, it is said, you may spot sea lions cavorting. This sounds very appealing until you discover that the three islands offer only one anchorage between them; that it is approached through scattered rocks and is recommended for daylight hours only, in ideal weather conditions and with a crew member left aboard during any shore leave because of the unstable holding. We decide to give Ilhas Desertas a miss.

Much further south there are also the Salvage Islands, about which more later.

MADEIRA

2

Under the Volcano

It is a sparkling, blue-and-silver, soft-aired motor-sail to Madeira. Its coastline is striking as you approach because the island is a volcano and its sides are very steep. Even Fora, the large rock at its eastern corner, with St Laurence's lighthouse perched on it, rises steeply to a point. This white lighthouse gives every appearance of having been iced onto the top, like a bride on a wedding cake, with the white icing running downhill to cover every last walled inch of the tiny summit.

Although only 31 miles apart, the two islands could not be more different. Brown and treeless, Porto Santo's low hills are flat at the bottom, providing the island with its spectacular beach. Madeira in contrast has virtually no beaches, rises steeply up from the sea, and its mountainous peaks and deep ravines are covered in lush green forests. From out at sea the lower slopes appear bright green thanks to the terraces of vines, while large tracts of the coast road give the impression of being suspended over rocky gullies.

Off Caniçal, the first town we pass, we are met by a pod of orcas, visually striking in their black and white. There are seven of them, moving very slowly, sending spray languidly from their blow holes and watching us with as much concentrated interest as we are watching them. When we get closer we can see there are actually nine of them. Two small calves are swimming close to their mothers' sides.

Orcas have a roundness to them that other whale species do not. It makes them look almost cuddly and, combined with their distinctive colouring, is why they are often a model for soft toys. Add moist-eyed memories of the movie *Free Willy*, and it is easy to forget that their common name is *killer whale*. They do, in fact, kill and eat other whales. They also snack on seals and penguins and like to play with their food, the way that cats do, before killing and eating it. The pod waits for us to get level with it and then sinks effortlessly, only to reappear moments later in our wake, watching us go.

The coastline between Machico and Santa Cruz is dominated by the long runway of Madeira Airport and over our starboard rail we can see planes landing and taking off. A glance to port, meanwhile, causes us to stop and stare at what appears to be one of Henry the Navigator's three-masted caravels floating in the shimmering blue haze of the far horizon. It is like being in a time warp: on one side of us the world's fastest and most convenient form of transport, making Madeira only a ninety-minute flight from Lisbon; on the other, the wraiths of 15th century Portuguese navigators like Zarco and Teixeira who spent months on their wooden ships, in uncharted waters, seeking new and exotic lands.

A few miles further down the coast, Gaula's white-walled houses and terracotta roofs soar almost vertically up a precipice and over a mountain ridge. Craning your neck to look up at them, the thought occurs that should a householder trip over his doorstep *up there*, within seconds he could be swimming for his life with orcas *down here*.

Porta do Garajau, the last headland before Funchal, is dominated by an enormous statue of Christ with arms outstretched, like the ones at Lisbon and Rio de Janeiro. In 1927, when it was built, Madeira's visitors arrived by boat, and the statue was located here in welcome.

By the time we begin the approach to Funchal, the gap between ourselves and the ghostly vessel to our left has narrowed and we still might have bought into the time warp theory were it not for the large, bright blue, late-20th century RIB it is towing. This 15th century sailing ship's impressive turn of speed, on this virtually windless day, also betrays the existence of a powerful, non-standard diesel engine beneath its otherwise authentic wooden decks. It overtakes us at the entrance to the harbour and, as we follow it in, we can read its name. It is the *Santa Maria*, a replica of Christopher Columbus's flagship, its decks lined with tourists.

While the ship ties up to the sea wall, and its passengers disembark for their hotel and cruise ship dining rooms, we go in as close as possible to shore looking for a suitable place to drop our anchor. The harbour at Funchal is protected by a substantial sea wall, which along with the *Santa Maria* provides berths for visiting cruise ships and the Porto Santo ferry. But this is a roly poly anchorage when the wind is from anywhere other than the north, that is to say from the other side of the island, and it becomes untenable in strong southerly winds.

The holding at Funchal is poor, too, but we do finally get the anchor to bite at our fourth attempt, after a lot of shunting and shouting. It is now a little after 6pm. So, with our accommodation taken care of, we put out the cockpit cushions, fill two glasses with Madeira wine, settle back in the evening sunshine and gaze about us.

On our landward side we can see a rocky shore, a bit of the Old Town walls, part of an ancient fort and trees in pink blossom; while rising steeply above them are the densely-wooded, mountainous sides of Madeira's dormant volcano. On the ocean side of us, the cruise ships against the sea wall are bathed in the mellow tones of a sun due to set within the next hour or so. There are shearwaters and terns here, too. Birds have been noticeably absent lately.

Next morning we dinghy into the crowded little marina and complete the entry formalities. When we have officially registered our engine number and the colour of our sails again we stop off at the nearby tourist office for a town map and then catch a Number 31 bus.

In the cruising guide David has read about another little piece of Portuguese territory he thinks we might enjoy, the Ilhas Selvagens or Salvage Islands. They lie one hundred and fifty-five miles south of Madeira and ninety-five miles north of the Canary Islands – our next port of call – and being almost on our course anyway, will make a welcome and enjoyable break in our journey.

The particular Salvage Island which interests us is Selvagem Grande. Although less than two square miles in extent, it is the largest in the group and has for some years now been a nature reserve and bird sanctuary, especially for breeding colonies of Madeira petrels and Cory's shearwaters. It has recently been declared a marine reserve as well, which means that along with other human predators it also keeps fishermen away, who used to take birds' eggs as well as fish. This isolated scrap of land has a human population of four: two wildlife wardens and two lighthouse keepers.

To visit this tiny island, yachtsmen must obtain a visitor's permit before leaving Madeira. These are issued without charge by the National Parks Department from their office at the Botanical Gardens, north of Funchal. Having already experienced Portuguese bureaucracy, we suspect getting one may take a while. Which is why, after clearing in with the authorities, we are on a Number 31 bus on our way to the Jardim Botânico.

The road up to it is very steep and the view across the harbour on this glorious sunny day is breathtaking. So is the two-mile drive, but for different reasons. The road skirts the edge of the mountain and the bus seems to be in the hands of a homicidal maniac. Or perhaps breakneck speed is the only way to keep an engine going up such a steep incline. Perhaps reducing speed for blind corners or stomach-churning chicanes would cause the vehicle to stall, roll backwards and tumble down the almost vertical mountainside. Mostly we avert our eyes and observe that this would not be a place to cycle, or even walk unnecessarily unless you were exceptionally fleet of foot.

We stumble off the bus at a sign saying *Jardim Botânico*, in that confused state which is a mixture of euphoria at having survived a challenging experience and shock at having been involved in it in the first place. We enter the gates, pay our entrance fee and set off in pursuit of a permit to visit Selvagem Grande.

We begin our search in the main building but the first person we ask denies any knowledge of the island's existence. After a few more attempts, someone admits that it exists but says you can't go there. We persist and are gradually directed from one office to another until the outstretched fingers point us away from the main building altogether and into the gardens' interior. Ultimately we find ourselves edging between delicate plants lining tiny paths leading to small offices, half-hidden by foliage, where the public clearly is not intended to go. Then, just when we think we may be getting somewhere, someone suggests we try the marina down in Funchal Harbour. We smile politely, nod and head back towards the main buildings. We are beginning to flag.

More by accident than design we wander into the museum, with its antique maps of exotic places, exhibits of the paraphernalia of specimen-gathering, giant seed pods and exquisite drawings of plants. There are also some atmospheric sepia photographs of the intrepid explorers responsible for some of the wonders now gracing the verdant hillsides of Madeira in general and the *Jardim Botânico* in particular. Inspired by their endurance we renew our pursuit of the secret office from which the rare and exotic permit to visit Selvagem Grande flowers unseen by all but the most persistent of foreign travellers until suddenly and unexpectedly we stumble upon the right person at the right moment.

We follow his careful directions and enter a long gallery of large free-standing panels of plant illustrations. Then we make a sharp, unmarked turn taking us behind them and arrive at a staircase of polished wood and marble bearing a large sign saying 'Private'. As instructed, we ignore this sign and mount the stairs. There is a man at the top sitting at a large desk with nothing on it. His expression changes from bored to startled at our sudden appearance. We are equally surprised to see him. We nod in his direction but do not falter in our progress. In all probability he will not speak English and if he stops us it will get complicated and time-consuming and most likely he will order us downstairs again. So we stride purposefully past him, down a corridor smelling strongly of camphor, and enter a large office containing two women.

They also look startled at our unannounced arrival. We explain what we desire. They deny any knowledge of the island. We persist. The senior of the two, very small and with a persistent cough, looks at us intently: wondering perhaps how we managed to penetrate her inner sanctum; or, perhaps, if it *might* be necessary for us to be accommodated after all.

Portugal's political and social structures have undergone seismic changes within less than half an average life span. The long dictatorship of General Salazar was followed by a military coup in the 1970s, but even this allowed only limited and gradual democratic reforms. In essence the country has had little more than a decade in which to adapt to the political dictates of the European Union and the market forces of mass tourism. It is therefore not surprising that, faced with officialdom, you can sometimes see a flicker behind the eyes as the traditional response to an inconvenient request – a dismissive wave of a uniformed arm – reluctantly gives way to a present where it is no longer an option to simply say, 'No!' With a final long look at us, the woman with the cough applies herself to her computer.

Even her computer programme which produces the permits appears to consider our intrusion unwarranted, however. It is, she explains, refusing to allow her access. Nevertheless, she gives every indication of trying to key required data from our passports and ship's papers into its apparently resistant boxes. While we wait it occurs to me that of all the offices in all the world that I've ever been in, this one, in a botanical wonderland, is the only one that doesn't have a single pot plant in it.

Finally, after what seems a very long time, a printer across the room rumbles into life and, with much smiling and thanks, we take possession of our permit. It is not until we get back to the boat and actually read it that we discover it is valid for one week only.

In the meantime, still light-headed with success, we lunch al fresco at a shady table overlooking the gardens' sunny terraces. Two peacocks, one the more familiar variety of luminous blues and greens, the other pure white, wander gracefully among the tables. I have never been so close to a peacock before and to have two of them – especially the rare and almost-mythical white – undulating past one's elbow in such glorious surroundings is truly magical.

A middle-aged man settles at the table opposite, putting down a cup of coffee with one hand and a plate with a large slice of Madeira cake on it with the other. As he reaches for his slice of cake, however, the white peacock, with a swiftness obviously honed by much practice, darts a long elegant neck forward and snatches it from the plate.

The man, with an equally surprising turn of speed, slaps the bird hard across the side of its head. The cake falls to the ground. I gasp in shock. The crest of delicate white feathers crowning the peacock's regal little head has been bent sideways by the blow. Other people look up from their plates and stare. Man and bird are frozen, eyeing each other.

The spell is broken when the man turns away and reaches sullenly for his coffee cup. The peacock continues to glare at him a moment longer. Then it raises its head, turns and stalks slowly out of the restaurant with all the dignity of a dowager duchess, albeit slightly the worse for wear and with her tiara askew.

3
Funchal

We spend the following day discovering the island's capital, Funchal. After tying up the dinghy in the harbour our first stop is at the small public garden whose pink blossoms we can see from the anchorage. To my great delight there is also frangipani.

I met my first frangipani tree in Australia when I was twenty. It was love at first sight. Related to the magnolia, its branches form a huge umbrella of long, oval leaves. Among them nestle clusters of small, waxy flowers, ivory in colour shading to yellow and finally to apricot at the very centre. They have five petals and unlike most blossoms fall from the tree long before they wither, so the grass under a frangipani looks as if it is littered with tiny stars. But it is when you pick one up that you discover the ultimate joy of the frangipani tree – its perfume. For each little star smells of marzipan, that soft paste made from ground almonds, sugar and egg yolk that Christmas cooks use to cover a rich fruit cake before coating it with white icing.

The longer I spend adrift in the natural world, the more I wonder if culture is a blessing or a curse. How much of our history, myths, art, religion and education is really a means of instilling fear and loathing? It is always easier to control frightened people, after all. Why else do we terrify children with tales of cannibalistic old women living in ginger-bread houses, or invent a place called Hell?

Frangipani is a good example of this. Look it up and you will learn that in one culture the tree is linked to ghosts and demons. In another, its flowers are associated with death and funerals. Another connects the shedding of the tree's flowers with the woes of the world. How depressing. When without knowing any of this beforehand, you can stand under a tree that looks like heaven, smells like Christmas and sends you on your way feeling even happier than when you arrived.

On the main boulevard, the Avenida Arriaga, another old favourite from Australia awaits. Jacaranda. With their dancing, fern-like leaves, and blossoms like oversized bluebells, jacaranda trees make a wonderful contrast with the stately palms lining the avenue. We have coffee in the sunshine of this blissful mid-October day, on a pavement of the kind beloved by the Portuguese. These black-and-white mosaics can be hard on the feet when their tiny, square tiles become uneven, but they are always a pleasure to the eye.

The newspaper stand opposite has a thatched roof. Beside it, a low, shady fountain has been commandeered by a duck for the ablutions of her minute offspring. They wave their stubby wings in delight as jets of water rise above their heads and cascade over them, rolling off their waterproof feathers in glistening droplets. *Water off a duck's back*, my father used to say of people impervious to criticism or shame. And you never truly appreciate the metaphor until you watch it happen.

Step off the main road, and you are in gardens of more palm trees, frangipani and jacaranda, flowering shrubs and a tree festooned with the most extraordinary blossoms. Each flower is several feet long, narrow where it joins the tree, fluted at its open end, and resembling those long graceful trumpets favoured by musical angels in Renaissance altar paintings. And later, when I look the tree up in a book, *angel trumpet tree* is in fact its common name.

Meanwhile, at ground level, are spider plant and tradescantia, the kind of plants I nurtured at home in a northern climate, in small pots, indoors. Only here they are many times the size and flourishing out of doors as exuberant borders.

We walk on, past a circular bandstand and stone seating, out of the gardens altogether and into streets with buildings reminiscent of a 1950s Hollywood version of the artists' quarter in Paris. *Daddy Longlegs*. Fred Astaire and Audrey Hepburn. A bit seedy but deeply picturesque. We wander through it eating ice cream, step around workmen re-cobbling a stretch of road using only water and wooden mallets, and visit a church with a blue and white tiled interior.

Funchal is said to have been named after the abundance of *funcho* – fennel – found growing here, and nestles in a natural amphitheatre with a southern exposure. It was founded five centuries ago, with its cathedral dating from 1493. It is also an absolute delight. Its squares are lovely and its architecture varied, old and beautiful. Especially pleasing is the traditional Portuguese use of black basalt to frame white buildings, which somehow manages to make them look elegant and solid at the same time.

There are fountains, too. Fountains add sparkle to a city because they catch the light, and water splashing on stone is cooling on warm afternoons.

A couple of rivers run through the capital as well. Only small ones, it must be said, and they end their journey at the anchorage in a state of exhaustion, although doubtless they are more robust when the rains come. Even now, though, in their off-season, they still add lustre.

And everywhere there are trees. I have never seen a city with so many trees. Or so many bearing so much blossom in so many varieties, or so many flowers or simply so much *green*. Visit anywhere else and it is natural to assume that the founding fathers stripped the land, built their city, and then added trees and shrubs to beautify it. Here it is as if the flora never gave up its tenure of the land in the first place and that the people, when they came, simply arranged themselves around it. So when you pass a small bungalow in a side street with a huge banyan tree filling its front garden and beginning to overwhelm the dwelling, you get the feeling that when space really becomes an issue the final decision will be for the tree. Or perhaps I am simply unfamiliar with the effect of a Mediterranean climate on fertile, volcanic soil.

We visit the two-storey flower and vegetable market. It is a colourful place, not only from the variety and exotic nature of the flowers, but because the women selling them wear very pretty national costumes and head-dresses.

There is also a large fish market which, at this time in the afternoon is empty apart from us and two men behind one of the tables. Unlike Porto Santo, however, they have cool boxes. And they are offering swordfish, a particular favourite of ours. We indicate two slices, please, and the size we want. One of the men cuts and weighs them, eyes us thoughtfully, and then keeps cutting further pieces off the fish with a lethal-looking knife and adding them to our slices, observing us between times. The two men look so much like pirates that we say nothing, pay what they ask and wander off clutching the little black plastic bag they hand us. It will turn out to be not only the cheapest, but also the freshest and most delicious swordfish we have ever eaten.

In the vegetable market upstairs, the man serving us drops part of our change and creaks picking it up off the floor.

'Forty-five years,' he says mournfully as he hands the coins to David.

'Fifty-six,' says David.

'Ah,' says the man, eyeing him. 'You've had an easy life.'

'No,' says David, nodding meaningfully at me.

I may kill him.
But *slowly*.
Like an *orca*.

We wake next morning to a golden sunrise and a calm sea. After breakfast we make an early start for Monte Palace Tropical Garden and a bus-ride even more hair-raising than the previous one. The journey is roughly twice as long as the one to the Botanical Gardens. The bus driver seems to be even more maniacal than last time and the twisting road seems to get even more precipitous as it winds ever upward and seemingly closer to the edge.

At one stage a pedestrian skitters across in front of our windshield and lands against a wall. He's attempted to cross what only moments before had been a deserted corner. Unfortunately, he is only halfway across when our bus accelerates to get around it, and he nearly ends up under its wheels.

At a bus stop, a woman gets off and teeters on a curved ledge only inches wide, beyond which is a deep, sloping storm drain and then a low concrete wall. Her choices are: to balance where she is until the bus has gone; stand on the road and risk being dragged under its rear wheels; or take her chances in a storm drain whose angle could easily send her over the low wall and headlong down the cliffside. It is teeter, get dragged by the bus or go swimming with orcas. She teeters, and my last sight of her is crossing the road behind our departing bus. They're nimble, these Madeirans. Like mountain goats.

After the hot road, concrete walls and vertiginous glimpses of the sparkling bay hundreds of feet below, you suddenly find yourself in cool, sweet air surrounded by stillness, lush greenness and towering trees. The enormously tall tree trunks are like the pillars of a living cathedral and encircle a space so shady and tranquil that it is almost a religious experience. Indeed, there is actually a shrine among the trees. I buy a candle for 100 escudos, light it and put it with all the others burning inside. I'm not sure why, exactly.

Monte Palace Tropical Garden boasts 100,000 flower species from all over the world. It is also a testament to love and/or duty, to self-sacrificing volunteers, a surplus in the labour market or the Portuguese equivalent of workfare, because the weeding needed for the flower beds

alone must be *astronomical*. While the miles of dirt paths must take thousands of man-hours a year to maintain, with their shallow steps, each one
edged with slivers of stone. Or the sloping paths paved in semi-circles of
round pebbles so you don't slip going downhill. Or the ones done in sliced
stones...

And yet, notwithstanding the welcoming shrine, and the spectacular
number and variety of plants, this is a place to drift and dream; to ignore
words like *species* and *genus,* and simply surrender the senses to the smell of
freshly tilled soil, warm foliage and the colour and perfume of flowers; to
the play of light through giant branches; limpid pools of koi carp; and
shady paths between cascading foliage, especially after the green-free zone
of an ocean passage. It is more a pleasure garden than a *jardim botânico* and
nowhere more so than over by the baroque church of *Nossa Senhora do Monte*
where the wicker sledges of the *carrinho do Monte* are lined up and waiting for
customers.

This might best be described as a 19th century version of the Winter
Olympics' luge event only without snow. Two people sit side-by-side on a
high-backed wicker settee on runners, and hurtle down a winding, cobbled
street. The sledge is controlled by two *carreiros*, or drivers, wearing white
shirts and trousers, short leather boots and straw hats who initially pull the
sledge from the front by ropes, to gain momentum, and then leap onto the
back to steer it during its precipitous mile-and-a-half-long descent at speeds
approaching 30mph.

We consider it briefly, then decide the bus is marginally preferable.
Once embarked on its white-knuckle descent, though, we are not so sure.
It is also very crowded and we miss our stop by the market, ending up on the
waterfront of the Old Town, near the ancient fort we can see a bit of from
Voyager. A man is laying a mosaic pavement, placing each half-inch-square
tessera individually in a grey powder.

We amble down a narrow alley behind shops and restaurants, their
back doors wide open to let in air. Anyone could walk in and take whatever
they wanted but it seems nobody does. Stray dogs lie sleeping in secluded
corners. Somebody has left food in shady places for them. We wander
narrow, cobbled streets of little restaurants and ancient houses with flaking
shutters in the process of renovation. A ladies' college is selling delicate

embroidery. A shop is offering exquisite wicker work. On the quay, small fishing boats lie beside the walls of the old fort with its characteristic little towers.

In a small square near the quay two short, stocky men wearing curly cowhide chaps and leather waistcoats play haunting music on long, Andean pipes. We dinghy back to *Voyager*, to thick slices of tiger bread and blackberry jam and large mugs of hot black tea. The musicians play late into the evening. Around bedtime the pipes are joined by a muted guitar. It would be easy to linger here, but if we are to visit Selvagem Grande before our permit expires we must make a move.

SELVAGEM GRANDE

4

Salvage on My Mind

We rise early to be at the marina's fuel dock when it opens. We are joined shortly afterwards by a lot of anxious tour boat owners, loading trays of sandwiches over our heads off the quay and eager to be off. One of them has that glazed, rumpled look of someone who has seriously overslept. We let the anxious ones have the fuel gun first. We have a large, slow-filling tank. They have small boats with small tanks and a living to earn.

In the meantime, I begin filling our water tanks. Both of them are slow fillers, too. If hurried they will gush out water and appear full, even though they are still half-empty. The starboard tank has a gauge in the bathroom cupboard so you can easily check if it is full. The port tank's gauge is under the forward cabin's bunk and inaccessible under the great pile of heavy stuff we store on top of it.

I am over-zealous filling this tank – sending in a bit more and a bit more after each small gusher in the firm belief that it can't be full yet – and will pay for it later. For now, though, we bid Madeira a reluctant farewell and sail off into a gentle, blue day. The wind is light but we put up all three sails anyway, to get the most advantage from what there is, and motor-sail using just one engine, turn and turn about.

A three-quarter moon is well risen before sunset, and by 8pm the wind has all but died away. A warm, gentle day turns into a warm, starry, moonlit night. I do the 8pm and the 3.30am watches. About half an hour after beginning my first one, there is one of those inexplicable events you sometimes get at sea. In the distance something brilliant crosses the sky very fast, slows, and then tumbles into the sea. It is a radiant green, a long curve like a scimitar that circles as it falls. But as with many things seen in the night sky at sea I will never know what it was.

Later in the morning, when the starboard engine warning light comes on, David goes below to find out why and discovers a loose fan belt. He traces the problem to the pulley wheel that drives the water pump for cooling the engine. The bearing has disintegrated and it is not the sort of thing for which you would carry a spare. One of the advantages of having two engines, however, is that we can still make progress on just one. Manoeuvring in tight areas might be a problem but having cleared away the debris we could still use the starboard engine in short bursts if necessary.

Going barefoot into the workshop for tools, David notices that the carpet in there is wet. The port water tank that I filled at Madeira without due care has overflowed into five lockers containing a wide range of items including spare parts, electrical equipment, board games and a briefcase full of personal records and documents including our birth and marriage certificates.

They say bad things come in threes. Our next stop will be a cramped, rocky bay in an area the cruising guide describes as 'inadequately surveyed'. It has reefs lying just below the water and, as a reminder that they are not called the Salvage Islands for nothing, the photograph accompanying the navigational data in the cruising guide shows a broken-backed French cargo ship draped across one of them. I am not filled with optimism. In the meantime I set about some salvage work of my own.

I spread the damp paperwork from the forward port cabin around the saloon where it cannot blow overboard, and carry everything else that is wet and portable up to the cockpit to dry in the sun. Then, while mopping up the cabin, I prepare my nervous system for arriving at Selvagem Grande, and my Portuguese for meeting its wardens.

Having read all the warnings about the necessity of keeping the environment here pure, I am shocked to see long ribbons of brown sludge and foam off the island's southern shore. Only it is not floating on the tide as flotsam or jetsam usually does. It is spinning rapidly on the spot.

Instead of recognising it as the result of conflicting currents around a very small island, I perceive it as the effect of one of those reefs I've been reading about, very near the surface, and panic, getting David to change course and losing us temporarily. In an area full of dangerous reefs that is 'inadequately surveyed' this is potentially disastrous. But, after a few moments of chaos, we calm down and simply do as we always do. That is to say, David slows the boat right down and studies his chart and instruments, I go and lean over the bow rail and shout my observations of the seabed back to him, he ignores me totally and re-establishes his original course, and we enter the anchorage safely. Dozens of shearwaters escort us in.

The anchorage is very small. Even if we drop our hook in its centre, to allow for any wind shifts, our stern will still be very close to the rocky shoreline. There is also a very heavy swell.

To get ashore you have to first identify the wardens' house and then locate the concrete ramp below it at the water's edge. We had managed to spot the wardens' house from out at sea, although with some difficulty as it is a low building in the same shades of pale brown as the island. But we never do see the ramp that we are supposed to land the dinghy on because of the amount of surf roaring onto the shoreline. This is a calm day, so heaven knows what it is like here in even moderately bad weather. A warden appears and observes us through his binoculars.

It is now 3.15pm. Our plan had been to anchor here for the night and go ashore in the morning. Along with all its other warnings about inadequate surveys and treacherous reefs, however, the cruising guide also says that on no account should the island be approached in the dark. Given the present turbulence in the anchorage, our anxiety is that if it should become untenable during the night, we might be put in a position where we need to *leave* it in the dark.

We are tired from a night at sea and the day's mishaps, and looking around the anchorage we will need to keep another night watch. Observing the surf crashing over the spot where we suspect the dinghy ramp might be, and wondering how on earth we are going to land our aluminium one, it all looks like a disaster waiting to happen. One of the wardens calls us on the VHF to ask our intentions. David tells him, with great reluctance, that we shall not be staying.

' 'Til next time, then,' says the warden.

And so we turn our boat and sail away, escorted out by shearwaters and a solitary gannet.

I had found the combination of tiredness, the approach to the island and the anchorage's roaring surf unusually stressful. An individual's response to stress is often unexpected, but mine now is irrational by any standard.

'They must be so disappointed,' I wail, as the tiny, low-lying island diminishes behind us.

'Who?' says David.

'The wardens!' I snap, as if anyone with an iota of sensitivity would know that without my having to explain it. 'They must have been able to see us coming for the last five hours.' I sag miserably into my corner of the cockpit with my eyes fixed on the small dot disappearing into an otherwise empty sea. 'They probably had the kettle on ready.'

Doubtless these are men who enjoy isolation and their own company. I can't imagine why I should think they would need ours. But in my current state of tiredness and anxiety I feel we have let them down dreadfully and am depressed for the rest of the evening.

We see nothing throughout a long, calm, moonlit night beyond a tanker that quickly passes and a lot of shooting stars. Venus, when she puts in her morning appearance, is stunning.

THE CANARY ISLANDS

TENERIFE

5

Santa Cruz

There is an unpleasant smell in the galley reminiscent of drains and the stench of diesel in the cockpit. Neither has any apparent source. We shall be really glad to stop, find the cause and enjoy some fresh air. Our priority, however, will be to locate a new bearing and get it pressed into the existing water pump housing so that we can use the starboard engine again and with it our freezer.

From what David has read, marina places are at a premium in the Canary Islands but Tenerife's capital, Santa Cruz, appears to be the most likely place to find one. It also offers a good chance of finding a replacement bearing or, as a last resort, the ability to order a new housing complete with a new bearing.

There are seven major islands making up the archipelago known as the Canary Islands, a name which probably derives from the large dogs, or *canes*, found living on the one which subsequently became known as Gran Canaria. Canary was also the name bestowed on the small brown and yellow native bird with the sweet song when it was first imported into Europe. The islands are Spanish territory and Tenerife is the largest. As we approach Santa Cruz harbour we become aware of a smell that makes the ones we have on board pale into insignificance.

When we get inside the marina, the 'friendly, helpful staff' described in the cruising guide appear to have taken the day off. In their place is an offhand adolescent with a ring through his nose whose attention is permanently focused on some indefinable point above our heads and whose only two words of English turn out to be, 'No problem'.

We prepare to berth bows-on to the quay and as we approach we can see that the youth is holding one end of a lazy line aloft on an extended palm in a somewhat theatrical pose. The harbour has a high concrete dock and it is currently low tide so, with a two-metre tidal range, the quay on which he is standing towers above us. It is worrying to see a lazy line pulled up as high as this. It may work for a monohull, with a single propeller in the centre of its stern. But on a twin-engine catamaran like *Voyager*, the propellers are close to the sides of the boat.

Standard practice in marinas is to tie up the bow first and only then pull up the lazy line, so as to avoid wrapping it around the propeller. Pulling it up at such an acute angle is putting our port prop at serious risk. This propeller also happens to be connected to our only functioning engine and our only means of propulsion. I explain our anxieties to the youth on the quay above us.

'No problem,' he says.

Using the simplest of sign language, I try to persuade him to *lower* the lazy line.

'No problem,' he says, continuing to hold it aloft.

We decide our best option is for David to turn off the port engine as we approach and simply drift in. I will throw a bow rope up to the youth and fend our bows off the wall with the boat hook while he ties the rope around a cleat on the quay. Then, while I keep our bows off the wall, David will leave the helm, take up the lazy line and tie it to our stern.

A bonus of visiting the Salvage Islands had been the prospect of a full night's sleep. Instead, we have done two night passages and two tiring days since leaving Madeira and I am weary. To make matters worse, Santa Cruz is hot and humid. I too am hot and humid. And itchy. And somewhat irritable.

The higher the quay, the longer your rope has to be to reach the cleat on the top of it. And the longer the rope, the heavier it is. Our present bow rope is pretty heavy. It is also a long way upwards to have to throw it. But I do, and it flies directly up in front of the youth. All he has to do is reach out his free hand and take it. I turn away and pick up the boat hook to fend us off the wall. The bow rope falls at my feet. I assume he has missed it, gather it up and throw it again. And again. Until perspiring and furious I realise he has no intention of catching it. He is ignoring me and my rope, and simply standing there, head on one side, gazing impassively at the horizon while holding out the lazy line on his outstretched hand like some over-the-top thespian declaiming the Bard's immortal words.

'Take the rope!' I yell at him.

He shakes his head, just a single half-turn, and waves the lazy line at me.

Every country has its stock types and eccentrics. A French one is the Adult Boy Scout: never without a penknife and a piece of string; addicted to being practical but, above all, *hyperactive*. In his yachting incarnation, while in port he is more often to be found on someone else's boat, being practical, rather than on his own.

Unfortunately for us a member of this manic breed just happens to be visiting the French boat on our starboard side. He invites his host to join him in clambering over our rails and with neither of them speaking a word of English, or Spanish either, proceeds to take over the berthing of our boat. It is like watching *Monsieur Hulot Takes a Holiday* as a tall, thin Frenchman accompanied by a short, fat one sprint back and forth across our decks, tripping over cleats, colliding with each other, waving their arms about and shouting instructions which neither we, nor the Spanish malcontent up on the quay, understand.

Meanwhile, with our one remaining engine switched off and the Spanish youth rejecting my bow rope, *Voyager* has begun drifting backwards, away from the harbour wall. If our French neighbours had simply stayed on their boat and rested a hand on our starboard rail when we had arrived, all would have been well. *Voyager* would have remained stationary, I could have climbed up the portable steel ladder hanging off the quay and tied us up, and David would have had all the time in the world to take up the lazy line and tie it onto our stern cleat.

Instead, we have a Spanish adolescent above our heads with his eyes fixed on a distant planet, two crazed Frenchmen on our foredeck, and *Voyager* drifting so far back out into the harbour that David has no option but to restart the port engine and steer us back towards the wall again. Inevitably, the event we had both worked so hard to avoid occurs and the lazy line goes around our port prop. So now we have *two* unusable engines.

The adolescent on the quay makes a downward cutting motion with the hand that has just let go the lazy line and walks off. The two Frenchmen address us witheringly from behind a flurry of dismissive hand gestures which despite the language barrier leave us in no doubt that as far as they are concerned we could have handled things *very* much better. Then, apparently satisfied that they have done their best for us under the circumstances they climb back over our side rails and return to their bottle of wine.

Unravelling the lazy line from our port propeller will require some time spent under the boat. Neither of us considers going into this water without proper diving apparatus (which we do not possess) as the pungent smell that was so noticeable on approaching the harbour now reveals itself on closer acquaintance as unmistakably raw sewage.

David vaults up onto the portable steel ladder that hovers above our pulpit, climbs up onto the quay and ties on our bow ropes. These will stop us drifting out. The lazy line currently wrapped around our port prop will hold us off the wall for the time being. Then he goes off to find the office, clear in, pay our marina fees and book a diver.

Meanwhile, I turn off the instruments, put all the equipment away, tidy up the galley and start work on a meal. On his return from a very long wait in a very hot marina office David gives me a shout and I go out and throw our electricity cable up to him so that he can plug us into the mains. It takes quite a while because most of the sockets don't work. Then he has to walk back down the quay the way he came and clamber over four other boats to get back on board ours. This is because while I have been busy in the galley the French Boy Scout has moved the steel ladder from in front of our boat to further down the quay, where it will be more convenient for the two French boats on the other side of him.

At least we have electricity and after dinner, too tired to do anything else, we unpack the television and shove in the only video within reach that we haven't watched recently. The script is by a celebrated and very prolific English writer and as it unfolds I wonder sourly whether, had he been prescribed counselling or anti-depressants at an early age, all our lives might have ended up that much brighter.

Two Swedish boats and another French one join us to port, however, so we are spared the movie's melancholy finale when a marina attendant unplugs our electricity supply in his search for working sockets for the newly-arrived boats. We go to bed. At least we can have a good, long lie-in tomorrow morning.

We are woken at 6am by two marina attendants in a dinghy talking at the tops of their voices a couple of feet from our bed. With reluctance we get up and greet the new day. This is not the best berth we have ever rented. Just beyond us, the inter-island ferries load and unload, while above us there is an enormous parking area for cars and commercial vehicles waiting to board the ferries. Their combined diesel fumes waft over us and merge with the odour of sewage rising from the water around us.

The marina office provides us with an address where we might get our broken bearing replaced. It is at the furthest end of a very long tramp through narrow, airless back streets lined with tall, featureless buildings to the eastern end of the town. It turns out to be a chandlery which naturally enough does not do machining, but they know a man who does – in the opposite direction, at the westerly end of town at the top of a very long hill. We get to see a lot of Santa Cruz in the process. But the man is very kind and without our even asking offers to do the work while we wait, so that we won't have to walk all the way up here again tomorrow. He also charges us a very modest amount for a new bearing and for pressing it into the old housing.

It is interesting how little it takes to affect the way you feel about a place. Our chaotic arrival at the marina yesterday, this morning's rude awakening from much-needed sleep and the long dreary climb up here, gives way to a generous man with a warm smile and a downhill return to *Voyager* through streets that are wide, airy and often pedestrian. This is actually a *very* pleasant capital, with beautiful open spaces, attractive buildings, lots of trees and big wooden tubs of old-gold mini-chrysanthemums everywhere. Down at the quay, even the bad smell has gone.

On our return to the boat, David fits the housing holding the new bearing back onto the starboard engine which means we can get the freezer working again. A diver arrives and frees the port prop. We cook a particularly pleasant evening meal, watch one of our favourite videos and feel altogether better about life generally and Santa Cruz in particular.

You also feel better when something that had appeared to be rather a waste turns out to have been in your best interests after all. In particular, we had loved Madeira and should undoubtedly have stayed longer had it not been for the short sell-by date on our permit to visit Selvagem Grande. Now, it seems, Madeira is experiencing very bad weather and, given the anchorage's poor holding and lack of shelter, our departure had undoubtedly been for the best. It was, if the weather we now experience is anything to go by. Gale-force winds and torrential rain batter Santa Cruz for days and we are grateful to be tied securely behind the high protective sea wall of this moderately-priced marina.

It is part of a huge rectangle, a former commercial dock whose high walls were not only designed to accommodate large ships and a two-metre tide but also provide protection from Atlantic gales. Unfortunately there are not enough ladders by which to scale them. To get ashore we can either clamber over three French boats to starboard, or two Swedish and one French to port. A trip to the supermarket means over-handing down a steel ladder with fully-laden shopping bags dangling from each wrist and then negotiating the decks of three monohulls before reaching *Voyager*.

After the spaciousness of a catamaran, a monohull's deck always seems to be full before you even set foot on it. Everything is closer together for a start and, unbalanced as you are by the weight you are carrying, you constantly crunch your ankles against cleats, trip over vents or walk face-first into shrouds. After our first attempt we abandon the ladders, let down our dinghy and go ashore by motoring round to the marina's ramp.

The gale is ferocious and looks set to last indefinitely. It ends after only a few days as suddenly as it began, leaving behind it a rainbow so large, so low and so vivid that it turns the hills behind us into shimmering layers of violet and green.

It is now the last week of October. The Atlantic hurricane season is approximately between June and early November. Mostly these hurricanes begin on the eastern side of the Atlantic, just south of the area we are now in, and travel west towards the Caribbean where we are intending to go. Thus the optimum time for us to set out into the Atlantic is anywhere from mid-November onwards, depending on prevailing conditions, naturally, and not forgetting El Niño.

This is the name given to a weather pattern which occurs across the tropical Pacific Ocean every few years causing a warming of the ocean's surface and a change in air pressure. Its impact is not confined to the Pacific, however. It alters temperatures and wind patterns on a global scale resulting in severe weather extremes including floods and droughts. This is an El Niño winter and in our small corner its effects are manifesting themselves in heavy cloud, hot sticky days, heavy rain and strong winds. *El niño* is Spanish for *the boy*, and refers to the Christ child because this particular weather pattern was first identified one Christmas.

So, until we can safely depart, we need something to do to fill in the time. It is too soon to begin provisioning for the crossing, but with electricity and water available *Voyager* gets a thorough cleaning, inside and out, and a backlog of laundry is taken care of. We sanitise our bilges, get our gas bottles refilled and David services the engines. We also revisit the chandlery up in the town – via the pretty route this time – to buy new rope for our topping lift, along with charts and courtesy flags for the countries we intend to visit.

We find the correct thickness of rope for our topping lift and get it cut to the required length without difficulty. And we have no trouble at all in finding all the charts we need. But the courtesy flags are in dozens of small, brown, obscurely-labelled boxes on a long shelf at floor level.

Throughout our travels we have always been touched by the courtesy of the Spanish. What has particularly charmed us – given a tendency among northern European youth to treat the no-longer-young as if they are at least invisible and at worst expendable – is that young Spaniards are not only aware of older people but mindful of them.

Accordingly, the young man behind the chandlery counter, spotting two middle-aged customers moving slowly down one of his aisles on their hands and knees, comes over to assist and ends up sitting on the floor, opening each of the brown boxes in turn and unfolding a flag, which we either accept or reject depending on whether we plan to visit that Caribbean island or not. He holds up a familiar one and we shake our heads vigorously.

'No?' he says, surprised.

'No!' we say, emphatically.

That particular island has a dual reputation. One comes from its tourist industry, which describes a Caribbean paradise of friendly people and warm welcomes. The other is from the international press reporting tragic holiday encounters and frightening statistics.

'That's the murder capital of the world,' we tell him. 'And we're getting older. We don't run as fast as we used to.'

In the following days we also take a trip around Our Lady of Africa market which sells traditional island products, stock up the wine locker, and post our latest newsletter to family and friends. In between times we also become acquainted with some more of our neighbours.

6
The Neighbours

To our left are Ulrika and Johan, a Swedish couple roughly our age, another Swedish boat, and a Frenchman who has commandeered the only other ladder on our stretch of the marina wall. But no-one begrudges him, for several times a day he carries an enormous woolly dog up and down the ladder over his shoulder.

The man had found the dog, only a few months old, running with a pack of strays on a Greek quay. The life of a stray is often harsh and brief. And a thick, curly coat in a hot climate soon becomes matted, filthy and a haven for vermin. The man had had little idea at the time just how big the dog would grow, but he carries him cheerfully to and from his exercise and bathroom breaks. Depending on how the light catches him – as he rises majestically up and down the wall – Champy appears as either an untrimmed Standard French Poodle with a touch of something more muscular in his genes, or as a champagne-coloured Old English Sheepdog only leggier. Whatever his lineage, he lies over his man's shoulder in a state of perfect trust and composure. For like many a rescue dog before him, he knows that he has landed on his feet.

On the other side of the marina, there is an all-nations of fellow travellers including Norwegians, Danes, a South African, a couple of large American yachts, a very small sloop called *Down Under* with seven very amiable Australians on board and a Dutch couple called Piet and Else cruising with their young son. After sailing from the Netherlands the latter had followed a similar route to us. In fact, we recognise each other's boats from Gibraltar and Madeira although this is the first time we have actually met. Piet and Else intend to cruise the Caribbean for a while before going through the Panama Canal and into the Pacific. At present they are trying to decide if they need an extra pair of hands for the Atlantic crossing.

There are also a surprising number of Swedish yachts. Our next-door neighbour, Johan, looks across at the long line of them tied up to the opposite quay and draws thoughtfully on his pipe.

'Is there anybody left in Sweden?' David asks him.

'Not many,' says Johan. 'Only eight and a half million to start with. Most of us are under sail now.'

Like us, and so many others from northern Europe, Johan and his fellow Swedes are looking for a bit more warmth and sunshine. Migration appears to be of two distinct types these days. One is younger and economic: moving north in search of a better standard of living. The other is older and climatic: going south for warmer weather and a better quality of life.

With regard to our own southern migration David does a few calculations. We covered 951 miles in the eighteen days between leaving Gibraltar on 2nd October and arriving here at Tenerife, with the layover at Madeira in between. And in the four and a half months since leaving The Balearics on 16th June we have done 2,400 miles. Since leaving England last August we have completed 4,360.

When we get up this morning the sky is clear and the day, after all the rain, is preparing to become humid as well as *very* hot. In anticipation of the latter Ulrika does some laundry, a pair of jeans plus a few items of underwear, and pegs them out in the rigging to dry. The Coastguard, meanwhile, is preparing for some air-sea rescue exercises. A helicopter has landed down the far end of the dock, while tied up not far from us is a huge orange search-and-rescue ship.

The two crews stroll past the line of yachts tied to the quay. The rescue ship's crew is clad in bulky, heavy-duty, sea-going foul-weather gear in that lurid shade of orange that is most easily detectable in a violent sea and poor visibility. In contrast, the men from the helicopter are dressed in black, close-fitting, one-piece flying suits with epaulettes, apart from the one sporting a wet suit, ear protectors and a pair of green plastic flippers tucked into his belt. They speak faultless English and apologise for any inconvenience they might cause during three proposed takeoffs and landings.

The big search-and-rescue ship leaves first. Then the helicopter takes off. A few of us troop out onto our decks, shade our eyes and peer down towards the end of the harbour to watch it go. Sometime later, the characteristic sound of rotor blades can be heard coming back. Only this time a glance upward reveals that instead of returning to its original spot, down the far end of the quay, the helicopter is planning to land on the car park above our boats. It is a dramatic moment and, with so much noise, impossible to ignore. Everybody on the yachts goes out to watch. It is low tide at present, so to raise our sights above quay level we are all balanced on coach house roofs or booms or teetering on pulpits as the helicopter begins its slow, controlled descent.

I spot a smiling face at one of its windows and raise an arm to wave – but then duck into a crouch instead and run whimpering for cover along with everyone else. It is regrettable that the helicopter crew, with its immaculate English, had not thought to use it to warn us about the effect of the downdraught from their rotor blades. High-velocity dust from the car park blinds our eyes while a hail of grit, gravel, loose tar and cigarette ends peppers our faces and bare limbs like airgun pellets. As I grope my way down to the cockpit, and the shelter of the saloon, I am overtaken by the pair of jeans from Ulrika's washing line. I grab them and take them inside with me. The underwear that had accompanied them she retrieves later from somebody's rigging.

We all remain below for the remainder of the Coastguard's manoeuvres, with our boats battened down and not a little resentful as the morning gets hotter and stickier. When it is finally safe to open the hatches again I spend ages vacuuming grit and cigarette ends from everywhere, including our bed, while David sweeps our previously spotless decks before it rains again and the whole disgusting mess gets wet and walked indoors.

On our way into town during the afternoon we bump into Piet and Else, the Dutch couple who have been debating whether or not to take on extra crew. A young man called Jan, who has recently completed the passage here aboard a Scandinavian boat, is looking for a berth across the Atlantic and has approached them. Since we last spoke to him Piet has been making enquiries about the business of taking on crew for the Caribbean and discovered the same daunting facts as we had in Gibraltar when faced for a time with the choice of extra crew or being refused insurance cover.

'You have to buy them a ticket home,' says Piet, his hand moving involuntarily towards the general area of his wallet.

We nod sympathetically.

'And if they get drunk,' adds his wife, 'and wreck a bar or something, you have to pay the owner compensation.'

We know, we know.

'And if they haven't anywhere to go once you get to the Caribbean,' says Piet, 'you're stuck with them!'

We spend the evening over a glass of wine with Ulrika and Johan and some of the other Swedes. Like us, they have been disappointed that there are so few good anchorages around. We should all like to be at anchor again, away from the dust and dirt of the huge car park and the pervasive smell coming from the waterfront. There is *one* anchorage, apparently, at Los Cristianos on the other side of the island. We all decide to go there.

7

Los Cristianos

The Swedes set off very early, but we need to visit the fuel dock at Puerto Radazul, a few miles along the coast, and it won't be open until nine. So we opt to head for the anchorage at Bahia de Abona for the night, which is roughly halfway between Santa Cruz and Los Cristianos.

One thing I particularly notice on the way are some tiny fishing villages, clinging to the bottom of the cliffs, right on the water's edge, some of them with a small beach. Way above them, up on the clifftop and out of each other's sight, are huge, expensive developments. It is like a metaphor for so many beautiful places we foreigners invade: the indigenous, timeless and low paid at the bottom and the incoming affluent on the top.

By 4pm we are entering the anchorage. There is a heavy swell as David noses close into a corner of the bay to get as much protection from it as possible. I am on the foredeck making sure that the jagged rocks I can see on the shoreline do not extend out under the water. Suddenly we are approaching a wide ledge of yellow rock less than a couple of metres below us. With the present swell, I fear *Voyager* will be lifted up and brought crashing down onto it. I turn towards the wheelhouse and wave at David to reverse out. He smiles and nods back. I begin waving my arms madly in the direction from which we have come and yelling at him to get away from here. Even after all these years together he has never been one to take a hint, but fortunately the depth gauge finally takes an interest and he shoots into reverse.

A few minutes later we find a suitable patch of water and the anchor sets very nicely. During the early evening the small Australian sloop, *Down Under,* joins us. When the wind shifts, it turns into a very bumpy night. With the heavy swell still coming from the east, and the wind now from the north, *Voyager* is buffeted unmercifully between the two so that every time you drop off to sleep you find yourself jolted awake again.

Unable to rest I get up for a while and go out on deck. Bahia de Abona contains one small and one tiny village, at either end of the bay. I settle down in the cockpit and gaze out at the lights in the windows of their houses and wonder about the lives lived within. Further out in the bay *Down Under*'s anchor light is bobbing violently. A monohull, and needing deeper water than us, she is bouncing even worse than we are. But turbulence is soon forgotten when you lie back and look upwards into a vast sky full of shooting stars.

We leave the anchorage early next morning with *Down Under* not far behind. Unlike them we are a little too casual in setting our course, given the strength of the wind and tide and find ourselves being swept rather dramatically towards the Point de Abona lighthouse and a rather nasty reef. It takes us quite a while to get clear of it, all the time convinced that despite our best efforts we are not actually making any headway. Once out of the bay the sea settles and we begin what turns out to be a very pleasant sail to Los Cristianos.

Spain's highest mountain isn't in Spain. It is here on Tenerife and it is a volcano. We are sailing under it now. Pico de Teide is 3,718 metres high and its peak is white with snow. Below it, on the beach directly opposite us, is what looks like an old-style power station, while to the left of it stand a large number of new, hi-tech wind turbines.

The coastline itself provides evidence of a very much older power surge, its volcanic rock elaborately fluted and full of distorted holes like partly-melted Gruyere cheese, or something from Salvador Dali. In fact, the landscape is quite surreal along here. This includes multiple peaks above the shoreline that are smooth, dark brown and scattered with low, round shrubs which look as if most of their colour has been bleached away. The effect is of brown spoil tips covered in pale green polka dots.

At around 11am our depth gauge shows 4.3 metres which is worrying as our chart says it should be closer to a thousand. We ponder on whether a dolphin is practicing close-shave swimming against our hull, just where the echo sounder's transducer is located.

By 1.15 at Punta Rasca, the southernmost point of the island, we are in a Force 6 with the tide from behind and the sea becoming very large. Then the wind shoots to the bow, drops to Force 2 and the sea becomes calm, making the genoa flap, so we take it in. There is a very odd effect to the sea here. It is mostly quite flat but with odd areas splashing up quite violently, the way fast-moving water does when it has rocks just below its surface. There are none marked on the chart, however, and it is most likely the result of two currents meeting at the point; something we met with frequently during our early sailing days in Wales and known there as 'outfalls'.

Los Cristianos has a large harbour with berths for cruise ships and ferries. Once a departure point for yachts heading for the Caribbean, nine years ago the authorities outlawed anchoring here because of concerns about beach pollution. Nevertheless there will be somewhere between 15 and 25 yachts anchored in the harbour at any one time during the coming days. Since you are illegal, however, the authorities do not require you to clear in. At the same time no-one bothers you for being there illegally. This is Spain.

The weather is delightfully warm with just a light breeze. From the anchorage it is only a short trip into town by dinghy, where we tie up at the northern end of a long sandy beach in a convenient corner created by the harbour wall.

Behind the beach is a large tourist town with a lot of shops and a very long promenade. At one end of it African men and women are selling leather goods and wooden carvings out of suitcases or from rugs spread on the ground. At the other, Spanish men, with a little wooden tray hung from the neck by a piece of string, are working the three card trick. In between, small groups of Britons are offering timeshare apartments.

We stop to watch as a Spaniard invites a newly-arrived holidaymaker to *find the lady*. He seems rather inept as cardsharps go, and makes it easy to see where the Queen is. After several correct guesses, the visitor decides he is ahead of the game and agrees to do business. The Spaniard shows him the Queen once more, puts her face-down with the other two cards and turns all three slowly to the right. It is obvious where she is. The cards stop moving. The visitor points to the one that both we, and he, and his wife know is the Queen and the Spaniard makes that universal gesture of rubbing fingers against thumb that says it is time for money to change hands.

But in the instant that the man takes his eye off the cards to reach for his wallet, the Spaniard gives them a further small turn to the right. In consequence, when the man has handed over several hundred pesetas and the Spaniard turns the cards face-up, the Queen is no longer where he knew her to be, and he is utterly bewildered that he could have been so wrong. We return to the beach to find a small child energetically using her bucket and spade to fill our dinghy with sand.

However, it is a delight to be at anchor again, with an open aspect after the enveloping walls of the marina. We spend quite a few days here. On one of them, a topic of conversation among Johan and the other

Swedes is an area called Los Gigantes, just along the coast. Dolphins, it is said, sometimes gather there and people swim with them. We go out for a sail, on the off-chance, swimsuits at the ready, but there are no dolphins about, just lots of replica galleons full of tourists. But it is worth the trip for the scenery. The cliffs are dramatic: high, sheer, dark and thickly wooded. And at the very top of them, hidden from the sea, and indeed from everywhere else, is an ancient secret we will discover a little while from now.

In the meantime, Navtex gives a coastal warning about a plague of locusts heading towards the Canary Islands from Algeria. Mariners are asked to notify their nearest Coastguard station of any sightings.

Our second water tank runs dry. We still have an emergency supply in five-gallon containers but we need to think about refilling our tanks some time soon. From Los Cristianos, looking south, you can see the neighbouring island of La Gomera. We decide to visit another island and fill our tanks at the same time.

LA GOMERA
San Sebastian

We arrive at La Gomera's capital, San Sebastian, at around 2 in the afternoon and are glad to get into the shelter of the harbour. In a mixture of sun and cloud, most of the four-hour sail has been very enjoyable. The last part of the journey has been most unpleasant.

There is around these islands a phenomenon called an acceleration zone. It is created by an island's height and the way this causes the wind to funnel around it. For a yachtsman it means that when you leave the shelter of an island's mountain the wind hitting your sails can increase in strength from five knots to as much as twenty-five in as little as 200 metres. Accordingly, having sailed down the east coast of Tenerife and across its southern tip in a moderate breeze, on beginning the approach to Gomera we had been hit by a Force 6 funnelling between the two islands and a rough sea.

Voyager is the only boat on San Sebastian's quay. A muscular marina attendant with a pony tail, a very deep voice and excellent English all but takes a ruler to the concrete dock. When he is satisfied about exactly where our bows should be – to allow the local water taxi adequate space to berth – he helps us tie up. It is a small marina, with most of its pontoon space taken up by local boats and only the quay, where we are, available for visiting yachts.

We shove the water hose into one of our empty tanks and are just feeling very relaxed and comfortable when a small, plump Frenchman called Georges, with a drooping moustache and a handheld VHF, arrives on the quay and says he hopes we haven't planned on going anywhere for a while as he has a rally of twenty or thirty boats arriving. I can't help feeling as he says this that as the organiser of such an event he ought to know *exactly* how many boats he has. But I don't have time to dwell on it as the first of them begin to arrive.

We help them to berth along the length of the quay behind us, Georges having disappeared to the ferry dock where the balance of his fleet – those yachts too large for the marina – is to be berthed. In no time at all we have three boats rafted up to us and similar rafts are forming behind.

Our own raft consists of another 40-foot catamaran, only much wider than ours. Almost square, in fact, with four Swiss aboard comprising father, two adolescent sons and a young woman whose relationship to them is not defined but who is very nice and seems to do all the work. Next to them is a ketch with four Germans aboard, while the outside boat is a small sloop containing an Italian couple and their six-year-old son.

Like us, their destination is the Caribbean. Unlike us, they have chosen to cruise in convoy, as members of a rally. They are here to provision their boats, after which they will be setting out across the Atlantic. 'A bit keener on the calendar than the weather forecast,' one of them will grumble subsequently. And, given that we have barely edged into the month of November, the organisers do indeed seem to have settled on the very earliest possible date recommended by weather experts for an Atlantic crossing if you want to avoid the hurricanes. And not forgetting the vagaries created by El Niño, of course.

For our part, we are simply grateful to be tied up securely to a quay, because these are not good days for sailing or even being at anchor. One of them is particularly blustery and by evening it has also begun to rain. Everyone is battened down, including us, although for some reason I wander out into the cockpit. From there I can see a solitary masthead light plunging in the blackness beyond the harbour entrance.

It is a truly horrible night to be out, not to mention a very crowded marina to have to enter in darkness and find a berth. I climb off our boat onto the quay. The young man at the helm of the small German sloop looks relieved to see someone in the gloom offering to take his lines.

'I go in here,' he shouts above the wind and rain as he begins his approach into the water taxi's berth in front of us.

It is a very little thing to catch a rope and tie it around a cleat, but to those on board on a bad night it can mean a lot and as I reach for his second rope I catch sight of a fraught young woman in the shadows with two small children clinging to her. This little yacht has not only come through a dark, blustery night but also Gomera's vicious acceleration zone.

'They won't let you stay here,' I tell him as he jumps ashore to complete his tying-up. 'This space is reserved for the water taxi. But you're safe for tonight and they'll find you somewhere else in the morning. Oh, and mind this,' I add, pointing to a broken manhole cover David and I have been avoiding for days. 'You could lose a foot down there in the dark.'

He thanks me for my help. I leave him out in the rain to adjust his lines and put on springs while I return to *Voyager*'s warm, dry, lamp-lit saloon. I have done only what many a yachtsman has done for us, their kindness remembered if not their faces. By the time we are abroad next morning his boat has gone. It does not occur to me for a moment that I will ever see him again. We were not quite the ships that pass in the night of Longfellow's poem, but near enough. And given the darkness and the anonymity of hooded wet weather gear I wouldn't know any of them again if my life depended on it. But six months from now he will recognise *Voyager*, and provide us with one of our most memorable experiences ever.

In the meantime, our days echo to the bangs, thumps, scrapes and rumblings of our neighbours. We wince hourly at the outrages committed against our boat. Things are not helped by a two-metre tide and the difficulty this presents to people trying to get between our boat and the quay. We suggest politely that at low tide, regardless of sailing protocol, we are more than happy for them to pass across our stern instead of our bow – down the ladder bolted to the quay wall and onto our stern steps. But the two Swiss adolescents prefer to stand on the quay, hurl their purchases six feet down onto our foredeck and then take a running jump after them. The four Germans prefer to stand on our wire rails. I begin to empathise with the Australian yacht-owner at Porto Santo who tied *NO RAFTING UP!* signs onto his rails. Not that this is an option for us, of course. But given the amount of traffic, I do toy with something to the effect of: *IS YOUR JOURNEY REALLY NECESSARY?*

Also, in terms of traffic, is the ongoing mystery to us of how the little Italian sloop on the outside of our raft stays afloat under the endless trolley loads of groceries, canned goods, gas tank refills, wine, bottled water and other supplies crossing our decks daily, all purchased and loaded by the wife; her husband needing to discuss sailing essentials with another Italian man on a boat behind. Although to his credit he does give her a hand with the seven or eight 25-litre diesel containers that have to be heaved on board.

Gino, their 6-year old son – although so pretty he should surely have been a girl – is a perpetual satellite to these activities. Although even when his mother is below decks, stowing all the provisions she has so stoically hauled aboard, this child is not still. All day we listen to the sound of his feet thumping ceaselessly back and forth across our decks, between Mama on their boat and Papa on somebody else's.

If we happen to be sitting in the cockpit, he fixes us with large, liquid brown eyes and raises his arms appealingly for one of us to get up and lift him over our rails, twice: once onto *Voyager* so that he can patter across her, and then up again and over onto the quay to visit Papa. In what seems like only minutes, he will be back again for the process to be reversed so that he can return to Mama. There is something almost demonic in his angelic looks combined with his certainty of getting whatever he wants. As the days pass we rename him Damien and begin to fantasise about ways of destroying him.

We had intended to hire a car and see something of the island but are not inclined to leave *Voyager* to the mercy of our neighbours and their provisioning. And, having watched the process at close quarters, La Gomera does seem to be an increasingly odd place to do this. To begin with, there is no convenient fuel dock which means that, as the stoic Italian woman can testify, all the diesel required on board has to be brought to the boat in cans. And the shopping facilities are those of a small rural community that cooks and bakes, catches fish, grows its own fruit and vegetables and keeps a few chickens but which does not run to much in the way of long-life packaged goods.

In particular, there are two long, narrow shops, almost next door to each other, selling a limited range of foodstuffs and general goods. And on Wednesdays and Saturdays there is a small street market selling home-grown vegetables and fruit. There is also the local co-operative above the fish and meat market which never has fewer than three hopeful cats sitting outside it. At the front of this building some steps lead down to the market traders' bar and restaurant, which is below street level. Whenever someone opens its door to enter or leave, there is a delightful gust of hot, tasty meals and *bon ami*.

It is, in short, typical of a small, self-sufficient community on an unspoilt island, and one of the things that makes it so attractive to a visiting city-dweller. But suddenly injected into this village is innumerable boats and their crews, and for a number of these yachtsmen this is their first-ever experience of stocking a boat for such a long voyage. The result is a shopping frenzy.

Not finding what they want locally, people hire cars and take them on the ferry to Tenerife from where they return laden with enough to stock a small supermarket and shouldering whole hands of bananas. A hand averages a hundred bananas, according to one cynical old timer. 'They'll all ripen together,' he mutters gleefully. Someone even takes the ferry all the way to Los Cristianos just to buy a cabbage.

Directly behind us is a very expensive yacht crewed by an Englishman and his twin teenage daughters. Unwittingly I become a sort of galley guru for the two sisters. Without their mother along they feel very keenly the weight of responsibility for provisioning the boat for their father, and also Uncle Jeremy who will be joining them any day now as the fourth member of the crew.

Each time I emerge onto our afterdeck they are up to their young elbows in some sort of preparations, mostly washing things at present. Large quantities of fruit and vegetables, from a recent trip on the car ferry, have been immersed in water during the last few days. Today it is apples.

There are two reasons for all this washing. One is to do it while there is fresh water on tap and thereby save onboard supplies for drinking and cooking during the voyage. The other is to keep your boat free of cockroaches which, once aboard, are not only deeply unpleasant but difficult to get rid of. By washing fruit and vegetables you remove any eggs they may have laid on it because while adult cockroaches may be easy enough to spot sprinting through your Cox's orange pippins, their progeny are not. Although they soon will be if the eggs are allowed to hatch and develop undisturbed among your supplies.

For the same reason you are advised not to take on board any cardboard, including the large outers you have used to carry goods from the supermarket to your boat, or the trays holding cans of beer and soft drinks, since their corners and crevices can also be fertile breeding grounds.

One of the twins bites her lower lip thoughtfully and then asks, 'Should we wash the onions?'

I'm not sure what to say. I've never been in this situation before. But I do have three decades of housekeeping at my back.

'I think they'll go mouldy if you do.'

The question is: how easily could a cockroach breach the bulb's tight layers and outer skin, as against how long does it take to dry an onion to its core once you've immersed it in water? The thing about washing everything is how do you ensure that it is all properly dry before you stow it away for anything up to three weeks in a humid atmosphere? One of the problems is the current unstable weather. One day it will rain, the next it is hot and sticky, sometimes it is heavily overcast with high winds, at others sunshine and a gentle breeze. Most of it, however, is not good food drying weather.

Next day the sisters lift between them a whole hand of bananas for me to admire.

'There are supposed to be a hundred to a hand,' says one.

'But we've counted them,' says the other. 'There are only 97.'

I can't help thinking that 97 bananas will be more than enough for four people to get through in quick succession if, as Old Jeremiah down the quay insists, they do indeed all ripen together. I don't know whether they do or not. I've never bought a hand of bananas. But I'm not going to be a Jeremiah myself and spoil their pleasure. There is, however, another problem with bananas purchased this way that I feel I must mention.

'You do know about...?' I begin.

'Big hairy spiders?' says one sister, waggling the fingers of her free hand.

'Yes,' says the other. 'The man who sold this to us inspected it before he handed it over.'

They look thoughtful. 'Should we put them in the fridge, do you think?'

'No!' I cry involuntarily, envisaging 97 lovingly-acquired bananas all black by morning.

At the same time, I can't help wondering exactly what size refrigerator their yacht contains that could accommodate a whole hand of bananas as well as everything else they will be taking with them. But concentrating instead on four people with 24¼ bananas each to consume in short order I add, 'Just keep them as cool as possible.'

They look at one another, two peas in a pod, as the same thought strikes them at the same moment. 'We can put them on top of our wardrobe!' And I wonder again at the interior of a yacht which has sufficient headroom for a full hand of bananas to sit on the top of a wardrobe. I return to my own boat wondering if theirs might be the ocean-going version of Doctor Who's Tardis.

One afternoon a day or so later, when this massive effort of theirs is virtually complete, there is a loud thump as two expensive seagoing bags hit the concrete dock just beyond our stern. They have been dropped there by a slender man in his forties wearing a linen suit, a scarf draped around his shoulders and a panama hat. The crew of the Tardis, still busily employed in the cockpit, looks up at him in delight. Uncle Jeremy, the fourth member of their crew, has arrived.

'Darlings!' he cries, thrusting a hand theatrically towards the sea bags at his feet. 'I've *brought* the *Marmite*!'

9

The Garden of Eden

This is only the second migration I have ever witnessed and it is very different from the first. This one is full of activity, excitement, anxiety, moments of tension and not a little apprehension because, on a journey such as this one, you will be tested.

The other occurred one English autumn afternoon thirty years ago. The narrow path through the trees opened into a field and, suddenly, there they were. Perhaps they chose that particular spot because it was so secluded. They couldn't actually be seen unless you stumbled in among them. The field was lying fallow and full of weeds. The railway line on top of the embankment had been closed for years. Nobody had any reason to go there any more except ramblers or someone with a dog to exercise.

Swallows are such active birds and normally when you see them they are in rapid flight. But none of these moved. That was the eerie thing, the stillness. That and the silence. Even a dozen small birds can be deafening when they want to be. Yet here were thousands of them and there wasn't a sound. They just stood, silently, side-by-side. Waiting. Every fence rail, telephone wire and tree branch, black with swallows.

I just stood there, as well. Unsure what to do. I wondered if crossing the field would spook them and what effect the sudden beating of all those wings would have on the young, rather nervous collie beside me. Even I was having a Hitchcock moment. But it was a long walk back to get home the way we had come. So I bent without haste and clipped the lead onto my dog's collar, patted her head for reassurance, then led her gingerly across the field towards the gateway on the other side. It seemed to take a very long time.

I remember wondering, as we neared the middle, what the signal might be that sends them all off at a particular moment on their long and hazardous journey to Africa for the winter. Whatever it was, I hoped it wouldn't arrive for just a few minutes more.

When we had finally got to the far side of the field and passed through the gateway I turned and looked back at them all. Waiting. Silent. *Eerie*.

Then suddenly, like swallows rising from telegraph wires in response to some unheard signal, all the boats around us untie their mooring lines and leave. All except the little Italian sloop which would be going a day or so later than the others. 'Because we are tired,' Papa informs us solemnly, without a trace of irony. But, if the rally's time has come, so at last has ours. We hire a car.

Just beyond the edge of town we embark on a wonderful new road. At San Sebastian our surroundings had been rocky, volcanic and barren but once out of the capital the island quickly becomes lush and green. We meander upwards for a little while and then the wonderful new road ends abruptly at unmanned road works.

'It'll be lovely,' we stammer, bouncing in our seats over pot-holes and patches, 'when they finish building the road.' But, of course, improved roads bring greater access which inevitably leads to change. And with just a cursory glance around you, the last thing you would want to see on this island is change. This is a little piece of Paradise, a green mountain rising out of a sunlit sea, its slopes dotted with small, whitewashed villages that have red poinsettia trees growing wild at the roadside and yellow snapdragons blooming in the gaps between the kerbstones. It is Shangri La built on the sides of a volcano in the Atlantic Ocean, 200 miles off the North West coast of Africa but Mediterranean Spain in character, only before the developers got to it. And not a single block of concrete apartments to be seen.

In one place, a couple of men are building a wall in the same way and with the same kind of stones as the ancient terraces that climb the slopes of the mountain. A donkey grazes. The little native finches Europe named canaries and kept in cages and took down coal mines to test for the presence of gas, fly wild here. A solitary seagull circles overhead.

We skirt the edge of Parque Nacional de Garajonay, the national park which contains the volcanic peak and centre of the island, and then turn right down a secondary road to the village of Hermigua. It lies in a fertile valley, its white houses bright against dark green banana groves.

For anyone enjoying the simple life there is everything here, on these terraced slopes and fertile valley bottoms, that a person could want – olive groves, date palms, vineyards, banana plantations, orchards, orange and lemon groves and neat little market gardens of herbs and vegetables. Melons on the vine trail over the roofs of tool sheds, ripening in the sun. Flowers bloom in the gardens of the small houses while every conceivable shade of bougainvillea climbs their white walls.

Just outside Agulo, we stop for coffee and then onto Playa de Hermigua, a black sandy beach that you reach through banana groves. A hand of bananas, as it ripens on the tree, produces a long brown fibrous pigtail at its base and a large, mauve flower that adds patches of colour to the valley's greenness.

At Vallehermoso we stop above the town. There is a delightful smell up here, like warm cinnamon, while below us a man in a loose white shirt and a straw hat wields a long-handled hoe. Around him: pampas grass, herb plots, vines and the ubiquitous bananas. It is idyllic.

Involuntarily comes the memory of a short story about a couple who stop their car, look down into a Californian valley, and say that it is *so beautiful* that the people who live there must be *very happy*. The reader is then taken down among those living in the beautiful valley, people who spend their days embroiled in spite and pettiness, guilt and shame, because a place cannot make you happy, no matter how beautiful, if you or those around you are sour. I find myself hoping that the misery gene is missing here.

From Vallehermoso we spiral upwards towards Valle Gran Rey, where we plan to stop for lunch. Just past Epina, however, the road sign must have been knocked out of alignment because instead of continuing along the present road we find ourselves taking a sharp corner rather too fast over a large, loose, temporary manhole cover and skittering onto an unmarked dirt track that takes us down a very steep incline. At the bottom, a tiny village sits just above the water's edge, on a black volcanic beach. One of the handful of buildings is a restaurant. We decide to lunch here.

We cannot understand the menu board and the owner speaks no English, so I ask him in my most basic Spanish to choose for us. He looks startled, then says tentatively, 'Fish?' We say, 'Si,' and in time a large platter of fried fish, green chilli sauce, homemade bread, baked potatoes and salad arrives. The fish is salty and delicious with Dorada beer.

As we walk back to the car we are approached by an elderly German tourist clutching a map, the only other motorist we shall see all day.

'Where am I?' he says.

Like us he has been snatched from his intended route by the faulty road sign. David fishes our lunch receipt from his pocket, reads out the name of this tiny place – Playa de Alojera – and then finds it for him on his map.

We leave him to ponder his own lunch and retrace our route back up the mountain track, back over the loose, temporary manhole cover to the junction with the treacherous road sign and then head for Valle Gran Rey once more. We descend a very long road into another tranquil valley. It is Utopia. Out of time. Still untouched. Except for the new road, of course.

To return to San Sebastian and *Voyager* we have to go back up the mountain and into the national park, not just skirting the edge of it this time but deep into it. We abandon the car for a while and set off down one of its footpaths. Although you expect valleys to be fertile, the rest of the island surprises you. For while the soil exposed by these paths is thin and dry and the mountains are volcanic rock, every outcrop has trees clinging to it and the forest floor is thick with vegetation. Sunlight slants through the leaves of deciduous trees and palm fronds, fallen trunks have been turned pale green by succulent moss, a mountain stream gurgles over boulders.

The car journey through the forest is cool and shady, until you emerge at the highest point, the road spiralling around a rocky summit. A little dizzy from our dramatic ascent and blinking into the sunlight, we gaze down upon the tiers of dark green ravines dropping away towards a glittering sea. As if to reinforce the loftiness of our perch, quite some way below us a solitary bird glides upon the thermals and we realise with a shock that we are so high we are looking down onto the back of an eagle. As the gods on Mount Olympus looked down, perhaps, admiring their creation before they played havoc with it and spoiled it all.

With the long descent towards San Sebastian comes the gradual return of rocky barrenness, and a stop at a small empty café overlooking a treeless but nevertheless stunning panorama. Volcanic activity did not continue on La Gomera as it did on some of the other islands, so natural erosion has produced extraordinary profiles in places like this one. A stark contrast to the lushness elsewhere, its sculpted beauty is breathtaking. So has our day been.

Back at San Sebastian's marina next day we get news of another rally on its way. We have no desire to be trapped under the provisioning process of another three or four boats. Added to which, we shall need to think about provisioning our own shortly but see little point in travelling back and forth by ferry to Tenerife lugging foodstuffs. And it is easier to take on diesel direct from Puerto Radazul's fuel dock than heaving it on board in cans and then decanting it into our tank.

It would also be nice to have a sail again. So we decide to go back to Los Cristianos for a while, swing at anchor, gorge on English newspapers, have a sail when we feel like it, and then return to Santa Cruz to stock up at one of its large supermarkets. There is also that most essential of items when preparing for your first-ever two-handed Atlantic crossing – Christmas cards. We top up our water tank, pack up and with the first of the new batch of boats approaching the harbour, we cast off.

10

At Anchor Again

We arrive at Los Cristianos at sunset and anchor in our old spot. This is largely because no-one else wants it. It is too shallow for the average mono-hull's keel but ideal for our one-metre draught. It is heaven to be at anchor again and away from the madding crowd.

Today is 11ᵗʰ November. Remembrance Day. I may not be in a place to buy a poppy any more, but I do remember their sacrifice. And what might have been, had they not made it.

Next morning, in a blissful quiet uninterrupted by the ebb and flow of yachtsmen across our boat, we remove Gomera harbour's black oily stains from our fenders and topsides and scrub the footprints off our decks. *Voyager* has also lost a certain amount of paint off her foredeck from unsuitable shoes and abnormal wear and tear.

In the afternoon we paddle into Los Cristianos to buy our first English newspaper for a while. A beach party is just packing up as we arrive. When we return we find that rather than take their refuse home with them, the party people have dumped their food containers and empty bottles in our dinghy. I can only suppose that it is because it is aluminium that people would mistake it for a skip.

Although we haven't spotted so much as a small grasshopper yet, Navtex is still much exercised by plagues of locusts, to the exclusion of weather forecasts even. And David has finally noticed that the female anglers in the anchorage fish topless so I have hidden his glasses. He doesn't need them for anything important at present.

On a subsequent trip into town we bump into some of the Swedes from our previous time here and at Santa Cruz. As usual, the talk centres on weather, departure plans and boat insurance. There is a lull in the conversation following the latter as everybody ruminates bitterly for a moment on battles fought, and usually lost, with marine insurance companies.

'Piet was thinking of taking Jan on,' we say to lighten the mood. One of the men rolls his eyes eloquently.

'Lazy, selfish and greedy,' says another.

'Lars was glad to be rid of him,' says a third.

'Does Piet know?' we ask.

There is a degree of chin-rubbing and gazing thoughtfully into the middle distance.

Saturday 13th November turns out to be the date of the England v Scotland football match. Since first setting out I have wondered if, when recruiting agents, national security services should tap into the average football fan's capacity to find a game involving either his national or his home team no matter where he is or what he is doing.

David seems able to receive intelligence through the ether. His ability is positively uncanny. I mean, here we are, at anchor, on a small Spanish island out in the Atlantic, without access to local newspapers or radio, no television and not another British football supporter in sight, yet without any apparent effort he has located the only public venue in town which will be showing the match.

Accordingly, in the afternoon David dinghies into Los Cristianos to the Full Monty Nightclub – no entrance fee and a pint of San Miguel beer at pre-war British prices – to watch the match live on satellite TV. England rewards his efforts to support them by winning 2-0. And when he gets back to our dinghy it is still afloat, but only just, no thanks to the small child currently filling it with poly bags full of sea water. One wonders about the parents.

II

A Tragedy

A woman is taken from the sea today. I'd heard rotor blades passing over the anchorage earlier, en route to the harbour, and thought nothing of it. But when we paddle into our usual corner the helicopter is parked on the jetty while a large group of people stand around watching paramedics at work.

It seems intrusive to remain and callous to walk away. With no way to be of use, however, we are simply adding to the crowd. We trudge off into town.

When we return a covered stretcher is being lifted into an ambulance. In the helicopter a man in uniform is sitting in the front window seat, laughing with a colleague in between sucking an ice cream on a stick in a contented, leisurely sort of way.

Before we can get into the dinghy and paddle away, the helicopter pilot starts his engine and leaving is not an option for a while. The pain on bare skin is intense but the threat to the eyes is of greater concern and all any of us on the beach can do is go into a crouch and try to shield our faces from the sandstorm caused by the downdraught from the rotor blades.

Back on *Voyager*, as I shampoo sand and grit from my scalp, I wonder at the depth of my sadness and anger at the death of a stranger. Is it purely selfish, to do with my own mortality? Or the thought of her dying alone; yet in such a public way amid the indignity of attempted resuscitation and all those curious onlookers?

Even in a culture where violent death is a nightly form of entertainment on our television screens, someone's life suddenly snuffed out on a bright morning at a pleasure beach is profoundly shocking.

Or was it the laughing man in the helicopter, enjoying his conversation and his ice cream? I have never saved anyone's life so I am in no position to criticise. He may save hundreds in his working lifetime and recover bodies that families desperately want returned to them. A barrier for the emotions of some kind would be essential in a job like his. But the mechanism is better kept from public view.

12

Return to Santa Cruz

It is now mid-November and officially the end of the hurricane season. Not only are we safe to set off for the Caribbean in terms of insurance cover for our boat, but the weather is becoming more stable. There are two things we want to do before we leave, however. One is to provision our boat for the crossing. The other is to take a tour of Tenerife. For both we need a car.

David rings the marina at Santa Cruz to ask about a berth. They have a lot of boats in at present, a rally, but they can take us tomorrow. We decide to go halfway again, to Bahia de Abona, but leaving the mild conditions of Los Cristianos proves to be a mistake.

The wind gradually rises and shifts to the nose. For a time it reaches 39 knots, the top of a Gale Force 8. Inevitably the sea becomes rather larger than is comfortable, with *Voyager* ploughing her way into it. We average only three knots and take eight hours to do 23 miles, arriving at 5.30, half an hour before dark. David looks tired. He's stayed at the helm for much of the day.

He tucks us as far into the north-west corner of the bay as he can but still can't get us completely out of the waves currently surging in from the Atlantic. While he battens down the boat for the night I start an evening meal. The body needs food to maintain its energy levels and the brain is cheered up by it. But after a passage like today's there is little enthusiasm for eating, and none at all for cooking. This is just the sort of occasion for which packet pasta and bottled Italian sauces were invented. The resulting meal is colourful, tasty and on the table in no time. The penne rattles metallically on its way into the boiling water, like the pen nibs it resembles. The chillies in the Picante sauce make their presence felt on lips subjected to wind and salt spray for most of the day. But it is hot and filling and most welcome.

With so much turbulence in the anchorage we mount a night watch. I do the first one, at 7pm. There is supposed to be a meteor shower later tonight but with so much cloud about it probably won't be visible.

By the start of my second watch, at 1.15am, the cloud has all gone leaving the sky brilliantly clear. And when I step out into the cockpit I find David lying on his back watching the meteor shower. I grab a cushion from the saloon to put under my head and join him.

According to the newspaper we bought yesterday it is the result of Earth crossing the path of the Tempel-Tuttle comet, a huge ball of ice and dust thought to have been orbiting the sun for over a thousand years. Its glowing silver head, shooting across the night sky, leaves a vast tail of red, green, blue and silver specks behind it which is known as the Leonid meteor shower. We only get this close every 33 years, apparently.

At the end of my third watch, as I trudge wearily from bathroom to bed, I reflect that the trouble with night watches is that you either clean your teeth every three hours or not at all.

The wind has lessened a bit by daybreak. It has also shifted direction, so when we set off for Santa Cruz after breakfast – despite ominous cloud cover and a pervasive greyness – we have a following wind, a following sea and a very much better passage than yesterday. As we approach the entrance to the marina a line of nine French boats comes billowing out.

Something you become aware of here is the danger of following a calendar rather than the weather, of setting off into potentially bad conditions for all sorts of wrong reasons. For instance, even though a rally has a scheduled departure date, individual boats are under no obligation to set off then. But some people are driven by their place in the rally's record book – nobody wants to be the last to arrive. Others have arranged for friends and relatives to join them for Christmas in the Caribbean and want to be sure of getting there in time and having everything ready.

Another reason is boredom. A safe crossing from Europe to the Caribbean all comes down to timing and unfortunately a safe arrival at the Canaries is not the time to then embark on a crossing to the Caribbean. Not unless you are prepared to take serious risks earlier in the voyage, by attempting the notorious Bay of Biscay and the Atlantic coasts of France, Spain and Portugal at unseasonable times.

The best time to sail from northern Europe to the Canaries is May to mid-August, which can result in a long wait in the Canaries. This is not to say that these islands are not a wonderful place to spend a winter in themselves. But for cruisers they are simply one stage of a much larger journey and the most challenging part has yet to come. As a result, impatience begins to set in and the urge to set off takes hold.

Over time we will encounter more than one apprehensive crew member untying mooring lines, with the wind tearing at his oilies and waves crashing over the harbour wall and ask, 'Do you *really* have to go *today*?' In answer he will shoot a furtive glance at his skipper, busy at the helm. Then, with a sigh and an air of predestination, gaze mournfully back at you from his stern as the boat beneath him disappears into a roaring gloom.

However, while sailing by the calendar can have a negative effect on the mental health of inexperienced crew, it can have quite the reverse effect on more experienced yacht owners. As with any situation involving a group of men, an external challenge and something under power that they can steer, a kind of group machismo emerges.

A catamaran is at its best with wind and sea behind it, so as we approach the marina we are fairly bowling along. In contrast, the rally of French boats currently leaving it have wind and sea against them. We are surprised, therefore, that given the conditions they are all under full sail rather than reefed.

Every yachtsman knows that vessels at sea are required to pass port-to-port and only then make any desired turns. To get out to sea, the French boats will need to turn to port and I watch them bouncing and billowing towards us with growing mistrust. The first boat in the approaching line is getting quite close. I have one of my bouts of intuition. Or maybe in this case it is cynicism based on growing experience.

'He's going to cross in front of you,' I say.

Despite all evidence to the contrary, David retains a maddening belief in another yachtsman's intention to do the right thing.

'No,' he says confidently. 'He'll go behind.'

'For crying out loud!' I yell at him. 'This is the *French* we're talking about.'

And sure enough, *whoosh*. Responding to a messianic wrench of its wheel, the leading yacht lurches left, straight across our bows. Inevitably, changing course slows a boat. Sails being changed over, as a vessel makes a 90° turn, inevitably lose their motive power until in a position to take up the wind again. Accordingly, the hull now very close in front of us shudders and wallows as the combined force of wind and wave hit its starboard beam.

Vindicated, I listen to the sound of David cursing under his breath as he takes avoiding action while all nine of them – Adult Boy Scouts to a man, no doubt, with a penknife and a piece of string in every pocket – swerve left in front of us into a churning, battleship-grey ocean under a seething leaden sky.

It is not unusual, when one of these jamborees takes place, for a boat to limp back into harbour a day or so later, a victim of too much pressure of wind on sail and in need of repairs to its forestay. Although when we enter the marina we become aware of one with something rather more serious than a damaged forestay. It is a large German yacht with a vibrant and quite unmistakable design on her hull and the last place we had seen her was La Gomera, from where she had set out on her Atlantic crossing some days ago. She has been dismasted and her once-exuberant hull, now much damaged, is currently patched with plastic sheets and duct tape to keep out the elements. He is not insured, her distraught skipper tells us later. It is going to cost $50,000 just to replace the mast.

We are berthed on the opposite side of the marina from last time, against the sea wall. On our port side there is an expensive yacht called *Carpe Diem*, a 42-footer with an American couple aboard. Gene and Erica tell us they are lawyers. They are both rather aggressive in manner and Gene in particular has a very loud voice. He also seems at a loose end and tends to pop up onto his deck, as though by chance, whenever we emerge onto ours. Unfortunately, his attitude does not encourage either of us to linger, delighting as he does in anything negative he can find with which to confront us.

'Jeffrey Archer's resigned,' he bawls, wafting the latest piece of British political sleaze across at us from the newspaper in his hand. Another less than endearing habit is to put a negative spin on anything we happen to be doing whenever he manages to take us unawares. As when we are bent double replacing a frayed shore line before it has a chance to break and send *Voyager* sprawling into either his boat or that of our neighbours on the other side. 'Having trouble tying up your dinghy?' he bellows, creeping up behind us.

Gene and Erica have been cruising for three years, they tell us, but seem very negative about it. In fact, they don't appear to care much for sailing. Nor do they have a good word for any of the places they have visited either. They have been in this marina for several months already and do not intend to leave until just before Christmas, indifferent about reaching the Caribbean in time for the Festive Season or the Millennium celebrations either.

We say how lovely La Gomera is. They haven't been. They have seen nothing of this island either, apparently, beyond the supermarket and the newspaper kiosk. Although they did take the ferry to Gran Canaria, they say acidly. 'To observe the ARC's preparations!'

Gran Canaria is one of the larger islands in the Canaries group. It is also the starting point for members of the ARC – the Atlantic Rally for Cruisers – as well as a major jumping-off place for many independent yachtsmen embarking on an Atlantic crossing. With so many boats gathered together, provisioning there is a major event.

'A zoo!' sneers Gene.

'Mass apple washing!' snorts Erica.

I think wistfully of the twins and their youthful enthusiasm.

Happily this is the only occasion we are favoured with Erica's presence as she appears to spend much of her time horizontal in the saloon. I know this because during the first couple of days we cross their deck a few of times to get ashore and there is a hatch directly over her favourite roost. As with our earlier stay at this marina, there is a severe shortage of aluminium ladders to get you onto the quay. Gene and Erica have commandeered one of the few, and it is securely tied in front of their bow, but our using it means having to cross their boat and getting waylaid by Gene. We avoid the risk by going ashore in our dinghy as we had during our previous stay here.

I finally decide I've had enough when, brandishing yet another newspaper one morning, he informs me with a larger smirk than usual, 'President Clinton has requested that Mr Blair return the Elgin Marbles to Greece.' I nod at him thoughtfully and then ask if that means Mr Clinton will be returning Texas to Mexico. There is a lot of spluttering. If you can't take it don't dish it out, I always say. After a couple more face-offs in similar vein we rarely see him.

On our starboard side there is a catamaran with four young Frenchmen on it. One of them lives in Trinidad and during the following days there is a friendly exchange of information. David lends them our Atlantic Islands pilot so they can get SSB radio frequencies for their new receiver, while the one with the local knowledge provides us with maps of the island and directions as to where to find Trinidad's best Millennium party. 'Pier One', he tells us, 'is the place to be!'

The unfortunate thing about Frenchmen is that nobody seems to potty train them. You can actually identify a French boat at a distance, without benefit of a flying tricolour, by the silhouette of yet another Frenchman urinating over the side of his boat.

Other nationalities simply roll their eyes, or sigh, or ask sardonically if French marine toilets are really so expensive that nobody can afford to install one. In truth, it is part of the culture and groups of Frenchmen turn it into a social ritual. With four of them next door it's rather like having one of those infamous open urinals that were once a central feature of French towns, and still are in some places. In all other respects they are delightful neighbours and when the time comes we are sorry to see them go.

In the meantime, with water and electricity available again, the laundry gets done and *Voyager*'s interior is vacuumed. Her woodwork is polished, her kitchen and bathroom sanitised, her decks and cockpit are washed and her helm, bright work and gelcoat buffed to a high sheen. In between times we fill the fridge and gather the ingredients for a large Christmas cake. Christmas cards, newly arrived in the shops, are selected – with one for David furtively purchased and sneaked away – and we treat ourselves to an English newspaper.

Behind the kiosk in town that sells them there is a small, weedy area rarely frequented by anybody. In it is a very small fountain, just a bowl on a pedestal with a very small upward jet of water. So small, indeed that it is more like a drinking fountain except there is no button to press. The flow of water is constant, suggesting a loop, and therefore not fit to drink. Standing in it is a pigeon.

I always feel sorry for urban pigeons. Seabirds always look so clean and healthy while pigeons spend their days pecking about in dirty streets and their nights roosting on the filthy narrow ledges of buildings. In consequence they tend to look rather seedy. This one, however, has found the ideal answer to personal hygiene. It is using the small fountain as a shower, rotating under it, fluffing and shuffling to wash itself thoroughly under the thin but constant stream of water. I have seen urban pigeons wash before, when they have an opportunity, usually in gutters or pools of polluted rainwater gathered in broken pavements. But what this one does now I have never seen one able to do before. After completing its toilet, it gracefully raises a wing to allow the fountain to sluice its armpit. This done, it makes a half turn and rinses the other one.

There is a running joke through one of Jacques Tati's films; *Mon Oncle*, I think it is. His character's snobbish sister-in-law, a French Hyacinth Bucket, is obsessed with demonstrating the superiority of her home. Her front garden contains a small dreary fountain which spends most of its time dormant but the moment someone rings the doorbell the lady of the house flicks a switch and the fountain leaps into life. Similarly, the marina has a fountain, just inside the entrance, and when a yacht of suitable grandeur arrives, it too is switched on. If its arrival occurs after dark, the jets of water are enhanced by coloured lights.

The space on our starboard side, vacated by the French catamaran, is quickly taken by *Mojo*, quite the most stylish and expensive yacht to grace the marina and the fountain goes on accordingly. She is 80ft long and so new and shiny that it actually hurts your eyes when the sun glints off her topsides. With a 120-foot mast she carries a lot of sail and to cope with it all she has the biggest winches (powered, naturally) that we have ever seen. Worth several million in anybody's currency she has a French delivery crew of two young women and five young men. No sooner have they tied up than the latter are to be seen relieving themselves over *Mojo*'s stern.

'A coupla million quid,' groans David. 'And they still can't afford a toilet?'

But they are a jolly lot and very polite. Surprisingly so, for the delivery crew of such an expensive boat. Our experience so far has been that the more grandiose the yacht, the greater the delusions of grandeur exhibited by its crew. Unless the owner is about.

Happily, not this lot. Although they do tend to forget that their monster of a yacht towers over the smaller ones on either side of them, and that what they do on their deck tends to spill over onto those of other people. Nor do they seem to be very practiced at what they do. Accordingly they make a complete pig's ear of filling *Mojo*'s water tanks and we only just manage to clamp our hatches shut before they flood our interior. While another day our laundry is drying nicely on the foredeck until they hose their boat all over it.

One afternoon, as we go into town, we notice that the Dutch couple's boat has reappeared in the marina, so on our way out we stop off to say 'Hi'. Piet is busy up his mast. He greets us cheerfully.

'When you off?' we call up to him.

'Next week,' he says. 'All being well. You?'

'The same.' Then we add tentatively, 'Jan going with you?'

Piet's round face, already glowing from physical exertion and a warm afternoon, deepens another shade of red.

'We had him aboard for a week to see how we got on,' he says, wrenching his spanner as if it were a garrotte. 'I am putting in self-furling gear instead.'

13

A Magical Mystery Tour

After all the hard work we have put into preparing *Voyager* we decide it is time for our promised shore leave. On our trips into town we have regularly passed an office on the promenade advertising car rentals. This morning we go inside. There is a man at a desk talking on the phone, so while we wait David picks up a brochure from a neighbouring desk and we sit and consider it. During what turns out to be quite a long telephone conversation we work our way through the Spanish descriptions of the cars and the prices and decide exactly what we should like.

When the telephone call ends, the man looks up at us, smiles and says, 'Yes?'

We point to one of the cars listed in the brochure and say, 'We'd like one of these, please.'

Two separate businesses share this office, the man explains. Then indicating the unoccupied desk as the half we want, adds, 'He's not here at the moment.'

One of the wonders of language is its subtlety; its ability to encompass the tiniest shades of meaning. It is *across* cultures where, with the best of intentions and the kindest of motives, this subtlety sometimes escapes. The key words here are: *at the moment*. For us, they have a specific meaning.

'When will he be back?' we ask, expecting the answer to be something like, 'In about 20 minutes,' or 'after lunch.'

The man hesitates for a moment, glances at the calendar on the wall and then says, 'December.'

This is Spain! This little island may be a long way from its mother country but to all intents and purposes this is Mediterranean Spain and time is merely relative.

We thank him, find another car hire firm up in the town, and emerge with a dark green Seat Marbella.

Our first stop is Candelaria, a small town just south of Santa Cruz. It has a big public square with the sea on one side, shops and cafés on the other and a large church at the far end. According to our multi-language guide book, the Church of the Holy Conception was the only parish church for

Santa Cruz until the 18th century. Completed between 1500 and 1502 it is one of the oldest on the island and has a rather splendid tower.

The church's beautiful interior not only contains its famous Black Madonna and Child but, unlike any other church we have ever visited, instead of sculpted stone or painted-plaster statues this one has dressed figures with porcelain faces, hands and feet. They wear rich apparel – satins, velvets and lace – except for the coarse habits of the monk saints. The crucified Christ lies in a glass coffin between white satin sheets with a satin and lace pillow under his agonisingly arched neck. Nor do the virgin and child simply stand on a plinth in a recess. They reside in a small furnished chamber with an elaborately-panelled ceiling. The Virgin of Candelaria is the patron saint of the islands and thousands of Canarians make a pilgrimage here every year.

The absence of conventional stone statuary inside the church is more than made up for on the beach outside. Much larger than life-size, they are the Garanches, mythical early kings of the island. Each one is an individual, towering above you on his rock, staring resolutely landwards, his bare bottom turned towards the sea. Huge and macho they may be, but also touchingly human somehow, and impressive in their monumental greyness with the sea crashing from behind them over the shoreline's smooth black rocks and up onto the black beach. Despite accepting that the area is volcanic, it still takes a little while to get used to the idea of black sand between your toes.

We buy coffee in one of the cafes opposite the Garanches. It pours with rain while we sit inside and drink it, and stops just before we leave. The air outside has become fresh and clean.

We drive inland, twisting and winding rapidly upwards until we are above the clouds. I don't know if it is the recent rain, or something special about the light up here, but we are startled by the greenness of the forests, and the brightness of the occasional village gardens bursting upon our retinas with the brilliant reds of bougainvillea, geranium and poinsettia trees. After decades of buying a poinsettia at Christmas in a 10-inch pot, which goes into a decline if your central heating goes off for too long overnight, I find poinsettia trees growing wild particularly beguiling.

We turn left and follow the road along the ridge which forms the backbone of the island. From it we look down between pine and date palm onto magnificent views of fertile valleys and the island's spectacular north-west coast.

We also make a closer acquaintance with El Teide, the volcano. Cloud covers its summit and there is snow visible beneath the cloud. Below the snowline there is a stunning crater and you can drive for miles around its rim. It is a journey of infinite and totally unexpected variety. At one point you look out upon a brown moonscape, at another the crumbling pillars of Arizona's Monument Valley. After that come miles of black clinker as if a giant has been burning cheap coal. Then it is as if the same giant has piled one giant-sized shovel-full of damp, black clay behind another for as far as the eye can see. Finally, incredibly, you stare out over a vast area of aquamarine stones scattered on soft golden sand.

We make a detour to Vilaflor, 'Spain's highest village'. It has a very old church with a wooden barrel-vaulted ceiling. It is also surprisingly cold up here. There are snowflake road signs next to warnings about forest fires. Today's fire risk is set at 4 on a 5-risk scale. And unlikely as it seems at present, with scattered showers and chilly temperatures, there is an ever-present reminder of forest fires in the acres of pine trees which, though apparently still alive, are blackened all the way up their trunks.

For whatever reason, they rake pine needles into big, low, square piles here. Despite the fire warning signs and blackened trees, however, the driver of the car in front of us flicks a lighted cigarette end into one of them. We stop at a cold log cabin for a hot lunch of chicken in garlic sauce. The middle-aged and very busy *maitre de* is multi-lingual and incredibly courteous in all of them.

And then it is on to Masca, a hill village hidden in a magnificent gorge. Built by pirates, originally it was inaccessible by land. It could be approached only from the sea, north of Los Gigantes where, it is said, in the right conditions you can swim with dolphins and where we had stared up from our cockpit at the dramatic and almost perpendicular cliff. The island's modern road now crosses the top of Masca. There is still no vehicle access down into it. Entry is via a cobbled path, which drops almost vertically between the first of the small houses. Descend, and you enter a place of lush vegetation, jagged rock formations, vegetable patches and banana groves.

Back on the road again, there is something different round almost every bend; and there are a lot of bends. In fact, much of the road around the island is a switchback. You spiral for miles down into a gorge and then back up the other side and sometimes the road is so narrow that you have to pull over when a large tourist coach comes the other way. The most worrying encounter has a courier wiping a streaming windscreen with a fistful of tissues while the driver hurtles blindly towards us around a hairpin bend.

For a land mass of only 785 square miles, this is an island of immense variety whose terrain produces a wide range of microclimates as well as its stunning scenery; from fertile valleys and the rich green of pine forests to dramatic seascapes and lava fields. The latter takes on many different colours, but one of the most arresting is simply black and palest cream. At one point the road has been cut through it, and although its sides look like soft sand, in reality it is as hard as stone, but so porous that the rainwater trapped behind it seeps through and trickles down the road to meet you.

After Masca we pass through the lava fields of Santiago del Teide, created by the last eruption of the volcano in 1909. We are on our way to Garachico, an area devastated by the 1706 eruption and a great, brown, dusty moonscape.

In complete contrast is Icod de los Vinos, a pretty Mediterranean town of white stucco houses, colourful gardens and what is reputed to be the world's oldest tree. Many a tree around the world has similar claims made about it but, as well as looking very old, this dragon tree is *huge*. It is also in a very pretty area of a town blessed with many beautiful trees, and an old church in a rather lovely square. Inside the church, with its splendid ceiling and wooden panelling, a small group of people on scaffolding discuss, in hushed tones, their current restoration of a fresco.

Before we return the car we stock up with supplies for the crossing, spending a small fortune and filling two-and-half trolleys, including a whole Edam cheese which is quite expensive but proves to be well worth every peso.

The rest of the day is spent sorting and cataloguing supplies and then storing them anywhere we can. And remembering to put an apple in with the potatoes. As long as potatoes are kept in the dark – ours live under the galley sink – an apple will inhibit sprouting. And after the potatoes have all gone, you can still eat the apple.

I also have our Christmas cards to write, ready for posting on our next trip into town. They will arrive far too early, of course, but it can't be helped. It will be too late to post them from the Cape Verde Islands and it gives me an opportunity to include a reminder of the last posting date for cards to reach us via David's brother Tony. I do so love a card at Christmas and a bit of news. And if family and friends leave ours until they post the rest of their cards, we shan't get them until sometime in January. Presents are nice, but Christmas isn't Christmas without cards.

14

A Spell of Bad Weather

We are having dinner one evening when one of *Mojo*'s crew calls down to us. It's one of their birthdays and they are having a party tonight. We are invited. I'm touched. It's undoubtedly that courtesy thing where you avoid offending the neighbours by inviting them to your party, but I appreciate the thought anyway. I also suspect we should seriously cramp their style. With the possible exception of their skipper, there is no-one on board even half our age. I thank her, wish her a great party, but say we are having an early night. She draws down the corners of her mouth and looks anxious.

'Don't worry,' I say, jabbing my forefingers at the sides of my head. 'Ear plugs. We shan't hear a thing.' She looks relieved.

It turns out to have been a good decision on our part. They are soon completely stoned and the music, to our ears at least, is *terrible*.

Next morning, they rise late and look frail. They totter around their decks in an unfocused sort of way and the men sway in unison as they make water together off the stern. Meanwhile the two girls begin banging their fists into large cushions with elasticised covers held over their side rail. They look like the upholstery from sofas and bunks.

'What on earth were you doing last night?' I ask the nearest girl, meaning the cushions.

She looks anguished and as she gropes hesitantly to form an answer her skipper, close behind her, winces.

'No, no!' I say. 'What I mean is, what's with the cushion thumping?'

Her face brightens and her skipper relaxes and wanders off.

'Glitter,' she says. 'Fancy dress.'

They had all dressed as angels, complete with blond wigs, cardboard wings and *lots* of glitter. For a moment my mind's eye is filled with the image of some yachtie returning from a local bar, perhaps a little the worse for wear, confronted by five glittering angels relieving themselves off *Mojo*'s stern. Smiling at the thought, I go below and close the starboard hatches before our galley and bedding become filled with glitter.

The thumping is obviously unsuccessful because *Mojo*'s engines go on, water cascades from her stern for an hour, then the elasticised cushion covers emerge from *Mojo*'s capacious washing machine and are hung in the rigging to dry.

The following day, David is completing our maintenance and I'm doing the last of the laundry when *Voyager* skews violently to port. David rushes to check our mooring lines. I follow him. But when we get on deck we find that we are not at fault. *Mojo*'s starboard shore line has sliced through on the concrete quay and sent her 60 tons lurching into us. As David and I hold *Mojo* off – as best one can hold off 60 tons of fibreglass and teak, fourteen stainless-steel winches, half of them the size of beer kegs, a 120-foot mast and an industrial-size washing machine – her skipper murmurs, 'Oh, how careless,' and spends the next fifteen minutes unhurriedly seeking new rope and tying it in place.

Quite early in this longueur there is an anguished movement up the mast. One of the crew is at the top of it, doing a maintenance check. In the search for a new shore line, he has been forgotten, and the more time passes, the more agitated he becomes. I note the wind direction and hope it's not his bladder that is causing his distress. As soon as I can, I leave their rail and go and close our hatches.

They are leaving today, they tell us, when I return. At around 5pm. 'We'll see you off,' I say.

They finally cast off at 10.20pm and then spend the next hour and a half lurching between one extreme of the harbour and another. Because of *Mojo*'s size the lazy lines had not been adequate to hold them away from the quay so they had used a kedge anchor instead. Unfortunately, it appears to have snagged on something on the bottom and they have difficulty raising it. At midnight I leave them to it and go to bed. I have grown fond of them and shall miss them.

Piet and Else and their young son stop by next morning, to say farewell before they leave for Antigua. The fountains are turned on and shortly afterwards a very large yacht arrives.

There is a saying that misery loves company. It is also noticeable that negative people seek out conditions they can be negative about. In particular, of all the days of all the many weeks that Gene and Erica might have hired a car to explore this beautiful island, they choose today. The sky is heavily overcast and promising rain and the wind is rising steadily. It turns out not to be the best day to have left their boat for other reasons.

Gene and Erica have a negligent attitude to berthing. While we have double bow ropes as a safeguard against chafing, they have a single, rather threadbare ex-genoa sheet now almost completely frayed through from rubbing against the quay. They also keep their lazy line slack so that when they want to get on or off their boat they can haul on their bow rope, pull the boat close to the quay, climb onto the ladder, let the bow rope go and the lazy line pulls the boat back off the quay again.

Carpe Diem is an expensive boat of a type coveted by many. But it is not a restful one. On more than one occasion we have noticed the design's mobile tendencies when at anchor – plunging stem to stern and rolling port to starboard – even to the point where it has pulled up its own anchor. This is the first time we have been berthed alongside one and have discovered that even when moored it worries at its lines like a terrier.

Because of their casual mooring habits, Gene and Erica's boat has been leaning against *Voyager* ever since we arrived. This morning has brought a change of wind direction, however, and it is now colliding repeatedly with the Beneteau on the other side of it, which is also currently uninhabited. Along with a rising wind, and rougher water in the harbour than any we have seen during our time here, its lazy line has stopped doing its job and *Carpe Diem* is currently butting the quay.

We attract the attention of a man in a dinghy checking lazy lines on the other side of the marina. He chugs over, takes one look at the boat and then leaps aboard. He winches up its lazy line to pull it off the quay and then addresses the frayed bow line.

The water in the harbour grows increasingly rough as the day wears on while outside it the sea becomes ferocious. It comes flying over the huge sea wall, landing only feet from *Voyager* and all the other boats on the seaward side of the marina. All motor traffic is banned from entering the quay for a while and anyone attempting to climb the stone steps with a view to looking over the top of the sea wall is prevented from doing so.

But the sea is not simply reflecting the wind here at Santa Cruz but of much further away. For despite the Atlantic hurricane season having officially ended, on 16th November a Category 4 hurricane named Lenny arrived in the Caribbean with devastating results.

We remain aboard for the day. While David makes his final preparations for the journey, I start work on a big, rich, fruit cake. I get the best part of the deal. While he compromises his ribcage hanging headfirst into the engine bays and wanders blustery decks fitting safety lines, digging out our drogue and tarpaulin and strapping the dinghy onto the foredeck, I get to sit at the saloon table with a the big mixing bowl and a wooden spoon. When cooked and completely cold the cake will be wrapped in foil and stored somewhere low down in the boat in the cool where it will mature nicely in time for Christmas and not go mouldy in the humid conditions of the coming weeks.

By evening the worst of the weather has passed for the time being and everything is settling down for the night. We are just beginning dinner when a familiar flat, negative and very loud voice hails us from the quay. We leave our meal and go on deck. Erica is standing sullenly on the quay with a quantity of supermarket bags around her feet. Gene is yelling that somebody has been tampering with his lines and that he can't get onto his boat. We tell them about it butting the quay and suggest they might like to drive round to the marina's manager and use his tender to get on board, but Gene seems rather more the worse for wear than usual and wants his lazy line released. There will be no peace until it is.

Carpe Diem is still leaning on the Beneteau and a full boathook's length away from us so we end up hauling the boat over between us, which is a great strain on the back but enables David to climb over and slacken its lazy line. Then while Gene staggers off to park their hire car for the night David helps Erica and their shopping aboard. Tomorrow is Thanksgiving, apparently.

We go back to our own meal which has now gone cold. We have not quite finished it when a loud crash sends us lurching to starboard and David rushing up on deck. Gene has loosened his lazy line further still, the wind has changed back to its previous direction and Carpe Diem is back leaning on Voyager again.

There are a few more days of high winds and rain but finally the time comes for us to leave. Gene is returning from town with his daily newspaper as David is reversing out.

'Where you heading?' he calls to me.

'Trinidad.'

'Maybe we'll see you there.'

My silence hangs in the air.

We do see Gene and Erica again, in the Caribbean, embroiled in an argument with a householder who objects to their using his garden to get ashore instead of the dinghy dock like everybody else. But under cover of the ensuing melee we leave the scene. And the anchorage.

In the meantime I catch a glimpse of a fellow traveller of an altogether different stamp. On our way out of Santa Cruz harbour we encounter a very small, single-handed yacht named after a very large star, whose benign skipper has, like some recording angel, been witness to our progress so far.

The little sloop *Antares*, which was at anchor beside us at Alderney in the Channel Islands during the earliest days of our setting out, and most recently at Porto Santo after our longest-ever single passage, appears before us now as we are about to embark on the biggest journey of our lives.

I wave to the tall, dark, young man in his small cockpit, and then go down into the cabins and rootle about for the poetry anthology I know is in there somewhere with the Longfellow poem in it containing that stanza about 'ships that pass in the night'.

Our last act before leaving Tenerife, around noon, is to fill up with diesel at Puerto Radazul's fuel dock, just along the coast. Our destination after that is the Cape Verde Islands, 870 miles further south, whose currency is Cape Verde escudos, and after that we expect to be in the Caribbean which trades in US and EC (Eastern Caribbean) dollars. Accordingly we have gathered together all our Spanish peseta coins so as not to have money lying around the boat going to waste because, like banks everywhere, those on the other side will exchange only paper money.

'Going across?' asks the man at the diesel pump, eyeing the growing mound of coins being counted into his cupped hands.

Our purpose in heading for the Cape Verde Islands is to break the journey in two: a short leg and then a longer one. The distance from the Canary Islands to the Lesser Antilles in the Caribbean is 2,800 miles and a typical passage time is three weeks. The journey from the Cape Verde Islands to the Lesser Antilles is 2,085 and typically takes just over two. Although adding around 150 miles to the overall journey, it will give us a break, the opportunity to pick up fresh food and fuel, collect our mail, and experience – apart from a brief but tantalising gust of heat and spiciness one dark night in the Strait of Gibraltar – our first brush with Africa.

TO THE CAPE VERDE
ISLANDS

15

Dolphin Delight

Once out to sea we find that our log is not working. This instrument, showing the speed at which a boat is travelling and the distance covered, is not as important as it was before the advent of the GPS. But if for any reason our GPS malfunctions, the information provided by the log will be essential for calculating our position and navigating by dead reckoning.

Our log's measurements are obtained via a tiny paddle wheel a little over an inch in diameter and built into our starboard hull. Occasionally this paddle wheel seizes up. The cause is sometimes weed, but more often it is because tiny shellfish have set up home on the only bit of hull below our waterline which is free of the antifouling we have so assiduously painted on to discourage them.

One way to unblock the paddle wheel is to go full speed ahead, come to halt and then go full speed in reverse. As well as causing more than one mystified cliff-walker to call friends over to watch, this will often be enough to free the wheel and the log will work again. Today no amount of roaring back and forth will do the trick and must look to the man on the Puerto Radazul fuel dock as if the two of us are having a violent disagreement about whether to make an Atlantic crossing after all.

Our only option now is to take out the paddle wheel and remove whatever is preventing it from spinning. This would be simple enough but for the fact that a) it is below water level and b) most working parts on a yacht are in barely-accessible places.

To be specific, taking out the paddle wheel requires, first of all, that you crawl head-first into the little cupboard under the bathroom wash basin, because that is where the bit of hull with the wheel in it is located. As soon as you remove the wheel there is a heart-stopping moment as seawater starts pouring in, which you have to staunch with a piece of rag in one hand while prising off a determined mollusc with the thumbnail of the other.

Given that the cupboard's opening is not wide enough to get both arms inside at once, and that its interior is full of sharp-edged obstructions such as stopcocks, hose clamps and wiring, this is quite a painful process after which there is a second heart-stopping moment when you have to remove the rag bung currently holding the Atlantic Ocean at bay and shove the paddle wheel back into its hole again. And as David rains down blessings on the yacht designer his head gets banged, his knuckles cut and his elbows bruised. And if the vanity door's hinges get bent during this struggle, the door will creak and groan and fail to shut properly for weeks afterwards until he finally gets around to taking off the hinges and hammering them flat again.

In sailing, as in any other area of existence, it is odd how often the really irksome moments in life seem to coincide with some of its most memorable. For no sooner has a cut, bruised and rather twitchy husband reversed out of a cramped and water-logged bathroom cabinet, than a family of dolphins comes to visit.

Dolphins, on the whole, follow a basic procedure when taking their pleasure with a yacht. There is the sheer joy of swimming in your bow wave, naturally, and of challenging your bows by barrelling along barely inches in front of them. But all of this is heightened for these extraordinarily sociable animals if they can only get somebody up front to watch them. To achieve this, they have to get you onto your foredeck.

So, there you will be, sitting in your cockpit with your head down, reading or preparing vegetables for dinner or, as now, applying sticking plaster to bleeding knuckles, and they have to get you onto your feet and move you from the centre of your boat up to the bow. To do this they first have to attract your attention so they materialise alongside your beam directly opposite you and begin arcing vigorously through the water in ones, twos and threes. They then swim very close to your hull, so that to see them properly you have to stand up. Once they have you on your feet they move forward, and naturally you have to follow if you want to go on watching them. By then, of course, you are committed and the moment they have you hanging over your bow rail, *that's* when they put on a show.

Today, though, having got us into the front stalls as it were, these half a dozen small, common dolphins swim between our bows in an almost perfunctory manner, giving more attention to observing us and the boat than enjoying themselves and giving a performance. Then, after a final glance up at the two of us, they shoot away.

It is like having a human guest leave your home looking disappointed but not knowing where you went wrong. Perplexed by the briefness of their visit and its patently unsatisfactory nature, and feeling that we must have somehow given offence, there is nothing for it but to return to the cockpit. We have barely turned away from the bow rail, however, before the dolphins rush back again, only this time there are more of them. They have another family member with them, and two very small calves.

It is as if the original group had reconnoitred us and our boat, to see if we were safe for infants to play with, and then being satisfied gone back to fetch them and their minder. One calf is maybe two feet long, the other less than three; two perfectly-formed, smiling-beaked miniatures of the mature dolphins surrounding them.

The latter usher the two calves close to the inside of our starboard hull, where they swim side-by-side as if joined by an invisible thread, at exactly the speed of our boat and closely shadowed by adults who rarely take their eyes off them. We can't see all the dolphins. Some may be under the boat, because in the unlikely event that these superbly capable little calves should fail to keep pace with our bows, and the boat went over them, they could be hit by our propellers. So there are no acrobatics by the adults today. They are here to see that the two youngsters come to no harm while taking an early lesson in swimming between the bows of a catamaran.

They stay for quite some time. The slightly larger, darker calf is cautious, almost a little anxious, as if being a bit older it has reached that moment in its development where danger has begun to impinge on its awareness. It is watching its mentors almost as carefully as they are watching it. But the little one! Its black eyes glow, and even its naturally-smiley beak seems to have acquired an extra dimension. Like an already happy baby suddenly presented with a new and delightful experience... well, call me anthropomorphic if you like, but it looks *thrilled to bits*. When it is time for them to leave, the two calves sink and sweep sideways under the starboard hull with the same easy grace as the adults. Then the family swims away in a tight little group.

It is nightfall before we clear the south-eastern end of Tenerife, but for hours afterwards we can still look back on the tiny lights from the islands shining out into the darkness.

It is Tuesday and our second day at sea. The wind is fairly light, although we manage to sail all day except for a couple of short periods where it becomes so weak that our speed drops below three knots and we motor-sail. To grab every bit of wind available, David hauls out our staysail, the small sail between our genoa and mainsail, but before it is even fully out it collapses onto the foredeck. The loop by which it is hauled up the mast has snapped.

Weather reports are a problem as usual. On our way to Madeira we tried various sources but found the only accessible one was Radio France Internationale. It still is, but unfortunately we find the forecasts increasingly difficult to hear, and their being in a foreign language compounds the problem.

It is not a nice day, gloomy and overcast and for a while it rains.

Heavy cloud produces an incredibly dark night. So dark that you step through the companionway doors and you can't even see the cockpit you are standing in. Four or five squalls pass through during the night. It is too dark to see them but we can follow their progress and measure their size on radar. One of them is six miles wide. I watch it coming towards us on the screen, but only the wind and rain at its outer edge actually hits us as its great bulk passes behind our stern. All we see during the night are two lights, one astern of us and one off our starboard beam, probably yachts but both on a more westerly course than we are.

David has toothache.

During Wednesday morning the sky begins to clear and the day becomes bright and pleasant. The wind is light and from the north to begin with and we motor sail with just one engine on. Unfortunately the wind slowly backs until by midday it is coming from the south-west, the direction in which we are travelling.

Wind on the nose slows our progress considerably as the sea starts to build. By evening it is most uncomfortable. *Voyager* bangs and crashes and we feel jarred and jolted all over. When it is like this, just moving about takes all your energy and all your muscles ache. To add to the discomfort, two squalls pass through.

We have a number of options. One of them is to continue on this course but that will require us to tack continuously. Catamarans do not sail well into the wind, however, and we could beat and tack about throughout tonight and all day tomorrow, constantly shifting sails, but at the end of it still be only a few miles closer to our destination.

It would be better to make one very long tack, either well out into the Atlantic or towards the African coast, but both have disadvantages. If we choose the former, and then the Trade Winds kick in before we are ready, we would have difficulty tacking back towards our destination. As for the latter, we do not feel comfortable about getting closer to an area of the African coast where there have been recent reports of pirate activity.

In the last few years there has been a lot of media coverage about pirate attacks on merchant vessels and yachts off the east coast of Africa, especially Somalia. Apart from the sailing press, there has been little written about piracy on the western side of the continent. Here the target is yachts which, being slow-moving and with a minimal crew, are particularly vulnerable as the pirate boats are fast and powerful.

By far the best option would be to forget about the Cape Verde Islands altogether and head out into the Atlantic because the present direction of the wind would allow us to lay a course straight for the Caribbean Sea. The problem is, we have arranged for David's brother Tony to send our post to Mindelo and among all the other things it contains is our Christmas mail from family and friends. We don't want to abandon it. We also want to make our first visit to an African island.

We decide to continue on our present course, with one engine on, and hope for a wind change before fuel becomes a problem.

The only thing we see in 24 hours is a distant light, off our port side during the night. For a long time it seems to be shadowing *Voyager* before finally speeding up and overtaking her. It is only much later that David admits how uneasy this particular vessel made him feel.

Once off-shore our VHF radio, with its range of between sixteen and twenty miles depending on atmospherics, is our only two-way contact with the outside world. Although we can listen to BBC World Service on short-wave radio, and to weather forecasts on SSB (single-sideband modulation) which is the marine equivalent of ham radio. Unfortunately both require the use of headphones because reception is so poor out here.

BBC World Service provides a full range of programmes but our listening is restricted to a half hour broadcast each morning made up of twenty minutes of world events followed by ten minutes of UK news. This is because thirty minutes is as much as you can take before you get a headache from the interference. Something like a play or a closely-argued debate is out of the question. One item that never fails to get through the static, though, is Aston Villa's latest result which, on the team's present form, inevitably casts a pall over David's day. In my innocence I had assumed that missing out on the English Premier League would be one of the bonuses of being cut off from the world.

Given our difficulty with the French weather forecasts, David trawls the wavelengths again in the hope of finding an English-language one and is delighted when he finds himself at last tuned into Herb. He has tried before without success but happily our receiver is finally within range.

Herb Hillgenberg, known to trans-Atlantic yachtsmen simply as Herb, broadcasts personalised weather information from his home in Ontario, Canada via SSB radio to any yachtsman who requests it and who has an SSB transmitter/receiver on board. Every evening he calls up individual yachts all over the North Atlantic with a detailed forecast for the course each one is following and as many as 50 yachts will have someone beside their radios waiting to talk to him. In addition to those with transmitter/receivers, there will be many more yachtsmen like us who have only an SSB receiver but who will also be listening in to get forecasts.

He begins with yachts in the north-west Atlantic, off the coast of Canada, and works down to the South Caribbean. He then moves to the English Channel, down to The Canaries and across to the Caribbean again. All this takes three or four hours but by around 8pm he will have reached our own area and David can tune in for the twenty minutes or so that it takes to get the information he needs, and which is as much as his ears and brain can cope with.

Herb gives his extraordinary expertise at weather forecasting and ship routing without charge and calls it a hobby although he is so good that a number of professional maritime bodies use his services. He is there every day except Christmas Day and probably spends as long in preparing ahead of each broadcast as he does in transmitting. When he calls up a yacht he will already have a good idea of the area it will be in from the previous day's transmission and will have already identified the best possible course for that particular yacht for the next 24 hours based on the latest conditions available to him.

As we have only an SSB receiver, we cannot communicate with Herb directly or receive a personalised forecast. Instead David listens out for the names of yachts in front and behind us and takes down their forecasts. He then has a pretty good idea of what weather we can expect in the next 24 hours.

16

A Lack of Stimuli

There is a squall just after midnight with the wind fluctuating from 25 knots to 12; not gradually, but *wham*, straight up to 25 and then dropping like a stone. There are two more in the next three hours. In between times, there is a bright quarter moon. The only other activity is a flickering red light which our radar shows as five miles away.

Today is Thursday and our fourth day at sea. The wind continues from the south-west but lighter than yesterday so that apart from the squalls we don't get thrown about as much. We continue motor-sailing on one engine although now on reduced revs to conserve fuel and progress is slow.

Sunrise is at 7.45.

During the morning David tops up the oil in both engines.

The day's third exciting event is a piece of polystyrene floating past. Unfortunately I am asleep when this occurs but, on learning about it later, demand a full description plus the reason why I wasn't told immediately. It was about eight inches by three, David informs me, off-white with dirty grey marks; and as I was sleeping soundly at the time he thought it was a shame to wake me. I am nevertheless quite resentful at having missed it. There is a distinct absence of visual stimuli at present.

We are not seeing as much of each other as usual either. We are both desperately tired and all we really want to do is sleep, so we have extended our dedicated watches and whoever is off watch goes back to bed until lunchtime. We have found in the past that after the first couple of days of a long passage our brains and bodies have adjusted to the broken sleep and we assume a natural rhythm. The present trying conditions, however, have left us exhausted.

One of the last things we purchased before setting out from England was a battery-operated kitchen alarm. It is small enough to slip into any pocket and during night passages we set it to go off at intervals of ten minutes. Having long ago timed the passage of super tankers from horizon to horizon, we settled on ten minutes as the optimum time between checks to avoid a collision.

At present I am so tired that for the last half of my final watches our little kitchen alarm goes off and not simply alerts me that it is time to make a check, but actually wakes me. I then go outside, make my 360°

inspection of the horizon, re-set the alarm, sit down and remember nothing more until it wakes me again ten minutes later. My head is like lead and my whole body aches. David's toothache is proving persistent and analgesics give little relief.

Wind direction is about as uncongenial as it can be. North-west through north to east would put the wind aft of our beam and be ideal. Instead it remains persistently south-west and on the nose. So we motor all day on low revs while we wait for the wind to change.

Tonight is very dark, the blackest of black, and we creep through the blackness as if we are the only creatures left alive on a dead planet. Midnight to midnight we cover only 33 miles.

Early Friday morning, while David is sleeping, a green plastic detergent bottle with a blue cap floats past. I don't wake him. After all, I wasn't given the opportunity to view that piece of polystyrene yesterday. But sometime later, when we are both awake and on deck, a flash of colour draws us to the rails. Below the surface of the water, for as far as the eye can see, there are skeins of what appear to be tiny electric-blue eggs. The colour is riveting. In amongst them tiny jellyfish, looking newly-hatched, maintain a precarious balance using their little frills against the roll and rush of the water.

The wind is still coming from the south-west, but getting weaker all the time. At 9am we decide our fuel supply is such that we need to do something drastic. Feeling we are now far enough away from the threat of pirates to tack in towards Africa we change course to get some drive from our sails. We turn the engine off, resolving to use one of them only twice a day, for the hour or so it takes to recharge *Voyager*'s batteries.

This new tactic pays off and engineless we manage to maintain our speed although not strictly on course. We stay on this tack for six hours and manage to cover 19 miles but by the end of it we are only four miles closer to our destination. David is not encouraged.

At least we have recovered our energy and our days now settle into a comfortable pattern. While I am asleep, after my last watch of the night, David listens to the BBC's half-hour news broadcast on World Service. When I get up, around 9am, we have breakfast together and he gives me the radio news highlights. We do chores during the morning, then prepare and eat lunch. Afterwards, if there are no further jobs to do apart from the washing up, we are at leisure and as long as the weather is amenable we spend the afternoons out in the cockpit, propped up on cushions reading, writing or sharing a crossword puzzle. We have our evening meal while watching the sun go down, at around 6.30, then I go to bed at 7pm leaving David to do the first watch of the night, which he combines with tuning in to the SSB radio at 8pm for Herb's weather forecast.

This morning I see a Leach's petrel close up for the first time, with the distinctive white V pattern down its black back and wings. It touches its feet to the water, dips its head to scoop up something and becomes airborne again immediately. At around eight inches long, and with a 19-inch wingspan, it seems a very small bird to live on the wing out here. Yet amazingly it has an even smaller cousin, the tiny storm petrel, with which we are destined to have a closer acquaintance in the not too distant future.

We are also visited by a solitary shearwater. It is a superb flier although, like the petrels, it is virtually helpless on land. Like them it also goes ashore only to breed, in burrows or among rocks, and even then under the cover of darkness which is why they are rarely seen except from seagoing vessels. Much larger and heavier than the petrels, and with a four-foot wingspan, the shearwater is using the air currents to fly just above the waves in long, graceful glides with stiffly outstretched wings. Petrels and shearwaters are the only birds we have seen since leaving Tenerife.

Around midday David notes the chart reference 23°26N. We have crossed the Tropic of Cancer and entered the tropics.

During the afternoon the wind drops to a barely discernible breeze and occasionally dies away altogether. By sunset we have stopped sailing and simply drift. In theory we are back to our original course but that means nothing under these conditions. The sails merely flap with the slight rocking of the boat. We are becalmed.

It is something not generally known to most modern sailors. Before the arrival of steam and diesel, however, anyone who went to sea could expect to be becalmed at some time. Its effect was indelibly imprinted on my child's mind thanks to the school board's enduring love affair with Samuel Taylor Coleridge's *The Rime of the Ancient Mariner*.

By killing the albatross, the poem's narrator had doomed his ship and fellow crew members, and even all these years later I still recall his evocation of the becalmed vessel:

> *Day after day, day after day,*
> *We stuck, nor breath nor motion;*

As idle as a painted ship
Upon a painted ocean.

Like the ancient mariner we have no idea when the wind is likely to return and a sort of listlessness sets in. Instead of reading or doing a few chores David and I merely slump in the cockpit and stare out onto a flat sea.

'We shall go quite mad, you know,' I tell him.

'It's only been a couple of hours,' he says.

My second watch of the night is very, very dark. Pitch black dark. As I turn my back on the tiny circle of light shed by the saloon's chart-table lamp and step out into the cockpit it is like falling into The Void. It is at such times that you ask yourself if being adrift on a 40 x 16-foot piece of fibreglass in thousands of square miles of sea is really a sensible thing to be doing. Tonight is the nearest I have ever come to sensory deprivation. There is nothing here except my consciousness. When I look down I can't even see myself. Then, in the preternatural silence, a few feet from our stern, a whale sends an explosion of air hurtling through its blowhole and I become momentarily unhinged.

A little while later the wind gets up. Perversely, despite our current desire to increase our speed, I should have preferred it to stay calm; because in the all-pervading darkness, and twitchy from the proximity of unseen whales, the imagination takes over. The wind begins to whip up the sea and the resulting roll of the boat brings up the horseshoe lifebuoy on the port side deck, right in front of my eyes and outlined by the eerie glimmer of phosphorous which has suddenly appeared around our topsides. For a few moments the looming black shape ceases to be a lifebuoy and becomes a ghoul from a horror movie. The worst thing now is to start thinking about alien abduction. At times like this I tend to bolt indoors for a bit.

When David takes over the watch again we are becalmed for the next four hours. During this period he becomes transfixed by the GPS. Its screen currently bears a dotted line representing our progress. The only time it shows us travelling towards our destination is when the engine is on. The rest of the time we seem to be drifting backwards, sideways, every which way except where we should be going.

Although he complains hardly at all, and performs all his tasks as usual, David's toothache is giving me cause for concern. The pain has extended to the whole of the right side of his jaw and down into his neck.

Apart from offering painkillers, and neck exercises to relax the muscles and help him sleep, there is little I can do.

Saturday's dawn is silver and a dozen shades of grey, from silvery white in the east where the sun is loitering, to the colour navies paint their battleships. There is every kind of cloud imaginable, too: flat, billowing, wispy mares' tails, shimmering mackerel and fluffy cumulus, but all of them in shades of grey. Grey everywhere, but sparkling in the east and incredibly beautiful. A Seascape in Grey and Silver. Whistler might have painted it.

Around 11am the wind fades altogether and in the next five hours the only time we make any progress – 2.8 miles – is when we run an engine to re-charge the batteries.

We are visited by a petrel and a shearwater again.

Finally in the late afternoon a light wind emerges from the west and albeit slowly we begin to make a little progress which is even in the right direction. From sunset yesterday to sunset today we get only 23 miles closer to our destination. The black line on the GPS, recording our drift and our battery charging looks like a bootlace tied into a ragged bow.

Sunset is at 6.30. The cloud cover is lighter than last night. The fixed stars are bright enough to be visible and there are some shooting stars. The bobbing masthead light of a yacht appears behind us and slowly, over a period of hours, overtakes us. Two commercial vessels pass on our starboard side heading north-west.

When David wakes me in the small hours, for my second watch of the night, he says that as he left the cockpit he could hear a whale breathing. This is troubling for three reasons. If you can hear a whale breathing it is a) on the surface; b) very close; and c) probably asleep. Being mammals, whales have to rise to the surface regularly for air. The explosive sound that comes from their blow holes is them clearing foul air from their lungs after all the oxygen has been used up. They are then ready to take in a supply of fresh air. As there has been no whoosh of stale air being expelled, and the foul smell that comes with it, the chances are that the whale we can hear is lying on the surface with its blowhole out of the water. This enables it to have a good long snooze without the inconvenience of periodically rising to the surface, emptying and refilling its lungs, and then sinking again.

Whales sleeping on the surface at night are a problem for yachts. A boat under sail makes little noise anyway but if the whale is asleep its first indication of the yacht's presence will be when it gets hit by it. It is worst with racing yachts because of their speed, and the impact can be enough to seriously injure or even kill the whale and destroy the yacht. The one consolation for our lamentable lack of speed at present is that while a collision might dent both the whale and us a little bit, it is not likely to be life-threatening to either.

We have no way of knowing what type of whale it is. It could be a relatively small Minke, a 50-foot Humpback or an 80-foot, 150-ton Blue. Or any other of the species which leave the Polar Regions annually to winter in warmer seas. There is nothing we can do in the darkness but hope for the best and keep plodding on and we gradually leave the sound of breathing behind.

Which is fortunate, there being no emergency services in the Atlantic. Help depends on whether you are close enough to another vessel that it can pick up your SOS on its VHF radio. As a rule of thumb, if you can see another boat you are within range of its VHF signal, supposing of course that someone is actually listening; and it is possible to spend days without seeing another vessel.

However, we do carry an Emergency Position-Indicating Radio Beacon. Once activated, an EPIRB sends out a signal to a satellite which is then directed to a search-and-rescue centre in Falmouth, England. This centre will then divert the nearest ship to you, but typically when it arrives it offers only one choice: to be taken off your boat and put ashore at its next port of call. If you refuse to abandon your boat, the ship will continue its journey without you.

Cloud cover gradually increases and the night becomes very dark again. With no moon or stars to relieve the darkness you become instantly aware of any illumination when it does appear. A small white light emerges, to the east of us, probably a yacht. You can usually tell because a heavy ship's light travels in a straight line except in the roughest weather while a yacht, by its relative smallness and lightness, gets buffeted up and down and sideways by sea and wind so that its light bobs about.

On David's last watch another yacht passes close enough for him to see that our fellow-traveller has his cockpit light on. Since he is overtaking us, he clearly has his engine on as well, because we are becalmed again.

17

Assorted Visitors

It is Sunday morning and the only things I can see are the planet Venus and a quarter moon. When dawn does come it is a reprise of yesterday except that instead of silver and shades of grey it is a Symphony in Silver and Blue. And breathtaking. At last the wind has gone to the north, which would be good for us if only it would strengthen, but unfortunately it is still very weak.

At 7.50 I suddenly notice a cargo ship on our port side, coming from the east and only about three miles off. It is rather worrying that I have not seen it until now and I am not even sleeping on watch. On the contrary, I have not simply caught up on my sleep but feel energised.

At noon David calculates that we are just about halfway to our destination. We had anticipated that by now we would have completed the whole passage. David's brother will be expecting to receive a telephone call about now from the Cape Verde Islands to say we have arrived, and begin to wonder why he hasn't.

Late afternoon a tanker passes to starboard, a mere two miles off and heading north; not long afterwards it is followed by a second. *Two* tankers *and* a cargo boat all on the same day! And as if that weren't excitement enough, between the second tanker and us is what looks like a loose buoy – either the navigation or weather kind – which appears to be travelling rapidly in the opposite direction to us. How or why we cannot say. It is almost as if it has some motive power of its own, but it can't have. If it is a buoy it will be made of steel and weigh several tons. Covered in seaweed and plunging forward like a monstrous wrecking ball it is not something with which you would want a close encounter. And at night, of course, you wouldn't even be aware of its existence until it hit you.

Some while later we spot water spouts directly ahead of us and go forward, David grabbing a camera. One thing we learned about whales on the southern coast of Spain was: change course to get a look at them and they will vanish; but keep your course and they will gravitate to a point directly ahead of you and wait for you to arrive so that *they* can have a look at *you*. Because whales are as interested by something suddenly appearing in their world as we are in ours. When you do get close to them, they begin to sink so that you pass over them. They will then pop up again a safe distance behind your stern. In this way they have observed your boat from four angles – from the side, in front, below and behind.

As we get closer, one-by-one they begin to sink as usual. All except the one lying exactly where our bows are headed. We get closer and closer until we can positively identify it. It is a sperm whale and around 60 feet long.

Its name comes from the spermaceti oil contained in cavities in its huge head which accounts for roughly a third of its overall length. Spermaceti was used to make candles, soap, cosmetics and machine oil until replaced by petroleum.

It was to obtain this valuable oil, along with other products, that these animals were slaughtered in vast numbers. Although thanks to its size and massive jaws the sperm whale could sometimes defend itself against whalers. In the most famous examples, a sperm whale attacked and sank the American whaling ship *Essex* in 1820; and thirty years later the *Ann Alexander*. The sinking of the *Essex*, and the killing of an albino sperm whale known as Mocha Dick which had fought off whalers for several decades, inspired Herman Melville's novel *Moby Dick*.

It is thought that the whale uses its spermaceti as a buoyancy aid as well as to execute rapid dives as deep as 3km, or nearly 10,000ft. Water at this depth is extremely cold, and spermaceti oil remains the only lubricant capable of keeping equipment functioning in the freezing conditions of space exploration.

We are now a couple of boat lengths away and on the verge of an incredible photograph. David aims the camera. I begin to panic. Why isn't it sinking? Is it sick? Dead? Asleep? One boat's length from it my nerve cracks and I bolt for the controls. David's camera jams and we never do get a picture. To add insult to injury, the moment I wrench the wheel violently to port to avoid impact with this great monster, it drops like a stone and all that is left on the surface are two huge, flat circles of spinning water where it had lain only moments before. The wretched creature has been playing chicken with us.

Sunset this evening is incredible, as if some celestial artist has taken the pink and gold light of the setting sun and used it to paint pictures in the sky. On the north-west horizon there is an island complete with palm trees, houses, hills and forests. While high in the eastern sky, the subject is a huge mountain range covered in snow above a wooded valley.

During the night, the planet Venus is so brilliant that the light it sheds on the sea is as bright as any moon. It is also a very starry night.

As our eighth day at sea dawns, the sky turns azure and all the stars vanish, although Venus and a narrow sliver of moon continue to shine. The sun rises in shimmering red and gold. Silhouetted against it, gliding slowly backwards and forwards on outstretched wings, is a solitary petrel.

The wind has increased a little and is now from the north-east, which is directly over our stern, so we have to bear off a little or the genoa flogs. But at least we are getting a slightly increased speed. The wind even reaches 10 knots briefly at times. Noon to noon we are 65 miles closer to our destination, so things are improving.

Since leaving the Canary Islands, *Voyager* has been following what is known as the Trade Wind Route. Traditionally, from late November until April, the Trade Winds blow clockwise in an oval shape in that area of the Atlantic Ocean between Central/North America and Europe/North Africa. Complementing this congenial wind is a gentle current flowing in the same direction and there is even a theory that, since both wind and water are with you, even if everything on your boat from rigging to rudder was ruined at the same time you would still, ultimately, albeit very slowly, fetch up on a Caribbean beach. It is not unknown for even abandoned yachts to do exactly that.

This is the same route that Christopher Columbus followed 500 years ago and mariners use it still. You travel south until roughly 20°N 30°W, then make a turn to starboard which takes you west to the Caribbean. And as you have entered the tropics, the weather is getting warmer. Accordingly, from as long ago as the days of the square-rigged sailing ships, received wisdom has been: 'Head south until the butter melts, then turn right for the Caribbean.'

For those of us from a chilly, over-achieving north *this* says it all. Ease. Warmth. Laid back. All that's needed to get you ready for the delights to come is Bob Marley in the background, a hammock slung across the foredeck and a long cold drink with a little parasol in it.

The only problem for us is that there have been no Trade Winds. No gentle current either. And no tropical warmth. Instead we've had lumpy seas, winds ranging from squalls to lengthy periods of nothing at all, and a distinct chill in the air. Whether the fault lies with El Niño, global warming or the start of the New Ice Age is anybody's guess, but it is frustrating.

We are about 300 miles off the African coast at present, opposite Mauritania. At 6.45 a not particularly impressive sun, sinking behind some rather mundane clouds, does something quite extraordinary and turns the whole of the western sky into red and gold molten lava.

It is a very dark night despite the stars.

Our ninth day dawns with us sailing due south. We should really be going south-west but the wind is preventing us. We also have heavy rolling waves which are much bigger than one might expect from the light winds we are experiencing, but which Herb says are the result of strong winds hundreds of miles to the north of us. He also says that we can expect these conditions – light winds and heavy seas – to last for the next three days. Our only sighting in 36 hours is a single light on the eastern horizon around 5am.

At daylight two petrels appear. I run inside for the binoculars to try and see if they are Leach's or storm petrels but by the time I get back they have disappeared. Something similar occurs about six hours later. The setting sun is an enormous silver disk which slowly disappears behind silver-grey haze and cloud leaving not the tiniest wisp of colour behind it.

And that's it for the day. Not even a small piece of polystyrene or an empty detergent bottle to excite the eye until 11.15 tonight as we change over the watch. With both of us on deck we use the opportunity to shift the sails and change course. We have been on our present one, with the wind over our port quarter, long enough now to be able to bring it onto our starboard quarter and head directly for the island of St Vincent and its capital, Mindelo.

As we sit together in the cockpit and chat for a few minutes, before David goes off to bed, a bright light travels on a shallow trajectory from east to west very fast and low in the sky. It is behind our backs, on our port side, but as I turn my head towards David to ask him something I catch sight of it out of the corner of my right eye.

In shape it resembles an enormous airliner. It has great holes in its side through which you can look into the blazing inferno of its interior and it is being propelled by a huge fiery red tail. It is also very obviously losing height until it is so low that at one moment I have to peer around David to continue following its progress.

Then suddenly its pace slows, and its fiery red tail diminishes, until it comes to a stop directly off our stern and the tail vanishes altogether. How far away, it is impossible to tell. It could be less than a mile. It might be much more. On a dark sea there is nothing by which to judge distance. What makes it seem close is being able to see through the gaping apertures in its shell into the roaring furnace of its core.

After hovering for a few moments, it breaks into roughly three sections and the great blazing pieces fall into the sea. The middle part is the biggest and drops first, leaving the outer ones momentarily suspended in space before they too drop into the sea, accompanied by gobbets of liquid fire. The whole thing is probably over in less than twenty seconds. Neither of us says anything. We are too startled. Reflecting on it later, we suppose it must have been something from a space programme, burning up as it re-entered the Earth's atmosphere.

It is some time after David has gone to bed before it occurs to me that, whatever it was, even a small alteration in our respective routes could have put *Voyager* directly under it when it fell. And no-one would ever have known what happened to us. It totally changes your perspective on all the times you've heard some expert in Houston saying blithely over the airwaves, 'Oh, it's perfectly safe. It won't hurt anybody. It'll just fall into the sea.'

As I go about my duties during the rest of my watch – checking the horizon and the instruments and filling in the log – I reflect that this has also been a prime example of that provoking adage: *Be careful what you wish for, because it might happen.* Earlier this evening I had joked about so little happening that an empty plastic bottle floating past our hull would be a major event. Within hours, but for the Grace of God and a mile or two, we could have been flat-packed on the seabed under tons of molten space debris.

Today is Wednesday and our tenth day at sea. A check first thing this morning shows that we are still 194 miles from Mindelo and there is still no sign of the Trade Winds or the current which normally accompanies them. Instead, as Herb predicted, the wind is a light nor'easter combined with big rollers. Except that at present we have rollers coming at us from both the north-east *and* the south-east which is making for a very confused sea. And when two of them collide just where *Voyager* happens to be, it makes for a very bumpy ride.

When the sun set yesterday evening it was a huge silver disk surrounded by silvery haze and cloud. It looks exactly the same when it returns this morning, as if it has been lurking just below the horizon all night and re-emerged for duty without bothering to change its clothes.

It sheds no colour, no warmth and little light and doesn't so much rise as float unsteadily upwards and sideways like a slowly deflating helium balloon. By 8am it is too bright to look at directly but there is still no warmth or colour, rather like a winter sunrise at home.

Half an hour later I am absently gazing at the water and think I see a flock of small birds flying away from our hull. But when I look more closely I can see that they are not birds at all. I have just seen my first-ever flying fish. There are about a dozen of them, around four inches long with black backs, silver bellies and transparent wings and they fly just above the waves for some distance before disappearing into the sea.

At 10am, when David starts the port engine to charge the batteries, a red warning light comes on. We have a broken fan belt. He fits a new one. A cargo boat heading north is the only traffic we see all day. But we should like it to be thoroughly understood by the Universe, please, that flying fish, a cargo boat and a broken fan belt is *more* than enough excitement for us after last night's fiery visitor and that we do not desire anything more. Although we do achieve 103 nautical miles in 24 hours which is the best we have achieved so far.

Thursday morning, just after dawn, a tiny land bird flies alongside us, close to our starboard rigging despite being so many miles from land. Whether it has come from the Cape Verde Islands, or is heading there, it shows no interest in landing on *Voyager* and I find that my admiration for the stamina of very small birds just keeps on growing.

There are also an enormous amount of flying fish today. They really are extraordinary. For a start, why do they do it? There are no insects to catch. And it can't be that pleasurable because they land with the kind of agonising belly-flop that put me off diving into a swimming pool for years. But they *do* do it. All day. Thousands of them, resembling sardines with wings, from tiddler to small trout-size. They steer with their tails dropped into the water. The tiny ones go briefly in a straight line, while the mature ones curve and dive, resurface and curve again over a distance of around 30 feet before crashing into a wave and disappearing from view.

The wind becomes lighter and moves to the east.

A check of the log shows that in eleven days at sea we have sighted only fourteen other vessels: seven as navigation lights at night plus the yacht with its cockpit light on, and six commercial ships during daylight.

18

Mindelo

Today is Friday 10th December. Light easterlies persist but now we are close enough to Mindelo to be able to put on an engine without fear of running out of fuel. At 2am we can smell land in the darkness. By 6am we can see lights from the direction of the islands. An hour and a half later we can identify São Vicente. Although we entered the tropics a week ago it has been very cool out at sea, with a high reaching only 22°C. But as we enter the big bay that leads to Mindelo Harbour, despite heavy cloud and no visible sun, the tropical heat hits us.

Within three hours of our first sight of land we are anchoring off Mindelo, capital of São Vicente and one of the ten largest islands making up the Cape Verde group. This archipelago takes its name from Senegal's Cape Verde, or Green Cape, which is the westernmost point of the African continent. Sadly the islands are no longer green due to prolonged drought. This particular one was discovered in 1462 by captains in the service of Henry the Navigator. The date was 22nd January, the feast day of St Vincent, and so it was named.

A former Portuguese colony, the Cape Verde Islands gained independence in 1975. Of the ten islands, São Vicente is the one which has traditionally had the most contact with the outside world. Originally this was through American whaling fleets, which took crewmen from here. Later from British bunkering – the loading of imported coal – onto Atlantic steam ships from the mid-19th century until the mid-20th.

At 10.30am, when we enter the port, our first impression is that some of them are still here, for Mindelo's harbour is home to a number of large, rusting hulks. Mother Nature, however, has a way of mitigating even the worst insults we humans inflict on her. Along with a number of self-seeded shrubs the hulks have been colonised by herons and little egrets. The latter, with their blistering white plumage and long black legs are as slender and graceful as ballerinas just so long as you ignore their feet, which are the avian equivalent of over-large, yellow wellies. But then, it is those enormous yellow feet which provide the stability that produces their gracefulness, even over slippery mud or rocks.

A garrulous, rather demanding man in an ancient dinghy appears from nowhere and says that for US$10 he will help us anchor. All we really want is a little peace in which to do it calmly and quietly by ourselves once our brains have stopped rolling from side to side, even though *Voyager* herself has stopped doing it. We tell him we're fine thank you and he rows away. We find a suitable place with the right depth, drop our hook and dutifully raise our quarantine or Q flag up our mast.

A yellow quarantine flag should be raised by any vessel arriving in a foreign country although yachtsmen from EU countries tend not to bother when visiting another EU country. Nor do the authorities. But this is the first non-EU country we have entered and we dutifully dig out our yellow duster and hoist it as a Q flag.

Its meaning, according to Reed's Nautical Companion is: 'My vessel is healthy and I request free pratique (dealings with the port). This is used universally as a request for Customs clearance when a vessel is entering a foreign port from another country and also when returning to her own country from abroad.'

The flag's purpose is to alert the authorities that the boat has not yet registered its presence with them and technically – although many countries do not bother about this either – no-one except its skipper is supposed to go ashore until the necessary documentation has been completed. Along with our Q flag we also hoist a Cape Verde Islands courtesy flag.

Then we unstrap the dinghy from the foredeck, lower it into the water and set off to clear in. Once that is done, our priorities are to find a dentist, arrange to fill our fuel tank and get our staysail repaired.

As we near the beach a large number of young men become visible, standing around talking or lying in the sand. After the eagerness of the man to help us anchor, we suspect a rush to mind our dinghy. However, according to our cruising guide, close to the beach a German has received permission to anchor an old freighter which he has effectively converted into a small floating marina. Yachts can tie up there and it has showers, a washing machine and water. For 100 Cape Verde escudos, or one US dollar, you can also leave your dinghy and the slender young African who is running the place ferries you to a small jetty on the beach.

'When you want to come back,' he tells us, 'just give me a wave and I'll come and get you.' We ask him where we can get a sail repaired and he points to a little French boat anchored nearby.

The Capitania dos Port and the Policia Maritima share an office in a large building across the road from the beach. As we enter a man observes us wearing deck shoes and clutching our ship's papers, gives us a wide grin and says, 'First floor.' A woman ahead of us on the stairs turns and gives us an encouraging look, leads us unasked to the first floor landing, then nods at the relevant door.

This friendly interest and polite concern for your needs is a feature of Mindelo's general population whose approach to life appears in our very limited experience to be African. Its bureaucracy, on the other hand, seems to be based on the Portuguese model with which we have become familiar in the past year, with all transactions perpetrated in triplicate and twenty-four hours' notice required if you wish to buy fuel.

The large open office has a deep counter running from wall to wall where you enter. Behind it are a number of unmanned desks and two clerks who open cupboards and inspect the contents of box files without any sense of urgency. At the open window, a generously-proportioned officer (whether the Harbour Master or the chief of Maritime Police, we do not know) sits like a statue of Buddha gazing out over the harbour below him. Very occasionally he drags his heavily-lidded eyes, briefly and tiredly, from the window to the two male office staff and then stares out over the harbour again as though something extraordinary is imminent.

Completing the necessary forms with one of his subordinates is a time-consuming business, because our vital statistics are pecked out one letter at a time by an index finger on an elderly, sit-up-and-beg manual typewriter which has two sheets of carbon paper between three printed forms wrapped around its roller.

In one of the longueurs between questions, while the man behind the counter tap-taps our details onto yet another triple-decker of forms and carbon paper, we ask the officer where we can find a dentist. He writes down a name and address for us and suggests we take a taxi.

By the time our documentation has been completed here, it is too late to get to Immigration, down on the harbour's main breakwater, before its office closes for lunch. So we decide to leave that until the afternoon and go to the dentist first.

We are glad of the taxi, not just because of the distance but because of the heat and the steep uphill climb. The spotless waiting room, with its chilly air-conditioning and television set, is a world away from the hot, dusty streets outside. The surgery itself is immaculate, if somewhat short on equipment. It has two dentist's chairs and a drill. No x-ray machine or anything else. The two dentists, a man and a woman, have virtually no English and we speak no Portuguese.

The man examines David's teeth by gently tapping them with a small hammer. He consults with the woman and she taps David's teeth, too. The man then explains, mostly in eloquent but rather painful-looking mime, that David has an abscess and will need root canal work under three teeth. He makes it clear that the abscess will have to be cleaned up before the root canal work can be undertaken. Apart from the time this is going to take, from their expressions they are not keen to do the job. They ask where he intends going after leaving the Cape Verde Islands.

'Trinidad,' says David.

They look relieved and say, 'Good dentists in Trinidad.'

We shall set off on Monday.

The man writes a prescription for antibiotics along with instructions on how many tablets a day to take and for how many days. We pay the bill, which is incredibly small, and go in search of a pharmacy.

Currently the Cape Verde Islands is classed as the poorest country in Africa based on a scale which uses a nation's resources as its criteria for measurement. It has no agriculture, no mineral deposits and its main source of income disappeared when ships stopped using coal and could carry enough diesel on board to be able to sail straight past. Most of the population here is under 30 years of age and much of the male part of it seems to be out and about. The streets, like the beach, are awash with young men, not a few of them in football shirts given to them by people passing through or visiting home, and all of them are thin. In fact, with the exception of the man presiding over the Capitania dos Port, everybody in Mindelo seems to be thin.

One man, somewhat older than the rest, hears us talking to one another in the street and speaks to us in English. It turns out that some years ago he had worked in the shipbuilding industry at Birkenhead, just across the Mersey from Liverpool where *Voyager* is registered. After a chat he gives us directions to the pharmacy.

On the way there we find an ATM with a policeman guarding it, who says not to count our money in an obvious way and to put it away out of sight quickly. We've never used an ATM with an armed guard on it before.

The pharmacy has a long wooden counter and wooden shelves and drawers lining its walls like the old country shops of my childhood. The pharmacist speaks English and, given the uncertainties of our situation, I ask her to sell us double the ten-day course of antibiotics in case the abscess flares up again before David can get proper attention.

At the *post restante* counter in the big general Post Office the clerk asks our name and then pushes a large box filled with envelopes across the counter at us. We rummage through it until we find the one addressed to us but when we show it to her and offer some ID she is not remotely interested.

To make a telephone call to England we have to book the use of a wooden booth against a far wall which contains a large, old-fashioned, black handset in it. Even with the door propped open, the booth is very hot. We then pay for the call at the counter. It costs a small fortune but at least Tony is pleased to know we may still be around to enjoy another Christmas.

Our next stop is at the Shell office to book diesel. We are assigned the first delivery on Monday at 10.30am. We are to tie up on the commercial dock at the black and yellow Shell sign. From the fuel office it is then only a short walk, along with many affable groups of young men, to the main breakwater and Immigration.

There are hundreds more men waiting in lines at the docks in the hope of being taken on for work. A few are lying on the ground and look as if they have been waiting all day. But, as everywhere else here, there is no sense of menace at the sudden eruption into their midst of two people from the white, affluent West. Not even vague resentment. Quite the contrary. You actually feel welcome. The armed guard on the ATM notwithstanding, whether it is on the beach, on the streets or here at the docks, these young men smile at you. Ask for directions, and they are polite and helpful and ask where you are from. And when they hear you are from England, say, 'Manchester United! Best team in the world!' A sentiment not over-enthusiastically received by the Aston Villa supporter in their midst.

There is a row of open-fronted wooden sheds down the left-hand side of the breakwater. Inside each of them a man in uniform sits at an ancient manual typewriter tapping in the personal details of the job-seeker standing in front of him. The place we want, one of the men waiting in line explains, is in one of the wooden offices on the opposite side of the pier. He points out the relevant one.

The official inside it contemplates our yacht registration. 'Liverpool,' he says, 'has a fine team, but Manchester United is the best in the world.' I smile and nod, and don't even glance at David. Villa just lost at home to Newcastle.

The amount of English spoken here is at first surprising for a former Portuguese colony, but for a century there was a strong British presence due to the bunkering of coal from British mines into Atlantic steamers. And working on foreign ships now, or finding work abroad and sending money home, is the only option for many. These islands are the first place we have ever visited where the majority of people are so poor and it makes us very sad. Not the absence of material goods, but the lack of opportunity; of young lives spent waiting on a dock in blazing heat in the hope of a day's work and doubtless a very small day's pay. And, most of all, the brevity of those lives.

At the same time you know that there are people far more deprived and at risk than those on this island. But you are here, not there, and you look at the wide smiles and thin bodies and the occasional football shirt and wonder at the unifying force of football and a shared language.

Somewhat weary we stand on the beach and wave to the young man on the freighter/marina who comes to pick us up and reunite us with our dinghy. Our last act of the day is to collect our small staysail off *Voyager* and take it to the little French boat anchored nearby. The woman on board inspects the damage and says she will have it done by Saturday afternoon.

Saturday morning we take a turn around the town before doing some essential shopping. Mindelo retains its graceful colonial buildings but they have gone to seed. Its high-maintenance Portuguese mosaic pavements have also crumbled, although the roads are well-maintained. A few new buildings have gone up among the old, banks mostly and a hotel.

We walk across the seafront, down a wide street into a large square busy with card schools and fish stalls. The men smile when they pass. The women look at you. The children are nice. Thin, light-brown dogs lie curled up in the shade. There are rows of small, neat houses fronting onto the pavements. Like the pharmacy, the shops are traditional: a bread shop, neighbouring meat shops selling chicken in one, beef next door and a covered fruit and vegetable market.

The supermarket is a more recent arrival, basic and DIY-style. As one would expect, the range is limited but also surprisingly expensive, even for an island, and especially for such a poor one. An unexpected find, and something I haven't seen in years, is a packet of six little cone-shaped sponge cakes known to me as coconut pyramids.

There is a wide disparity between the old and the emerging new here. We have lunch in the modern hotel's bistro. There are some luxury goods in the shops, like the huge, ultra-modern cooker sitting incongruously in the centre of an old-fashioned hardware shop. Nevertheless, everything here, including the most basic, is expensive. It is no wonder that so much of the wage-earning population works abroad.

For those who remain it is not only a life of limitations but of physical risk. From our cockpit we watch a ferry arrive. It is so rusty that it is hardly distinguishable from the hulks around it. It is listing to one side and groaning with the number of passengers arriving from the other islands, many of them poorer even than this one. And you wonder if, sooner or later, you will read about a ferry disaster off the Cape Verde Islands with a horribly familiar catastrophic loss of life. And you understand as never before why so many people in very poor countries take such deadly risks to become illegal immigrants.

We stop off on the way back to *Voyager* to collect our staysail but it is not ready. Sunday evening for definite, she says.

19

Preparing for the Crossing

On Sunday morning, given the failure of our staysail, and the voyage ahead of us, David does another masthead inspection. Fortunately our mast has steps up it so it is not a problem.

Then he turns his attention to the water maker. Water makers have been around since the 1960s and, like Teflon, are a by-product of the space race. But it is not something we would have installed ourselves. Like everybody else we should have loaded up with large plastic containers and bottled water. But like the steps up the mast and the radar, *Voyager* already had the water maker when we bought her.

The average yacht making an Atlantic crossing would be capable of carrying less than two weeks' water under normal usage. Therefore it not only has to be used with restraint during the voyage, but quite a large part of the supplies taken on board prior to setting out will be bottled water and/or plastic containers of tap water stowed on deck. Some yachtsmen also set up elaborate systems for catching rainwater during a long voyage and for channelling it directly into their water tanks.

We head out to sea until we are clear of pollution and make our first attempt at converting seawater into drinking water. We have not used it before because Europe's coastlines are so polluted and clean water was always available on tap.

David spends ages crouched in the stern locker where the valves prove resistant. Ultimately, with the help of a little oil, brute force and some choice language, they free up and the pump begins to work. The process is simple enough. Seawater is pushed through three sizes of filter to get rid of contaminants and then into the desalinator which removes the salt. The result is excellent and very drinkable. You also have the benefit of knowing where the water came from (well away from habitation) and that it goes into your tanks by the shortest possible route (avoiding contaminated equipment).

It is hot and by the time he is finished David looks tired. Fortunately the pain in his jaw has been reduced to a dull ache thanks to the antibiotics. I am concerned, nevertheless, having once read about someone who died in his prime when poison from an infected tooth was blamed for a fatal heart attack.

On our way back into the harbour a local boat sails in ahead of us. Its main resembles Jacob's coat of many colours until we realise that it has been patched so many times with whatever fabric has come to hand, that little of the original white canvas remains.

We collect our staysail at dusk.

On Monday morning we make an early start. We have a lot to do. The first job is to put up the repaired staysail. After that we make *Voyager* as secure as we can against big seas.

We put the storm boards over the front windows, lay out a safety line and the warps for the drogue. We put the tarpaulin handy in case a window gets smashed and when we return from our final trip into Mindelo we shall lash the dinghy upside down on the foredeck. Finally, when we leave the fuel dock, the fenders will be stowed away in a locker so that there is nothing loose bouncing around the decks.

Then we take a last trip into town in the dinghy. Since we are going ashore anyway, we go first to the main breakwater to make sure we know where the black and yellow fuel distribution point is, alongside which the Shell official has told us to berth for refuelling. We figure it will probably be easier to find on foot than from *Voyager*'s deck if the quay should be obscured by other boats. We walk the length of what turns out to be a deserted dock, twice, but still can't find anything remotely black and yellow and there is no-one around to ask.

So we carry on to our most essential stop: the Capitania dos Port to complete the necessary disembarkation formalities and get our ship's papers back. Although the office is empty apart from us, after putting in our request we have a long wait on a bench in the corridor outside. Ultimately we are handed a small printed form with the barest of details filled in by hand. Then we sit and wait some more, to pay for it, at the accounts office next door.

We go to the post office to send a reply to a friend's letter received in the package we collected from here on Saturday, and then to a large modern bank to collect cash for the diesel we are going to buy. I'm not sure if I find it intimidating or just plain silly to look up above the counter clerk's head and count seven security cameras pointed at us. Our last stop is the bread shop. Then we return to *Voyager,* haul up the dinghy, lash it to the foredeck, weigh anchor, stow it away and motor to the quay in good time for our 10.30am appointment.

As I throw a mooring rope around a bollard a large piece of concrete falls from the quay and crashes into the water. Fortunately it misses our hull on the way down. Once tied up we mount another search for the black and yellow distribution point but still can't find it. Ten thirty arrives. Sometime after eleven David sets off for the Shell office.

While he is gone a very thin man arrives and slides his hand out of the pocket of his ill-fitting trousers. He opens his palm and offers for sale three minute tomatoes. He is replaced by another man bearing the kind of brush which in a more genteel age would have been used to sweep crumbs off a tablecloth. He seems to be offering to clean our boat. Like his predecessor, he is very thin and has that kind of heartbreaking smile which despite stretching from ear-to-ear nevertheless has little hope in it.

A thin, exhausted-looking dog comes and curls up on the dock opposite *Voyager.* I throw it some food scraps which it ignores. When a man wearing a hard hat arrives and opens a lock-up the dog uncurls and wanders over to him. The man fills his hat with water from a nearby tap, the dog drinks it gratefully and then curls up again.

David returns. There is a delay. When the official finally arrives he says we are in the wrong place and must move to the black and yellow distribution point. We look at him expectantly. He frowns at us, then walks a couple of metres further down the quay and points at his feet. We move *Voyager* back a couple of metres. Then another man, in overalls, arrives and the elusive distribution point turns out to be a very small metal plate flush with the dock and covered with concrete dust like the rest of the quay. But when the man in overalls brushes away the dust, and we stare at it really hard, it might once have had black and yellow paint on it. He lifts the metal plate, pulls out a hose, and we fill our diesel tank.

We cast off at 1.30pm local time and embark on our longest-ever voyage.

THE ATLANTIC

20

A Vast Empty Sea

There is hazy sun and a very light wind. Since the wind also keeps changing direction we have the engines on for a couple of hours to make sure we are well clear of the islands before nightfall.

Early evening David tunes into Herb. From the yachts reporting to him, David estimates that one called *Amber* is about a day ahead of us and will be an ideal boat for him to listen out for nightly, since its weather should be similar to ours. Initially this does not appear to be very helpful since *Amber* is enjoying a 10–15 knot following wind while we have 5 knots on the nose. But within a couple of hours our own fluctuating wind also makes its final shift of the day – to the east, like *Amber*'s. David hopes, within the next couple of broadcasts, to identify several other boats, especially one behind us, thereby enabling him to establish a comprehensive picture of prevailing weather patterns.

We sail throughout the night except for the couple of hours between 9 and 11pm when the wind becomes too light. The sky is mostly clear with just a few clouds and shooting stars every few minutes.

Yet when I take over the watch at 5am we are becalmed in a darkness so intense that it seems to have a presence all its own. It feels as if it is pressing in against the boat and that only an act of will on my part is going keep it at bay for the next three hours. As I take a reluctant step further out into the cockpit an even closer threat makes itself apparent when something scrabbles in the corner beside my left foot.

I have always hated the dark and for a few seconds, standing here in this overwhelming pitch blackness, I experience what I can only describe as primeval fear; a moment of morbid dread of some unimaginable horror about to reach out and touch me. Then common sense reasserts itself and another sort of horror takes its place. A rat! From those rotting hulks in Mindelo Harbour, perhaps. Or the fuel dock. As well as strong swimmers, rats are adept at climbing anchor chains and mooring ropes.

David has not yet gone to bed and my shriek of revulsion brings him running with the torch. In its small circle of light, a storm petrel ducks its head, fluffs its wings and huddles closer into the corner in a doomed attempt to make its blackness invisible against what is now, thanks to the torchlight, a startlingly white background.

Smaller than a blackbird, but with a slightly larger wingspan, like the Leach's petrel and shearwater that visited us on the passage to Mindelo, storm petrels are only seen ashore when breeding or driven there by particularly bad weather, hence the name. This one probably collided with our rigging while napping on the wing and then landed in confusion. Its round head and a distinct lack of sleekness about the feathers make it look particularly vulnerable. Weighing only an ounce, the storm petrel seems an impossibly small bird to withstand the Atlantic's ferocious autumn gales. Yet surprisingly its lifespan can be as much as 20 years compared to a garden blackbird's five.

It doesn't seem to be injured – its legs and wings all appear to work – and we see no point in terrifying it further by trying to inspect it more closely. So David switches off the torch, turns on an engine to get *Voyager* moving again, and goes off to bed. I withdraw into the saloon, leaving the little bird to recover from its shock. To help this recovery along, when I go out into the cockpit every ten minutes to make my inspection of the horizon for other vessels, rather than walk close to where it is huddled against the cockpit sole I climb up onto the seating instead. And in the process of minimising the bird's fear of me, I quite forget my own dread of the surrounding darkness.

The petrel, too, begins to recover its equilibrium, and at one stage even hops to the companionway doors with a view to an exploratory mission into the saloon. There it eyes me speculatively as I sit in the tiny glow of the chart table lamp. I don't want to seem inhospitable but I have to shoo it away. A black bird wandering about in a black interior is a recipe for disaster in terms of the little bird's safety. Not to mention its potential effect on our pale blue upholstery. I don't know what part of a seabird's diet it is that produces that particular brown stain but, whatever it is, it never washes out.

So the bird returns to its corner and remains there, quiet but alert. After a further half an hour it begins to make its way to the stern, in small stages, pausing between times to gaze about as if absorbing the features of this totally alien world into which it has fallen. Although it probably has more to do with the fact that it is unused to walking and can only manage a few steps at a time. After a good rest, however, and with its fear overcome, it is ready to return from whence it came. It flutters and flaps up onto the afterdeck and then it hops down the two steps onto our stern, around the corner of the port cabin and out of sight.

It is such a very black night that I do not see it take off. But when David comes on watch I clip on a safety line and go to the stern to see if it is still on board. Happily there is no sign of it. It is back on the wing where it belongs, out in a vast empty sea.

That brief image of a tiny dark figure in a circle of light evokes another, because night watches encourage the mind and the memory to roam. The last time I visited the National Portrait Gallery in London one of its rooms contained an oil painting of a man called Max Wall. He was a comedian from the English music hall tradition who successfully made the transition into the new mass medium of television, which was where as a child I first saw him in the 1950s. He also became a serious actor but continued to perform his popular one-man comedy shows wearing his distinctive black costume of jacket, tights and heavy workman's boots.

Towards the end of his life in 1990 an artist did a series of oil paintings of him. The one in the National Portrait Gallery was small and monochrome and in sharp contrast with the much larger canvases, often in sumptuous colour, that surrounded it. Its background was black: the darkened auditorium. In the foreground was a white circle: the spotlight. And in the centre of this white circle, looking very tiny, was Max in his trademark stage costume of black jacket, tights and boots. So simple. Yet it captured so eloquently the solitariness of a solo entertainer, on a brightly-lit stage, performing to an invisible audience.

I hadn't thought of this picture in years until we left land behind us for the first time. For no matter how large the ocean, what you can actually see of it is unexpectedly small. This is because standing in your cockpit, at sea level, on a clear day, the horizon is only about four miles away. In poor visibility, of course, it is even less. What is even more unexpected is that the horizon itself is round, because there is no coastline to give it a straight edge. So there is your boat, in the middle of a perfect but surprisingly small circle – as small and solitary as Max Wall in his spotlight – with an enormous, unseen auditorium beyond.

Being able to see only a short distance out here is probably a blessing, because if you could look out over vast distances, and all you could see was a boundless expanse of water in every direction, I think it would be a fairly simple matter to go stark, staring mad.

Only occasionally does this huge, unseen auditorium make itself felt. Usually it is a clear, moonless night that does it; when the Planets and the Fixed Stars pulsate, the Milky Way winks two hundred billion stars at you and your mind turns to troubling thoughts about Infinity. Another, more prosaic, reminder occurs tonight when I do the log.

Mindful of our feathered guest I have nevertheless gathered all the data from the cockpit instruments located just above its small round head, plus the GPS above the chart table, and entered them into the logbook as usual, and am now about to mark our position on the chart. I do this by taking the latitude and longitude provided by the GPS, locating the point where they meet each other and marking it in pencil with a small cross. I then draw a line between my latest cross and the previous one so that we end up with a continuous line from our departure point to our present location. By this simple method you can see at a glance your boat's current position and whether or not you are deviating from your course.

Charts come in all sizes. This one is very large, much larger than our chart table, and is folded into four. The land on it is coloured beige and the water is white. What is showing on the quarter of the chart that is currently uppermost is the north-west coast of Africa and the Cape Verde Islands. This fills much of the available space in beige with just a little bit of white – representing the Atlantic Ocean – to the left of São Vicente, the island we left yesterday afternoon.

Naturally, when your pencil line reaches the fold, you have to turn over the chart. When I turn this one over I simply sit and stare at it. At all the white space. At the two thousand miles of nothing but water ahead of us. And suddenly the chart does what the small round horizon cannot do. It makes me comprehend in no uncertain terms what a tiny speck on an immense sea we really are. It is more than my mind can cope with at present, sitting alone in the darkness with only a pinprick of light from the chart table lamp, and I turn the chart back over to the way it was.

When David comes back up a couple of hours later, to take over the watch, I tell him that I will of course continue to record the data from the instruments and GPS every hour during my watches but should be grateful if he would take over the daily responsibility for pencilling in our position as I'd rather not look at the chart for the time being.

When the wind returns it is light and variable, shifting about until finally settling at east-nor'east. This is a good direction for us but from time to time it gets so weak we still need an engine on.

Today is Tuesday and our second day at sea. We are experiencing much larger waves than one would expect from the present wind strength, but according to Herb there are gales six or seven hundred miles to the north.

Unfortunately the light wind and this big rolling sea is not a good combination. The roll of the boat keeps making the genoa flap, and whatever small amount of wind it takes in is rapidly spilled out again. The result is that in twenty-four hours we have covered only 84 miles. At this rate, far from enjoying its combined New Year/Millennium celebrations our estimated time of arrival at Trinidad is currently 6th January.

Around midday, there is a huge bulk carrier to the south-west of us, probably headed for Brazil. This is the only vessel we have seen in the twenty-four hours we have been at sea.

In the afternoon there is a lull in the sea swell so we take the opportunity of starting up the water maker for the first time in earnest. It is not something you can do in a rough sea as the roll gives the unit an inconsistent pressure which prevents it from removing all the salt. After running it for a little while the water it produces tastes very good and we deem it fit to go into the tanks.

It has been 26°C and sunny here during the day and the sky tonight is full of shooting stars. Usually, at the start of night passages, it is the second watch that I have difficulty completing. Tonight I crave my bed by the end of the first one.

21

Life at Sea

Over the next few days the wind settles into a steady direction but the rolling sea continues to spill it from the sails keeping conditions bumpy and slow; although we do gradually pick up half a knot of current which helps increase our speed a little. Meanwhile, our days are enlivened by flying fish and our night watches by shooting stars. There is also an indignant squawking overhead at 3am one morning as an inattentive shearwater collides with our rigging, its white underside turned green by our masthead light. It soon recovers its equilibrium and flies on.

Aston Villa loses to West Ham in the quarter finals of the League Cup. Southgate missed a penalty.

One night there is a half moon so bright you feel you could read by it, but it is soon consumed by cloud. A ship passes from north to south on the horizon ahead of us; only the second boat seen so far. For a couple of days we get runs of over 100 miles a day despite the continuing big sea but by Friday, our fifth day out, the wind has begun to shift again and get weaker.

Herb says that these big rollers which are making life so uncomfortable out here are being generated by the gales currently hovering off the Canary Islands, a thousand miles away, and due to hit those islands this weekend. They will be the second series of gales to hit the Canaries since we left them, but so serious this time that Herb is suggesting that any yachtsmen wanting to set off from there should not even think about leaving until Monday.

No responsible sailor throws refuse overboard, even all the way out here. But since we no longer have the dinghy on the davits to use as a skip, we are storing our gash bags in the chain locker. Given the present confused and lumpy sea, carrying them forward requires David to clip on his safety harness. It would be particularly ironic if *Voyager*'s refuse was dutifully stowed for proper disposal upon arrival, but in so doing her skipper got tossed overboard.

During refuse duty one morning he finds a tiny flying fish on the foredeck, only one and a half inches (4cm) from nose to tail tip. It could never have flown so high on its own miniscule wings and must have been carried up on deck by one of the large waves constantly pounding us. A huge one over the starboard quarter today drenches the galley and the starboard bed. We mop up the galley and dry the bedding out on deck in the sunshine.

There is a dazzling half moon tonight but it is very dark in the early hours of the morning. Sometimes the totality of the darkness, after all that moonlight, simply astounds you.

David gets the world headlines and UK news on BBC World Service through headphones at the chart table each morning and then gives me the highlights over coffee and biscuits out in the cockpit. He does it because I have ears like Radar, the character in the American TV series *M*A*S*H*, who could hear the helicopters bringing in the wounded long before anybody else. Similarly, I hear sounds well before David does. The downside is that headphones concentrate so much static, crossed channels, people who go down into the basements beside BBC recording studios and chop up tea chests and other extraneous noises that my ears, or my brain, have difficulty separating them.

The temperature is around 26°C so it is shorts and T-shirts until nightfall and sometimes beyond.

We are using the water maker to keep our tanks filled and also the seawater pump on the galley sink. The latter is not something you would ever want to use close to shore because of pollution, but out here the water is probably as clean as it gets and ideal for rinsing crockery and pans before washing them in fresh soapy water, as well as flushing the sinks to keep them fragrant.

A cargo ship crosses the horizon from south-west to north-east at around 6pm. Another passes from west to east at around 10pm – only four vessels sighted in six days. And I put some laundry in to soak before going to bed. This has not been an eventful passage so far.

Inevitably people are going to ask what on earth you do on a long voyage like this. The answer is you eat, you sleep and you keep yourselves and your boat clean. Without electrical appliances, and on a rolling sea, housework and laundry take longer and require more physical effort. For instance, where you once walked briefly behind a vacuum cleaner, now you wield a dustpan and brush, on your knees, while intermittently head-butting the furniture. This in turn creates a quantity of dust everywhere which also needs removing from a living space inhabited by someone with a serious dust allergy.

As for laundry, apart from overnight soaking before rubbing through with hard laundry soap, hand washing also requires quite a lot of rinsing and wringing. Here also, the fresh water provided by the water maker is a boon because, as well as being resistant to soap, salt water rapidly destroys all forms of elasticity so that pretty soon your underclothes and swimwear droop most unbecomingly.

In between times you stand your watches, keep a regular eye on the weather, the horizon, the chart, the boat and all its equipment. You play backgammon, Scrabble and chess or share a crossword puzzle. And you sink joyfully into new books, revisit old favourites and lift the covers of those worthy tomes you've always intended to read, or previously failed to finish. For David: *War and Peace* and *Moby Dick*. For me: *Moby Dick* and *The Brothers Karamazov*. For entertainment during our watches we have a Walkman and a selection of audio books, radio plays, classic BBC radio comedy, homemade compilations of our favourite old records and our collection of music tapes. You also have *time*. Which can become a subject of fascination in itself.

Time, like the calendar, is a man-made construct. Created for convenience. Decided by committee. Even as late as the mid-19th century the English cities of London and Leeds – with only 195 miles between them – functioned six minutes apart. What ultimately unified the clocks of Great Britain was the expansion of the railways with its demand for reliable train timetables. By way of establishing order in the far larger land mass of North America, the USA drew three vertical lines down its map and divided the country into four separate time zones. This may appear somewhat arbitrary to those living in the Dakotas or Nebraska, where the eastern side of their state functions in Central Time while the western side operates an hour later, on Mountain Time.

When you live on land, Time in this abstract sense is not something most of us think about much, except perhaps to be aware occasionally of the small differences that occur daily in the sun's rising and setting. This is most noticeable as spring or autumn get underway; the latter always prompting my Mother to observe, with a dying fall to her voice, that 'The nights are beginning to draw in'. This small difference, totalling only a few minutes during the course of each week, does not become an issue in the northern hemisphere until late in the year when people start grumbling that it is beginning to get dark around four in the afternoon. It was to deal with this kind of inconvenience, among others, that Daylight Saving Time – another manmade innovation – was introduced.

The only other occasion when Time impinges on us is when travelling abroad, or interstate in countries the size of America or Australia. But if we travel by air this difference in time zones is speedily dealt with when a member of the cabin crew tells us by how much to alter our watches before we leave the plane. Sailing west, from the Cape Verde Islands to the Caribbean, we will pass through four time zones. At approximately 100 miles per day this means entering a new time zone every five days.

Initially, we stay with Cape Verde Islands' time, but gradually the problem becomes apparent. In particular, I have been accustomed to going to bed just after sunset, at around 7.30 or 8pm, just as it is beginning to get dark. Although I currently set off for bed at the usual time, it is now still daylight. It is not only difficult to sleep with sunshine streaming in through the blinds, but I also miss watching the sun set before I go to bed. And of course it affects the other end of the day too, in as much as we are currently eating breakfast in the dark.

So we declare Central *Voyager* Time (CVT) which, in essence, means declaring dawn to be whatever time we want it to be so that our night watches fall at the right time and, especially, that David's first one coincides with the relevant part of Herb's nightly broadcast. However, to be able to tune into Herb, as well as BBC World Service News, we also need a fixed time so that we know when to access these transmissions. We choose Greenwich Mean Time and we keep two clocks: one on GMT to connect us with the outside world, and one on CVT which is basically whatever keeps us comfortable and functioning effectively on board.

Radicals during the French Revolution redesigned their calendar, among other things, with ten days to a week because it was tidier. While creating timeless literature, Shakespeare and Danté reinvented and transformed their respective languages to give us the modern forms of English and Italian used today. Strange to say, even all the way out here, just the two of us on a bit of fibreglass, it feels quite liberating to invent your own time.

The journey goes slowly. I think David is disappointed that he won't get us to Trinidad for the New Year celebrations. The Millennium ones promise to be rather special. I don't mind. I like it out here.

We have settled into an easy routine. We catch up on our sleep in the mornings and do our chores before and after lunch. And now that David's course of antibiotics is complete we have introduced Happy Hour. At 5pm. Alcohol consumption is limited to one glass of red wine daily at this time. A glass before dinner is pleasurable, a small ritual to look forward to as evening approaches, but which is not going to threaten the boat's safety. You cannot afford to become too relaxed or unobservant, especially as a rolling boat makes you quite tired anyway, constantly having to maintain your balance.

Dinner is at 6pm. I am in bed from 7 until 10. It is not always easy to fall asleep on this first rest. It is only after my second watch that I fall into my bunk and sleep like the dead. David is abed between 10.30pm and 1.30am. I get my head down again from 2 until 5am. I like the 5.30–8.30am watch best. I like the way the stars fade away in the pre-dawn light and dawn gives way to sunrise.

There are voices in the port cabin, and occasional music coming from the forepeak. Boats in a big sea develop innumerable vibrations which the brain converts into sounds familiar to it. For example, the one in the forepeak which is reminiscent of a mad timpanist is simply the effect certain sea conditions have on our port water tank, depending on how much water is in there. The voices are harder to identify. And nothing can explain the smells. Yesterday it was pipe tobacco smoke. Today it is orange blossom. We have neither on board.

22

Peculiar Weather

It is Sunday morning, the nineteenth day of December and the beginning of our seventh day at sea. The moon goes down at 4am but within an hour the planet Venus is bathing us in a glow even brighter than the departed moon; only more seductively. For while the moon sheds a cool, silver light, Venus showers you in gold. This is a novel way to spend December: out in the open air, in sunshine during the day and under a canopy of stars at night. It's a bit bouncy, but a small price to pay for not spending the winter indoors under cold, grey skies and interminable rain.

I wash towels and night clothes before lunch and peg them out on the rails. And, as conditions are congenial at present, David runs the water maker to top up the tank since Herb is promising 22-knot winds which will make the process impossible. Then, with the chores done, we set up the tree.

Before we left England we bought a small artificial fir tree in the post-Christmas sales. It has been sitting in its box in the fore cabin ever since. We dig it out now, assemble it and begin straightening its wire branches. In the box is a piece of card headed *Tree Fluffing Tips*. Suitably fluffed, we prop it up beside the chart table, although we have to bend the top a bit to make it fit under the saloon ceiling.

There is squawking in the masthead again this afternoon from another inattentive shearwater. And there are more flying fish than ever. It has been a busy day and warm – 30°C. There are shooting stars again tonight. And a full moon, incredibly bright.

In his broadcast tonight Herb says that there is a huge high developing between Europe and North America and, as a result, he expects the stronger, more favourable winds he's been predicting to develop above 15°North. He also says that there is a trough of low pressure developing below that latitude and that squalls are expected in the area. So we alter course to stay above 15°North although this will take us further away from our course to Trinidad. We just hope we'll be able to head south-west once we get closer to the Caribbean. But some decent wind *would* be nice.

Instead, conditions over the next two days and nights prove to be simply more of the same, and increasingly frustrating. Typically, the wind will be weak all day and then suddenly, towards dusk, it will strengthen and we will pick up speed. Then in the early hours it lulls again before picking up with the approach of dawn. Essentially, for four hours around dawn, and four around dusk the wind increases before weakening again. It is particularly irritating because you just begin to feel you are making some headway only to watch it fall away again after four hours.

By Monday evening Herb is also giving very different forecasts for the boats in front and behind us, so there must be a weather front between them. Unfortunately we don't know which side of it we are on. Our problem is this: Herb is advising *Amber*, the American boat ahead of us, *not* to go south for twenty-four hours but to take advantage of her present good conditions; while *Van Dyke*, the Dutch single-hander behind us, is told to head south to get out of a rough sea. David decides to maintain our course, as things are not too bad – if only we had more wind. In the event we actually experience nothing like the forecasts given for either boat.

Tonight the moon is so bright that only the fixed stars of the higher magnitudes are visible and the whole sea, sky and *Voyager* are lit up as if by laser beam.

On Tuesday morning the sun is a glass globe filled with peach-gold liquid. As it rises from the horizon the colour drains to the bottom half, leaving pure gold at the top and glowing peach at the bottom. In only minutes it loses its crisp outline and sparkle, becoming fuzzy-edged, soft-focused and a typical yellow morning sun. I do some laundry and peg it along the rails. It rains.

Today is the third day of this tiresome weather pattern. As usual the wind falls away during the day but our frustration with the conditions is compounded when David tunes into our SSB radio during the evening. For the information we so gratefully glean from Herb's broadcast has suddenly become very confusing and for once we wish we had a transmitter instead of just a receiver so that we could ask him for information specific to us. In the event David decides to alter course by 25° to the north for a time in the hope of finding some of the stronger winds Herb is warning people about.

Lack of wind is clearly not the problem being experienced by at least one of Herb's yachts whose skipper, prior to tuning into tonight's broadcast, had found it necessary to change course. Now, Herb is very skilled and works very hard and gratis for those people who have signed up for his services. So, if they ask for his expertise, and he is willing to spend part of each day working out the best course for them, and his evenings broadcasting his considered advice to them, it is only natural that he would expect them to follow it and be approximately where he expects them to be. If they aren't his disappointment, though never spoken, is apparent in his tone. So when people deviate from the course he has given them they can be pretty apologetic; sheepish, even. In fact, sometimes they drop out altogether and are not heard over the nightly airwaves again. But tonight the recalcitrant yachtsman faces the music like a man and admits to having changed course contrary to the advice Herb had given him.

'*Oh?*' says Herb, with that inflection in his voice which can reduce middle-aged men to eight-year-old schoolboys. And then, after a pregnant pause, 'Why?'

'We… um… went looking for somewhere… a little… quieter,' mumbles the skipper, downplaying a night of untenable violence. There is another uncomfortable silence which ultimately the yachtsman feels obliged to fill with further justification. 'The rivets were dropping out of the mast.'

Our own sailing conditions tonight are not good. We have the same roly sea and lack of wind so that *Voyager* wallows and the genoa flaps, shedding what little wind is in it. There is a wonderful moon over the stern when I emerge on deck to begin my first watch, but by the time David is due to go below it has become obliterated by an approaching squall.

A quick dip into the radar tells us that it is around six miles long by four miles wide. He remains on watch with me. The rain is torrential. The only possible advantage of a squall might have been a decent bit of wind to drive us forward. But no. The wind whips from north to south while oscillating between 29 knots and two. The result is that one minute we're hurtling along behind a billowing genoa and the next there's zero on the wind gauge and we are hardly moving at all.

David is an hour late getting to bed.

After midnight the moon comes through again, and I have to put an engine on because, after all the fury of the squall, the wind is now too light and erratic to sail by.

Today is Wednesday 22nd December and our tenth day at sea. In the early hours I take advantage of all the rain to wipe down the cockpit. I have heard other yachtsmen complain about the amount of hair that gathers on a boat. You'd think it would blow away, but it doesn't. It gathers in corners, silently accusing you of slovenly boat-keeping. At dawn a petrel keeps us company for a while, flying low along our starboard side, up from the bow close to our toe rails and then turning on the quarter to make another fly-past.

The day, when it comes, is overcast and oppressively airless. We sleep a lot, taking it in turns. In between I decorate the Christmas tree and air the laundry that got rained on yesterday. David, with a look of quiet determination, embarks on Tolstoy's 900-page epic, *War and Peace*.

It is hot and stuffy in the saloon, so I open the small hatch beside me, a mere twelve inches by six and the only one on the boat currently not open. Immediately all the trimmings on board become horizontal. It is as if this one tiny aperture has sole access to all the wind on this stretch of the North Atlantic. It is very refreshing but, with our Christmas decorations in danger of reaching the Caribbean before we do, I have to close it again and continue to steam. The flying fish are particularly active today.

We also have a crew meeting. David has always anticipated that we would reef the sails at night but up until now the winds have been so light that it hasn't been necessary. However, after last night's activity, approaching squalls being so difficult to see, and so vicious when they arrive, we decide that in future we will put two reefs in the genoa at dusk each night. It will slow us down in the quiet spells but we need to preserve the safety of the boat. When dawn comes we can shake the reefs out as we shall be able to see any squalls coming.

Tonight, when David tunes into Herb he finds that his assumption about a front emerging somewhere between our three boats has been confirmed. It has swept *Amber* an additional 60 miles ahead of us, and put her in a completely different weather pattern from us. Fortunately *Van Dyke*, who had fallen behind, is catching up with us again so we still have a point of reference for Herb's forecasts.

At 1.30 on Thursday morning, when David takes over the watch from me, all the little squalls that have been gathering around us for the past hour have finally joined up into a very large one heading directly for us. It has been fascinating to watch the process on radar, although there will be no possibility of using it to dodge the individual squalls as we did on our passage from Gibraltar to Porto Santo. This time they have homed in on us like a flock of predators upon a solitary prey.

It is always a little eerie, waiting for a squall to strike, especially in the dark. You make your preparations: you reef your sails, you batten down and you wait. There is often a period of quietness then, in which you wonder if perhaps you might be lucky and it will pass over you before it breaks, although it rarely does and not tonight. The wind roars up to Gale Force 8 and the rain arrives.

David ends up doing a seven-hour watch tonight, much of it out in driving rain, initially because the rain is so heavy that he cannot see enough from inside the boat to be safe. But then our autopilot begins to go awry. It does this three times during the night. Each time he steers manually until *Voyager* settles back on course and he can switch the autopilot on again. Then he stays at the helm to watch the compass and ensure we stay on course.

Conditions also prove too much for the radar. Its screen fills with clutter, its scanner bedazzled by too much rain and crashing waves for it to pick up anything remotely useful such as a dangerously-close vessel. As so often happens, just when you need it most, technology abandons you. And, ironically, this turns out to be the only occasion on the whole voyage when another boat is on the same course as us. It is also the only other yacht we shall see during this entire voyage. She is, we shall discover, a 36-foot catamaran called *Summer Dream*.

By lunchtime, and with the weather recovered, we spot her behind us for the first time. Around 3pm her skipper calls us on the VHF for a chat. His autopilot will not hold a course in this following sea of 12–15 foot waves, so he and his wife are having to steer by hand. They have two young children on board and are heading for Barbados.

Their autopilot would have been the brand we should have installed on *Voyager* in Gibraltar, at considerable expense, had we finally lost patience with the repair facilities of the manufacturer of our own automatic steering gear. The only thing that had stopped us replacing ours with the brand on *Summer Dream* was that a friend back home had always been let down by it in a following sea.

We are grateful that we had persevered in getting our own repaired. Manual steering over these distances, with only two of you on board, is very tiring especially at night. It is not only the hours spent physically at the wheel but the concentration needed to maintain a course in a big sea and the strain on the eyes as you refocus endlessly between a dark sea and a lighted compass. To add to their woes, they are also having trouble keeping a charge in their batteries.

We have all been accustomed by equipment manufacturers – domestic and automotive as well as marine – to expect a life span of ten years. However, some time ago, when a yachting magazine published a survey of marinas in the UK, it concluded that the average yacht was used for only ten days a year. This meant that marine equipment, in a ten-year life span, was used on average for little more than three-and-a-half months. Yet take it in for repair aged 8 or 9 years-old and service agents will shake their heads and tell you it is cheaper to buy a new one. If electronics are involved they will claim the life cycle should really be only five years which equates to a working lifetime of only seven weeks.

Perhaps it is this limited usage by the average yacht owner that removes the pressure for equipment that is more robust. It is only when full-time cruisers buy it that it is given a thorough test.

A comparable situation was cars after the opening of Britain's first motorway, the M1 between London and the Midlands, in 1959. In its early years the motorway's hard shoulders were littered with broken-down cars, more than a few of them new ones and some very expensive ones, because cars were not then built to do long-distance, high-speed motoring. Reliability improved with increased demand. Unlike car-owners, though, long-distance yachtsmen are, and will remain, a small minority of marine equipment purchasers. The implications for their safety, not to mention their basic comfort, are considerable.

In the automotive world, the JB Power organisation does a ruthless annual survey of cars over three years old with at least average mileage. The only survey we are aware of in the marine world at this time has been when the magazine *Yachting World* surveys equipment used on the ARC – the Atlantic Rally for Cruisers – which takes about three weeks. Even then some new equipment fails to last the duration of the cruise.

Fortunately for us our autopilot's one night of aberration is not repeated, but these big rollers are having a novel effect on our Christmas tree. Everything else on board is fixed in place, and simply goes up and down with the boat. The tree, weighing little and only lightly tied to stop it falling over, rises with the swell but comes down slightly after everything else, so that it constantly undulates, gently, in its corner.

Summer Dream overtakes us during Happy Hour and we raise our wine glasses to its crew as they pass. Her skipper calls us up on the VHF while his wife steers. Before he signs off, and almost as an afterthought, he asks if we have made contact with the big fish net. With our entanglement in a massive drift net off Morocco still vivid in his mind, David says, 'Good Lord, they haven't put one out here, have they?'

But the Big Fish Net turns out to be a self-help network of yachtsmen transmitting for a limited period on a specific channel on SSB radio each morning. One problem from our point of view is timing: the Net transmits at the same time that we tune into World Service News. Another is that we have tuned into yachting networks in the past only to find them dominated by one individual complaining endlessly about people anchoring too close to him and the spiralling cost of Spanish marinas. Nevertheless, David says we will give it a try.

The night begins with a big, very bright moon over the port quarter. But after a while black squall clouds travelling north obscure it sporadically until finally a dense grey cloud settles in and obliterates it altogether. Before the squall reaches us I make my way to the galley and put the kettle on.

Before we left England I bought a collection of teas. I pop one of the fancy teabags into a mug and while the water boils I open the packet of little cone-shaped sponge cakes from Mindelo's tiny supermarket. Another name for a coconut pyramid, where I come from at least, is a madeleine. And it was a madeleine, though not shaped like this one, whose long-forgotten taste instantly transported Marcel Proust back to his boyhood and inspired a series of novels exploring involuntary memory. Just as the small black bird in the circle of light had sent my thoughts back to the performer Max Wall.

This madeleine of mine does not prompt a memory, however, so much as a reflection. Out in the cockpit, indulging myself with sweet sticky sponge cake and jasmine tea, I watch lightning explode inside a long low strip of cloud to the south-west. It says much about the distance I have travelled, and not just in nautical miles. In a relatively short time I have gone from mortification at the mere thought of being alone at night under sail in rough weather, to sitting here in the darkness observing an approaching squall like an aficionado – complete with refreshments.

Gradually the wind begins to oscillate across our stern, but not satisfied with simply wafting back and forth, its speed fluctuates wildly between 4 knots and gale force. Not surprisingly, *Voyager* is handling badly and in need of regular attention. Our desired course is 275° but the nearest I can get the autopilot to work consistently is 260°. That puts us 15° off-course but, with something the size of the North Atlantic in front of us, there will be plenty of time to correct it later.

In between times I am trying for as much *quiet* as possible. David was on watch most of last night and I want him to get as much undisturbed rest as he can tonight. While he is asleep in the port cabin I sit at the chart table in the saloon and prepare to write the Christmas card I bought for him in the Canaries.

Writing a Christmas card this far from where he is sleeping seems a quiet enough activity. But as I carefully remove its cellophane wrapper and open it there is a high-pitched hysterical screech. Even as I rush across the bridge deck to check the gas alarm I realise that it doesn't screech to the tune of *Jingle Bells* and that I have unwittingly bought a 'musical' card. I have a devil of a job writing in it while keeping it quiet. The inscription is very shaky.

David takes over the watch at 1.30am. It becomes an increasingly squally, difficult night and he ends up doing another 7-hour watch, mostly in the rain again. With the wind strength increasing, he decides that repeatedly shifting the genoa, our biggest sail, is too heavy a job to leave me with, and he doesn't wake me until 8.30. Although we don't know it yet, several hundred miles away these unpleasant conditions are afflicting other people with much more serious consequences.

When David does wake me, and with no respite from the weather in view, we take in the genoa, put on an engine, switch on the radar and briefly watch the squalls together in the dry of the saloon before David goes off to bed.

23

The Festive Season

It is Christmas Eve. We are halfway there and a thousand miles from land in any direction. David catches up on his sleep after breakfast and I take down the news. The saloon looks very festive. The tree is dripping with red and gold ornaments and small paper angels. The undulations of the tree give the angels an added dimension. Across the front windows we have tinsel, also red and gold, and a red velvet bow. The Christmas cards from family and friends that we collected from Mindelo's post office are strung between the boat hook and the barometer. There's a green bow and some artificial holly over our dining area and silver-green streamers over the radar. Everything is unbreakable. We can't afford shards of broken glass under bare feet. There are squalls throughout the day and a heavy swell over the stern.

We have a Christmas Eve lunch of salmon pâté, slices of the big Edam cheese we bought whole and which has kept beautifully, fresh tomatoes with basil in olive oil and a glass of red wine. This is followed by some of Santa Cruz's delicious marzipan cake. It should have been the Christmas cake I baked but for the moment I can't remember where I stowed it and we can't wait while I mount a search.

We also listen to the Festival of Nine Lessons and Carols from King's College chapel at Cambridge University. It has always been something of a tradition to tune into the BBC's Christmas Eve broadcast and, knowing that we should be unable to access this year's programme, we brought along a tape of last year's.

I don't know if being a thousand miles from anywhere concentrates the mind particularly, but I never really thought about the unquestioning obedience demanded in Genesis before: that Adam and Eve remain in ignorance, that Abraham sacrifice his son Isaac. I am particularly taken with the prohibition in relation to the fruit that would 'make one wise', prompting God's question: 'Hast thou eaten of the tree whereof I commanded thee that thou shouldst not eat?' And by Adam's response: 'The woman whom thou gavest to be with me, she gave me of the tree, and I did eat, saith Adam.'

Not unlike our encounter with the Portuguese Navy last year, stopping us at sea for obscuring the name of our boat. 'My wife's airing her

laundry,' saith David. And most of the items draped around the cockpit his.
That still rankles.

The sky tonight is heavily overcast with black clouds travelling north, but so
far no sign of squalls. There are, however, lightening flashes in the south-west
again and the wind fluctuates wildly, from almost nothing, up to gale force
and back again. And also like last night, the wind's direction is as inconstant
as its speed. With it fanning between our port and starboard quarters, the
genoa keeps backing. Meanwhile, not far behind us, *Van Dyke* is reporting to
Herb that he has clear skies and ideal conditions. We put in an extra reef.

We get a few squalls during the course of the night, but finally the
wind settles at east 4–5, occasionally 6. I'm becoming rather partial to
coconut pyramids and jasmine tea out in the cockpit around midnight.

It is a very rough sea during the early hours but with the present
wind, even with three reefs in the genoa we maintain a good speed. In fact,
even heavily reefed our night time speeds are faster than in the daytime.
It rains at 2am and is so heavily overcast and dark that it doesn't manage to
get light until after 8am. Then the sea becomes calmer.

It is Christmas morning. It is also two days since our conversation with the
skipper of *Summer Dream* and his mention of the SSB radio network. Perhaps
it is because of the day it is, with its sense of communion and goodwill to all
men, that we decide to give World Service News a miss this morning and
try the network instead.

Had we been bored with our progress, which we aren't particularly,
our first dip into the Big Fish Net would have chastened us. An elderly
English couple are making the crossing in a boat called *Nirvana* which has
spent the previous five years on the hard. Battered by squalls and big seas,
one of their shrouds has broken and they are having problems with their
sails. They are also having difficulties with their batteries and automatic
steering. They are exhausted and at the end of their tether. Other yachtsmen
counsel them; most importantly to heave-to and get some rest.

A roseate tern with a black cap and long white streamers curving
from its tail makes three circles above *Voyager*, looking directly into my eyes
before turning away and flying south. They do that, seabirds; get close up
to you when you are perceived as no immediate threat to them. They
concentrate on your eyes, taking the measure of you, assessing your

intentions. For myself I am just so happy to see it, looking so pure and clean and lovely, on this of all mornings, that like a fool I actually wave to it.

There are also masses of flying fish about today and another unaccountable smell. I have formed the theory that smells become encapsulated somehow and float across vast distances before shedding their fragrance on some unsuspecting mariner. This may apply to sound, too. A friend once told us that on a voyage between the Azores and England he and his crew stood on deck and listened to a party in full swing. It unsettled them not a little, they being many hundreds of miles from land at the time and with no other vessels in range. I have been spared ghostly knees-ups so far, but to the smell of orange blossom and pipe tobacco smoke of the last few days is now added the distinctive aroma of a barbecue.

We have a very happy day, with a tape of Christmas carols and a bottle of fizz. We have Charles Dickens' novels aboard and enjoy a reading from *A Christmas Carol* and Christmas at Dingley Dell from *Pickwick Papers*. We have a turkey dinner with sage and onion stuffing, sauté potatoes, carrots, sweetcorn, asparagus tips and gravy. There is pudding and tinned custard standing by, but we have no room left for more than coffee and a hoarded Belgian chocolate each. Our appetites are much smaller these days. Our waistlines, too.

The temperature this evening is 27°C. We listen to *Round the Horne*, classic 1960s BBC radio comedy, on the Walkman during our watches and, on my final one, fortified by jasmine tea and the last of the coconut pyramids, I read Dickens' short novel, *The Chimes*. It is in the same volume as *A Christmas Carol*, although I have never read it before. Set in the days surrounding New Year, its themes include new ways of thinking and new beginnings which seem rather appropriate as we enter not only a new year but a new millennium and a very different kind of life.

From midnight to midnight we cover 106 miles in what has been our best sailing day yet. It has been very overcast but there have been no dramatic wind changes, just really pleasant sailing conditions. *Van Dyke* has also caught up with us. Or, more accurately, the yacht is now in our general area which means that its skipper's nightly exchange of information with Herb will provide an accurate picture for *Voyager*.

After yesterday's respite, the rollers resume with a vengeance on Boxing Day. In these conditions you are always on the move. Whether standing or sitting you are simply another loose object and, like the Christmas tree in the corner, you undulate constantly. There is no relief from it. Even lying in bed you slide up and down inside your skin. I have begun to wonder what it will feel like to be on land again. *Voyager* has been at sea now for fourteen days and all things being equal we anticipate a further five or six.

Around 5am there begins a seemingly endless sequence of squalls. As dawn approaches you can see them in front and behind you, like black beads strung on a necklace, stretching from horizon to horizon. As one passes over your head, another gathers behind it, moiling and broiling with seething enmity. For every one or two that slowly passes over you another breaks directly overhead, drenching you in a rain that is physically painful, driven as it is by 25-knot winds.

It doesn't begin to get light until after 8 again today. Sunrise is around 9am at present, although we don't get to see it because of the heavy cloud. At least during the daytime you can see the squalls coming. The problem is the cloudy nights, when they are invisible in the pitch blackness.

Despite a surfeit of wind at present, our wind generator is unable to keep up with our power consumption. Therefore we still need to run the engines to recharge the two 110-amp domestic batteries which power the GPS, the navigation lights and all the other pieces of vital equipment, not to mention the one which pumps drinking water up from the tanks to the tap. And, of course, as back-up to get us out of trouble in the event of the kind of crisis with which we are about to become acquainted at second hand. It is difficult to tell on a rolling boat, but with concentrated staring at the fuel gauge we think we have somewhere between 110 and 120 litres of diesel left in our tank. This should be ample for our needs.

From now on David will don the headphones and listen to World Service News in the evenings in between listening into Herb, thereby leaving the early morning slot free for the Big Fish Net. With its boats scattered across the Atlantic, each reporting its individual weather conditions, he can get valuable information about what we can expect on our patch. There is, in addition, the human drama unfolding daily on this frequency. The elderly couple on board *Nirvana*, we are glad to hear, have benefited from heaving-to and found the strength to repair their yacht's broken shroud and carry on.

In the meantime, another English couple on a 33-foot sloop called *Wanderer*, have lost their mast and rigging. It happened during a squall in the early hours of Christmas Eve but news of it reaches the network only now. With their mast and sails gone, the couple had been unable to start their engine because of a broken starter motor and they had been left wallowing out of control 560 miles from Antigua. Another yachtsman had offered to come and take them off, but they had refused to abandon their boat. Then something extraordinary had happened. An Australian couple called Don and Sally, on their 40ft yacht *Jupiter* thirty miles ahead of them, had turned back and begun towing them.

The additional information that comes crackling through the static of the SSB radio headphones is that in the early hours of this morning *Wanderer* had overtaken the tow rope as she slid down a wave in a squall. The tow rope had got caught around the boat's Aries self-steering gear, spun the boat 180° and torn the gear away. We begin praying for a really boring passage.

Heavy rain soaks the bathroom and the bow window sills; the wingnuts holding the weatherboards over the front windows have come loose. It is not until the afternoon that we can take advantage of a lessening in the sea swell to go forward and tighten them. We also take the opportunity of running the water maker but after about an hour the sea swell returns and, with the boat now lurching violently from side to side, David has to turn it off. The wind is also lessening and we are again caught in that vicious cycle whereby the roll of the boat keeps shaking the wind from the sails which in turn prevents us keeping up enough speed to counteract the rolling. In the meantime, our current tank of propane gas runs out and we change over to the full one.

It is difficult to hear Herb this evening; World Service, too. Although one item of news does manage to squeeze through the atmospheric interference: Derby 0–Aston Villa 2 away from home.

This morning there are dark clouds in the early hours but by 6am there is a very bright moon while Venus, huge and low, hangs over our stern. By the time I hand over the watch at 8.30 Venus has disappeared and the moon is directly above our masthead, hemmed in by cotton wool clouds. They have reduced its glow to a diameter only twice the size of the moon, creating around it a narrow rust-red halo that is rather sinister.

Meanwhile, via our SSB radio the drama on the Big Fish Net continues to unfold. The news this morning is that *Nirvana*, with its repaired shroud, continues to prosper. And a yacht not far away from her is relaying the relevant part of Herb's nightly broadcast to the couple on board at a time when they, and their batteries, are most receptive.

Also, on another part of the ocean a solo sailor, Jim on *Freedom*, has arranged to rendezvous with *Wanderer* and *Jupiter* to hand over a jury rig that may enable *Wanderer* to sail independently. David had wondered briefly about the possibility of lending them one of our starter motors, as their engine is the same as ours, but a glance at the chart had shown that we had absolutely no chance of catching up with them.

Any such thoughts soon become academic, anyway, when an Englishman on a big motor-sailer, with a very big engine – its deep, throbbing note can be heard over its VHF transmissions – sets out from Antigua to take over the tow from *Jupiter*.

The stricken boat had been part of a blue water rally and along with gallons of extra fuel the motor-sailer is carrying gifts from their fellow-yachtsmen already in Antigua (Boddingtons beer, gin and ice cream are mentioned) plus extra crew. The new boat's ETA is Wednesday. In the meantime, at least three other yachts have begun converging on *Wanderer* and her tow, to stand by and offer assistance if necessary.

Fast on the heels of what appears to be a satisfactory resolution to the disasters that have faced *Nirvana* and *Wanderer*, however, comes a new cause for worry. A lone sailor on *Sea Shanty* has a broken finger and a badly injured leg.

An overcast morning turns into a lovely, bright blue, shiny day. A happy day. We have baths in the cockpit in the sunshine during the afternoon and corned beef with sweet potato for dinner followed by chocolate pudding. Cholesterol? Forget about it!

It is Tuesday 28th December and our sixteenth day at sea. Last night and first thing this morning the sea was very violent. Weary of it endlessly shaking the wind out of our sail we are travelling northeast at present to try and keep some in and, if possible, maybe find a little more. At the same time you feel guilty about wanting more wind, because the last thing *Jupiter* and the boat it is towing need is overly strong winds.

As well as news of specific yachts within its purview the Big Fish Net provides an overview of current weather conditions. All northern Europe, it seems, is enduring extensive wind and rain damage. On the Atlantic coast of north-west Spain there are wind speeds of 80–100 knots. A boat entering Barbados this morning experienced rain so heavy that the crew couldn't see their bow.

One of the few things missed during this voyage has been a newspaper and when I take over my second watch I find that David has produced one for me. In biro. It contains the latest news from World Service, plus some of his own like the British government banning Happy Hour on board yachts and cutting the crew's sleeping time – which in my sleep-befuddled state I don't twig immediately – and a crossword.

Due south, just before dawn, there is the most heavenly smell of a full English breakfast. After our own cholesterol-free muesli, we have a strategy meeting. Why did we settle on Trinidad ?

One: as the island at the southernmost end of the Caribbean's Lesser Antilles, Trinidad had seemed the natural starting point from which to explore the island chain. There was also Trinidad's New Year celebrations, but we are going to miss those anyway.

Two: we had arranged to meet Ian there. It had been Ian, a Royal Yachting Association instructor and professional delivery skipper, who had given us our first, compelling taste of catamaran sailing. He had also helped us, as sailing novices, to get *Voyager* home to England from southern Spain where we had bought her. In the process he had become a friend.

He is currently skippering *Spirit of Diana*, one of four identical yachts in a round-the-world Millennium Yacht Race. One of her layovers is Trinidad during Christmas and New Year. Unfortunately, conditions are against us. And not only are we becoming increasingly tired struggling with them, but we are not going to reach Trinidad in time to meet up with Ian before *Spirit of Diana* has to leave.

We had found the passage to the Cape Verde Islands, during which similarly adverse conditions had prevailed, equally tiring and had we not had several compelling reasons to go there we should have changed course for the Caribbean instead. So the sensible option now is to forget Trinidad and head further north, where the weather is driving us anyway and where, according to Herb's current forecast, we can expect better sailing conditions.

It has another advantage, too. We do not have unlimited time to meander up through the islands. There is the not insignificant consideration of the hurricane season during which a force of nature regularly and spectacularly trashes whichever islands and boats are in its path and for which our insurance company – should we be imprudent enough to remain within range – does not cover us.

The new course will mean a shorter, more leisurely trip with more time to enjoy the individual islands along the way. Accordingly, we decide to give up the battle to get to Trinidad and at 9am we change course for the Lesser Antilles and Antigua.

Lesser Antilles is the name given to three groups of islands lying in an arc between Venezuela and north-east of Puerto Rico. The two main groups are the Windward Islands, from Grenada in the south up to Dominica and so called because they were more windward to European sailing ships than the Leeward Islands to the north. The Leeward Islands consist of Dominica up to the Virgin Islands (Dominica being unable to make up its mind to which of the two groups it belongs). The third group lies off the coast of Venezuela. Trinidad does not consider itself part of the Lesser Antilles at all.

Just out of interest, and because wherever there is a lesser there will be a greater, the Greater Antilles stretch from Puerto Rico to Cuba. Those far larger islands consist of rock and are part of the North American continent, whereas the Lesser Antilles, to which we are heading, consists mostly of volcanic or coral islands.

On the Big Fish Net this morning, along with updates from those yachts already familiar to us, the bad news is from the skipper of a new one called *Lightship* who reports that his main sail was badly damaged in a squall last night when the wind reached 40 knots. The good news is that the replacement tow should reach *Wanderer* by tomorrow morning to relieve *Jupiter*. *Jupiter*'s skipper, Don, comes on air briefly. He sounds tired.

At noon we put our Central *Voyager* Time clock back an hour since, with sunrise currently at 9am, I am going to bed in bright sunshine again. Herb's forecast for tonight and tomorrow is easterly 20–25 knots. This is what we have been hoping for all along, but it has taken until our sixteenth day at sea for it to arrive. The sea itself is bouncy and horrible but by midnight the 25-knot winds materialise, along with another necklace of black squall clouds. We put an extra reef into the genoa. We will now have these winds all the way to Antigua, sometimes even a little stronger, but excellent sailing conditions.

24

One of the Locals Stops By

At around 1am this morning I walk out into the cockpit and am startled by the moon behind cloud off our starboard quarter. It is startling because it doesn't look like the moon at all, just an unexpected light that is very eerie. Sometime after 2am I get David out of bed to another sort of light directly in front of us, quite large and suddenly *there*. We conclude it is a large commercial ship of some sort, because it suddenly moves away to port and disappears very fast and I've got him up for nothing.

After he's gone back to bed I get to thinking. I know that yachtsmen sometimes sail at night without navigation lights to save their batteries; only switching them on when they spot someone else's light to prevent a collision. And I wonder if large ships ever do this, too. If so, it's rather frightening especially if, as the third officer on a tanker once lead us to believe, the lookout on the bridge is rarely looking out.

After breakfast the Big Fish Net reports that *Nirvana* had been going along very nicely but that her main sail was damaged in a squall last night. Also that *Jupiter* and *Wanderer* had their tow broken at 3am this morning and had heaved-to until dawn when they reconnected. The replacement tow boat is currently around three hours away. This must come as a great relief for the couple on *Jupiter* which, according to our calculation, has been towing for four days now.

Meanwhile, on our own stretch of the Atlantic it is a lovely sunny day. With our chores all done we spend the afternoon sunning ourselves in the cockpit until around 3pm when we get a visitor. Quite suddenly the saying *up close and personal* takes on a special meaning. This gets very close and the intention may even be amorous.

Our first inkling is a sudden flash of white, close to our starboard side. When we stand up and lean over the coaming to investigate we find ourselves staring at the white underside of a whale. After hovering a moment or two, the whale proceeds to carry out a minute inspection of us, circling *Voyager* very slowly on its back or its side, just below the surface of the water, so that from on deck it appears as either shimmering silver or silver-and-black.

It shows no fear, swims as little as a foot from our hull, and pops its head up beside us regularly to roll an interested eye over us. When we, and the boat, have been thoroughly observed it swims away like a torpedo to reappear, only moments later, as a large, dark head in the middle of the enormous wave rolling down behind us.

Since leaving the Canaries we have become reconciled to a big sea, with waves between 15 and 20 feet high. But even by recent standards it is *huge* today, with monumental rollers sweeping down onto our starboard quarter. Despite conventional wisdom about big, non-breaking waves on one of its quarters being ideal for a catamaran, these are so big that when you first stand in the cockpit and look up at one curving voluptuously down towards you, you are convinced that, despite being gorgeous, sooner or later one of them must inevitably sink you. However, far from overwhelming *Voyager*, each wave simply raises her up and propels her forward with gratifying speed.

The present conditions are not only the result of our change of course but of the Trade Winds, which have finally lived up to their much-vaunted promise and actually *arrived*. Combined with the sunshine, this is the best sailing day of the passage so far. It would therefore be one of life's great ironies – after all the squalls, high winds, and big seas pummelling our beam – if *Voyager* were to be sunk by a relatively small inquisitive whale.

While being thoroughly inspected by our visitor, we take the opportunity of doing a little research ourselves. According to our book on marine mammals, a fully grown adult male Minke reaches 36 feet from head to tail and weighs in at ten tons. Measured against our 40-foot hull this one is about 25 feet long, so not yet fully grown. He is dark grey, with a small dorsal fin and the large distinctive Minke head containing the baleen plates through which the species filters its food.

We watch the large dark head rushing down the wave towards us with trepidation, wondering if this exuberant adolescent is capable of controlling his momentum in such a force, or whether he will be smashed against our stern and destroy our steering gear, or worse. We need not have worried. Our young visitor turns out to be perfectly under control as he executes the first of his many extraordinary sequences.

First of all he bodysurfs down the wave behind us straight to our starboard quarter. Once there he rolls onto his back, presents his silvery white underside and outstretched flippers and proceeds to shimmy gently just below the water. He hovers like this for a minute or two, only inches from our starboard hull, then limbos underneath the boat where he registers 21 metres on our echo sounder.

While we are still squinting into the sunshine, trying to see where he comes up, he is already back behind us, surfing down another massive roller to our starboard quarter. Watching him do this, again and again, we feel we finally understand the saying *having a whale of a time*. He surfs, shimmers, shimmies and limbos, each time recording a smaller and smaller depth on the echo-sounder as he passes beneath us.

This increasing proximity to our boat's underside does begin to cause a little anxiety, though, because our book on marine mammals also tells us that a solitary, immature male Minke in these waters at this time of year is likely to be in search of a mate. And an offshore yachtsman once told us that a whale did in fact seem intent on mating with his boat and was only driven away by pumping out a whole bottle of pungent toilet cleaner through the boat's foul-water outlet. By the time our visitor passes beneath us at around 1.5 metres we have become concerned.

Perhaps it is at this distance that he discovers his mistake, or simply loses interest in this buxom but unresponsive creature he has been courting. Or maybe he is far too savvy to make such a mistake. Perhaps he has simply tired of the plastic toy he found floating in his bath. Or, like many a young male, perhaps he has been practicing his seduction technique on *Voyager*, or simply honing his athletic skills. For whatever reason, after making one last pass underneath us, at a little less than a metre, he disappears.

25
A New Millennium

Our fresh food is all but gone. Just two apples left in the fruit bowl and enough potatoes under the sink for one more meal. After this it is pasta or rice. The dried fruit from Tenerife is heavenly, the best we've ever tasted, but the nuts when we open the tin are stale. The marzipan cake, on the other hand, really is out of this world.

Aston Villa 1 – Spurs 1.

Herb forecasts solid Trade Winds out of the east for the next four days, mostly in the 21 to 25-knot range with a chance of rain and squalls tonight for up to five or six hours. Before my watch at 10.30pm we put a third reef in. As per Herb's forecast, the night degenerates into an endless chain of squalls passing remorselessly over us bearing an awful, howling wind.

Yachtsmen are not the only people enduring this bad weather, of course. People on land are suffering far worse. At least on a boat torrential rain runs down your coach house roof onto your decks and safely out through your toe rails into the sea. World Service tonight reports that in Venezuela, 500 miles to the south of us, flooding may have cost the lives of anywhere between 20 and 50,000 people as hundreds of landslides up in the mountains, triggered by the exceptionally heavy rainfall, bury coastal towns and villages under mud and boulders or sweep inhabitants into the sea.

Today is our eighteenth day at sea. The formerly exhilarating rollers on our starboard quarter have transformed themselves into a heavy swell on our starboard beam instead. It is making *Voyager* roll uncomfortably and the waves hitting the underside of her bridge deck are producing a loud and constant banging.

Unable to sleep David gets up at 1am, half an hour before I am due to wake him. He startles me, appearing at the companionway doors when I think I am alone on deck in the darkness. Within minutes yet another squall unleashes its violence over us and we retire behind closed doors to escape the torrential rain. Heaven help *Wanderer* and her tow if they are experiencing conditions like this.

I imagine most of us could identify within ourselves a particular stress factor which is far more likely to destroy our resolve or our performance than more obvious causes. In *1984*, George Orwell's 1949 novel set in a totalitarian future, the State breaks its non-conformists by finding and exploiting the one fear an individual cannot withstand. For Winston Smith, the book's main character, it is rats and on being faced with one, in a quite literal sense, he capitulates.

While for many it may be a physical threat that incapacitates, for others it is stress on the emotions, the nerves or the senses that does it. With me, it is sustained noise. I can cope with only so much before it begins to exert a malign effect. It probably has something to do with overly sensitive hearing and at 4.30 this morning I emerge from sleep into noise levels that have increased enormously.

Within a short time of taking over the watch it begins to prove too much for me: the howling of the wind, the endless single-note whine from the forestay, the erratic banging under the bridge deck, the rattling shackles, the slam of canvas and all the other extraneous rattles, thumps and bangs caused by the wind, not to mention the violent roll of the boat which keeps you physically off-balance all the time. Even so, the effect on me is quite irrational.

I have stood my watch under worse conditions than these, including squalls whose vicious gale-force winds have been enough to wreck a sail in minutes or bring down a mast. The wind at present is only 31 knots and with three reefs in the genoa we are under no threat. Even so I am consumed with fear for the safety of the boat; that I will fail to keep her safe. I have a duty of care, to the boat and to David asleep in the starboard cabin, but my brain is so addled by the cacophony assaulting it that I can't even begin to identify the threat, let alone deal with it. Soon this fear becomes overwhelming and even concern for the boat and David is subsumed into a mindless, all-encompassing need for escape. To cover my ears; to bury my head under something, anything as long as it will reduce this intolerable noise. In short, I get the screaming meemies and flee to the skipper, who immediately takes over while I bury myself briefly under the duvet.

I have not experienced anything like this before, or since. And it is only long afterwards that I remember this night when an article about the First World War makes me wonder if hypersensitive hearing could actually mean the difference between withstanding days, or even weeks, of heavy bombardment and being shot for cowardice or desertion.

I am back on duty at 5am. Half an hour later there is a strange phenomenon. The wind and the noise levels have been dropping steadily and I am sitting up at the helm. With the instruments in front of me I notice that despite 16 knots on the wind gauge, our speed over the ground is zero, and staring around me we do indeed appear to have stopped moving. The only time this has happened before was when *Voyager* became trapped in an enormous drift net off Morocco.

Unwilling to get David out of bed again unless I really have to, I sit and wait to see what happens. Initially *Voyager* simply wallows. Then, after a while, the log shows 0.7 knots, then 1.0, until finally it settles at 2.3. One of the engines is on tick-over at present, charging up the batteries so I put the engine into gear until we gain enough momentum to stop the boat wallowing and the sail flogging. Gradually our speed returns to normal and I take the engine out of gear again. It is very odd. We discuss it later, but David can only suggest that we became caught up in a something soft below the surface such as a clump of weed which slowly broke up, freeing us.

Around 7am I watch the sky turning from grey to blue. The stars begin to melt, all except the brightest ones until only Venus is left. She is very large and bright and accompanied by a half-moon.

A couple of hours later the Big Fish Net reports that yesterday afternoon, as expected, the relief boat took over *Wanderer*'s tow from *Jupiter*. A couple of hours later the tow rope broke; they reconnected and hoved to until this morning. *Wanderer*'s skipper is on SSB radio for the first time, emotional with gratitude. Asked if his wife has received her ice cream yet he says it is too valuable to risk a transfer in the present rough conditions. They will try later.

Nirvana's skipper also expresses his thanks for all the support he and his wife have received and is pleased to report that they have managed to repair their mainsail.

Above us, somewhere around 11am, another squall peaks at 34 knots. Herb warns we can expect more of the same until Sunday, today being Thursday. It is a hot, sunny day with a large swell and a rolling boat. The interior gets very stuffy so we open all the hatches. One particularly high wave catches the boat on the bottom of her roll and seawater soaks the starboard bed again. We dry it out in the cockpit. Again.

I take a photograph of David enjoying Happy Hour and looking very Caribbean in his shades and faded hat. I think he's a bit tired and looking forward to arriving, but he looks extremely well. And despite our broken bedtimes he is sleeping properly since finally being prevailed upon to use earplugs to filter out the squawk of the automatic steering, the engine noise from battery recharges and currently the whining of the wind in the rigging.

It is Friday morning and New Year's Eve. Forty minutes after midnight we get another squall. The rain is *awesome* and regrettably I've left the port cabin hatch slightly open. Fortunately, with the engine only inches below the mattress, the latest battery recharge dries out the bedding a bit before I fall into it at 1.45am. The alternative is the starboard bed, which has the squawking automatic steering under it.

Thank heavens for automatic steering, though. I've heard yachtsmen say they are happy to spend the whole day at the wheel. Just the *thought* of three weeks' hand-steering would be enough to send me over the side.

The moon is up by my second watch. It is the shape of an orange segment. At last! So much more satisfying, aesthetically – also psychologically for some unaccountable reason – than a section of moon with a straight edge.

Every time I take over a watch with cloud looming ahead of us David looks up at it and says, 'It was beautiful and clear until half an hour ago,' as if somehow it's my fault. The other one that drives me mad is: 'I haven't seen it go above 23 knots all night,' and he's barely got his second foot under the duvet before it's 31 and rising.

On the positive side, we've become rather good at reefing without turning into the wind. Perhaps we've both got physically stronger, or calmer, or more confident. I can even haul in the genoa sheet myself now simply by waiting for the sail to flap in the right direction.

It is 6.45am, 22°C and Venus is aglow behind our stern. No wonder yachtsmen love her, bestowing her gift of golden light, comfort and the promise of morning not far away after a dark night. So what if astronomers do say she's just a huge ball of poisonous gas. I don't imagine many astronomers go to sea in small boats with open cockpits.

News from the Big Fish Net is that *Wanderer* is currently being towed at 6 knots, which is faster than we are going by ourselves. *Nirvana* has more holes in her main and most of her ports are leaking. And the Royal Dutch Air Force is out looking for the yacht *Rebecca*, out of Porto Santo and long overdue at Martinique. A big sea behind us makes us fishtail all day.

At midday a shearwater comes and inspects us, gliding from side to side of the boat on the thermals, without any visible movement of its body or wings. And mid-afternoon a bulk carrier passes about 2 miles away.

At 7pm, before I go to bed, we put three reefs in the genoa ready for the nightly squall activity which Herb says we can expect for the next forty-eight hours. When I take over the watch – at 10pm Central *Voyager* Time but midnight in the UK – we raise a glass to family and friends, the New Year and the New Millennium, under an incredibly starry sky. Then David goes late to bed and shortly afterwards I settle down to Dylan Thomas's *Under Milk Wood* on the Walkman beneath the first of the promised squalls. Enveloped in its darkness, but impervious to its rain and bluster, I am transported by a mellifluous Welsh voice into a very different dark night; a still, moonless, summer night in a small, sleeping Welsh town with its 'sloe-black, slow, black, crowblack, fishingboat-bobbing sea.'

Today is the first day of January, the beginning of the Third Millennium and we are approaching Antigua. At 2am CVT we celebrate Caribbean New Year. It is still squally but we are so used to squalls by now that it is deemed an average night although this constant rolling is tiring to the brain as well as the body. At 6.45am we spot a ship off our starboard quarter.

David calculates that at our current rate of progress it will be after dark when we enter Antigua's Falmouth Harbour tomorrow, so we start to push quite hard, all sails up, for the first time not sailing conservatively. Although even after dark, with three reefs in the genoa, we still make very good progress. It is another very squally night.

On Sunday morning the news from the Big Fish Net is that *Jupiter* reached Antigua before noon yesterday, while *Wanderer* and her replacement tow got in just after dark. We also hear that *Summer Dream*, the boat whose skipper originally told us about the Big Fish Net, has arrived in Barbados. All the Net's other members reach their various destinations safely, too.

We experience rough seas and squalls all day. Around 11am, however, we get our first sight of Antigua. In the next squall we strip off spontaneously and have a shower in the cockpit. We feel lovely afterwards, ready to arrive all clean and fresh. There is something about rain on your skin. Perhaps it's because the temperature is cooler than you would normally shower at and it leaves you tingling afterwards.

Still a few miles out we receive a classic fisherman's welcome: a long skein of discarded net, drifting with the tide and kept trailing at propeller level by its accompanying string of small, round, brown floats.

Closer to the island we are surprised at how green it is and approaching Falmouth Harbour we become re-acquainted with other yachtsmen as a large and very expensive Italian boat, with an excitable 8-man crew in matching maroon polo shirts and beige shorts, skitters and criss-crosses in front of us like an operatic diva in her final throes.

We have been at sea for almost three weeks. We are tired. We know we are safe now. All we want to do is drop our anchor, abandon responsibility for our survival for a little while and simply *rest* in a patch of water that is not surging. And, should a squall arrive, we won't have any canvas up to worry about. We have already taken down our sails and are under power, because the cruising guide tells us that the narrow channel into Falmouth Harbour has a coral shoal stretching out for half a mile to starboard while the rest of it has very shallow patches.

As we make our approach a Frenchman chops us up twice, forces himself in front of us and then stops dead to take down both his sails, which seems to take him an inordinate length of time. I attempt to steer round him but immediately find myself in 1.2 metres and spend the next ten or more minutes shunting about trying to stay in the channel and not run into the back of him. We arrive at the anchorage at the far end of Falmouth Harbour at a little after 2pm, Caribbean time.

Life with the colour-blind necessarily involves occasional, sometimes lively, debate and never more so than when anchoring on this auspicious afternoon. David's is not the serious sort of colour-blindness, like a taxi driver I once met who saw the world entirely in black and white and who dealt with the red, amber and green central to his daily life purely on the basis of their hierarchy. Nor the osteopath denied the naval career he had craved because navigation lights, flags and charts had no meaning for him. David's is more a failure to distinguish between some colours of similar tone, of the kind that requires the help of a shop assistant to convince him that the socks he is about to buy to match his shoes are actually red and not the brown he supposes.

In the Mediterranean, with David hanging over the pulpit monitoring the seabed and me steering with one eye on the depth gauge, it was never a problem because while many of the buildings are white they are different in shape. So it was simply a matter of, 'Aim for the one with the big balcony,' or 'the two chimneys.' However, on this stretch of Caribbean shore the houses are similar in style but very colourful and an unseemly squabble ensues.

By the time we finally establish that the green one with the brown roof that he wants me to steer towards is really the ochre one with the red roof, we are fast approaching land and end up anchoring with only a couple of feet of water under us. But in *such* loveliness! On a solitary journey like ours you do not expect any kind of welcome when you arrive, such as yachtsmen on the ARC or other blue water rallies provide for one another. But I think there would have been a huge sense of anti-climax had our journey terminated among crumbling commercial buildings and oil terminals.

Instead, we are in an incredibly beautiful natural harbour, surrounded by tree-covered hills and scattered houses of the traditional, single-storey, wooden kind. There is not a high-rise apartment block or a take-away food franchise in sight. And, with regard to being safe and restful, it is also very sheltered.

We raise our Q flag. Then we take the dinghy off the foredeck and put it back on the davits because we shall probably be pretty tired tomorrow morning and will need the dinghy to go ashore and clear in with the authorities.

Our cockpit faces outwards, providing a clear view all the way down Falmouth Harbour to the distant heads where we so recently entered. The squalls appear to have gone somewhere else for the time being and it is sunny and warm. We get out the cockpit cushions, put up the awning, and our feet, and raise a glass to celebrate our safe arrival at such a lovely place.

In the twenty days since leaving the Cape Verde Islands we have covered 2,255 nautical miles in which time we saw only seven ships plus the hand-steered yacht. Our longest period without sighting any vessel at all was six days. We averaged 4.7 knots. Since leaving England seventeen months ago we have travelled 7,600 miles. We have a light meal and are asleep by 6pm.

THE CARIBBEAN

ANTIGUA

26

Getting Acquainted

During the voyage one thing we have really looked forward to – apart from an end to the constant rolling – is a full night's sleep. Unfortunately, after three weeks of night watches, neither of us manages to stay asleep for longer than three hours at a time.

We make a lazy start to our first day on Caribbean soil and set off mid-morning with a small itinerary: to clear in with Customs, Immigration and the Harbour Master and to buy some fresh bread for lunch.

On our way ashore in the dinghy David spots *Jupiter* anchored a short distance away and we stop by to tell Don and Sally how much we appreciated the weather data provided by the Big Fish Net and especially to say a personal well done for their rescue of *Wanderer*. They seem embarrassed that anyone should think they had done anything out of the ordinary.

Then we continue into the yacht harbour. It is a delightful marina complex and dinghy basin. All wood and lots of secure dinghy space in a completely enclosed area of water. It is bordered on two sides by a couple of boutiques, a cyber café, a supermarket, a bank, a chandlery and the marina office. On the third side are pontoons, currently filled with very large, luxury yachts. You enter under a low bridge ensuring that only dinghies can get into it. After tying up ours, we set off down the road on the half-mile walk to English Harbour to clear in. It is lovely to see coastal seabirds again, especially the terns sitting one to each wooden pile and just hanging out, separate but together, the way terns do.

Out on the road and a little way beyond the marina, a small herd of brown and white goats with long floppy ears overtakes us. They enter a dirt yard on the right, with a basketball hoop attached to a small wooden building at the far end. They give the place a cursory inspection, find nothing of particular interest, exit and go tripping down the road ahead of us looking for something better to occupy their morning.

For ourselves, we are enjoying the stroll, the first time in three weeks that we have walked on a surface that wasn't moving in several directions at once. The road has neither people nor traffic on it. We dawdle with the pleasure of children discovering a new world or, like the little gaggle of goats, just looking about us and with no urgency to be anywhere soon.

I am a short distance ahead of David, gazing happily up into a clear, brilliant blue sky when my eye is caught by a dark and very distinctive predatory shape overhead. That languid glide on the thermals, that small head between those large sharply-angled wings. I have never seen a real one before, only pictures. I am so excited. I turn towards David to share my discovery with him but the words, 'A frigate bird!' die on my lips. A one-legged man with dreadlocks has David by the throat.

From a subsequent review of events it would seem that the man had appeared from a building across the road and that the only recognisable word uttered by him had been 'bread'.

Now, this morning David *is* unusually dozy. Partly general weariness from a long and tiring journey, obviously. But also, I suspect, from simply switching off the brain after the demands made on it to get the three of us here in one piece. The only thing David is thinking about at present, apart from clearing in with the authorities, is buying some fresh bread for lunch. Lunch is as far into the future as David can currently get. And to give him his due, the wooden building across the road from where the man may have come could quite easily have been a small shop.

Like me, David has been charmed by the unexpected courtesy, kindness and helpfulness of the people we have encountered during our journey through Europe and the Atlantic Islands. For all our lives, however, we have been hearing about the warmth, friendliness and good humour of laid-back Caribbean folk, and here was one of them offering unasked to provide the only item on the shopping list of David's tired mind.

'Bread,' he had agreed. 'Yes, we need some bread.'

It is at this moment, as I turn around to tell him about the frigate bird, that a human predator with an altogether different interpretation of the word bread and enraged by David's apparently cavalier response to his demand for money, throws one of his crutches to the ground and shoves the thumb and fingers of his freed hand around David's windpipe.

Welcome to the Caribbean.

Someone will tell us later that the young man had lost his leg in a car accident. Having spent the compensation paid to him he is now on the look-out for another solution to his cash-flow problems, making it advisable to avoid him wherever possible.

David prises the fingers from his windpipe, steps back, and while his attacker gropes for his abandoned crutch to pursue him we sprint for English Harbour.

It is gorgeous. Quite simply, *gorgeous*. There is no other way to describe it. Set in another beautiful bay, English Harbour contains Nelson's Dockyard. Although this was already a well-established navy yard before the 26-year-old Captain Horatio was stationed on the island during his Caribbean tour of duty. His name adorned it only later, after his naval career had made him famous.

The dockyard retains many of the 18th and 19th century buildings from when it housed the British West Indies fleet. They have been beautifully restored and are now in practical, everyday use as sailmakers, bakery, Customs and Immigration, hotel, chandlery, restaurant, bar and local market. It has also been declared a National Park, so happily it should remain free of high-rise concrete apartments and take-away food outlets in perpetuity.

The harbour itself is one of the few Caribbean refuges against hurricanes, a natural phenomenon which enabled the British Navy to reign supreme in the region because its ships could hole up in English Harbour during the hurricane season while other nations had to flee the area.

Before we arrived here I can't say that either of us had given any thought to Caribbean sovereignty, or even diversity. The attraction had been a warm winter, a blue sea and lots of anchorages. In reality, each island or small cluster of islands that you arrive at in the Lesser Antilles is either a separate country with its own constitution, or a dependency or protectorate of either America or one of the major European nations; or, in the case of Sint Maarten/Saint-Martin, *two* European countries, the southern half of the island being Dutch and the northern half French.

Independent or not, each of these Caribbean countries still reflects, to a greater or lesser extent, the culture of the foreign nation to which it once belonged. They may retain its currency (guilder or franc) as well as using the Eastern Caribbean dollar and the US dollar (roughly EC$2 to US$1). They drive on the right, except in former British territory where they drive on the left – although usually in left-hand-drive cars which are cheaper because they come from the USA. This can make overtaking a disturbing experience for a passenger, however, as the driver doesn't have a clear view of any oncoming traffic until he is fully committed whereas the passenger does.

More pertinent for us, each country has its own Customs, Immigration and Harbour Authority. You have to clear in with each of them. Just as importantly you have to clear *out*, because if you don't have the appropriate clearing-out form from your last island, the next one you go to won't let you in. But at least you get to meet a lot of local people, even if most of them are wearing uniforms. And you can learn a lot about a country from its bureaucracy.

Antigua, and its sister island of Barbuda, constitute a single country, originally British. The attractive little building where we have to clear in is on English Harbour's truly delightful waterfront. The officer there observes us from under low-slung eye-lids, a study in well-practiced contempt. In a fairly long lifetime on the public's side of a counter I have experienced what I had assumed to be every variation of bad attitude. But what I have never before encountered is such an overt intention to offend.

'Next,' he snarls, shoving what we thought was our properly completed form back across the counter at us. We have failed to name the place to which we intend going *next*, after we leave Antigua.

We don't know. We haven't thought about it. All our energy has been concentrated on simply getting here. We stare at each other, our minds a blank. In the past, clearing in has always been a matter of who you are and where you've come from, basic details about your boat, plus: if the country of entry is Spanish they want to know your engine number, and if Portuguese, your engine number *and* the colour of your sails. Nobody has ever demanded we declare our next port of entry.

Unfortunately, the chain of islands on a chart that was once so familiar to us has now disappeared into the miasma that used to be our brains before three weeks of broken sleep, undreamed dreams, unrelieved motion and a one-legged homicidal maniac laid waste to them.

After a long inner struggle David cries triumphantly, 'Barbuda!' Against all the odds he has dredged up a name from the depths of his exhausted mind to pacify this large, hostile uniform in front of us. He has that hopeful sort of look you see on the faces of schoolboys under pressure to pacify a relentless tutor which in the circumstances, and drooping helplessly as I am beside him, I find quite heart-rending.

'That's *ours*,' says the man behind the counter, rolling his eyes towards the ceiling and exhaling heavily through his nose. 'Think of somewhere *else*.' After another long struggle we do, after which we are required to write down exactly how long we want to stay on Antigua which we also haven't thought about because nobody has ever wanted to know that before either.

With the formalities finally completed we totter out of the building, follow an arrow attached to the word *Bakery* and climb a flight of stairs to the upper storey of a beautifully-restored wooden building. The baker has a surprisingly young face given that his thick curls are liberally sprinkled with grey. He has perfect white teeth and a very pleasant expression.

'Just arrived,' he says to David. A statement rather than a question.

David nods, his energy exhausted by the clearing-in process. Keen to engage with the locals, however, after our first two abysmal encounters, I say, 'The squalls were amazing, this great long line of them night after…'

But I don't finish. His previously warm eyes cool as they turn slowly from David to me, like I was something the cat just brought in and dropped onto his newly-washed floor.

'I know, *Lady*,' he says, with a heavy emphasis on the last word. 'I used to be a sailor.'

I suppose it does get pretty boring for the people here, hundreds of us turning up every year banging on about our once-in-a-lifetime experience. But, conversationally, there is nowhere to go now, so we pay the baker quite a lot more than seems reasonable and descend the stairs. On the other hand, might they not make a *small* allowance for the fact that they already live in Paradise? Whereas quite a few of us have not had that privilege and have gone to considerable lengths to get here. And give them our money. Lots of it, as it turns out.

Apart from clearing in and the bakery we cannot do anything more today as it is a public holiday and everywhere else is closed, so we set off back towards Falmouth Harbour and *Voyager*. On the way we are confronted by an open air, harbour-side bar and decide to stop, mainly because the barman looks up at us and smiles. Although by the time we have ordered it is apparent that it wasn't a smile. The man has a mouthful of very large teeth and a nervous tic.

'A local beer,' he says, uncapping two bottles. 'You'll like it.'

We have barely got it to our lips when his two other customers, an average sort of couple who have been sitting on bar stools talking quietly together, finish their drinks and amble away still deep in conversation.

The barman stares at their backs with a look of intense loathing and expresses quietly but forcefully through the gritted tombstones of his unnervingly exposed teeth his disgust at having to tolerate *that* kind of trash. We watch them walk down the quay. They are undoubtedly off one of the yachts here. They are probably a decade younger than we are but in all other respects they could be us. Another visitor arrives and receives a beer. I wonder if this newcomer, watching David and I walking away down the same stretch of quay in a few minutes' time, will ask the barman what we have done to inspire such revulsion or whether, like us, he will simply drink up quickly and leave.

As we make our way back to *Voyager* we observe the various yachts, tied up and at anchor. We hadn't felt particularly at risk at any stage of the journey here, but looking at some of the boats which have also made the crossing we think how small and vulnerable they seem. One of them is the dismasted sloop towed so valiantly by Don and Sally. And yachts do disappear. As well as the one which failed to arrive at Martinique and is currently being sought by the Dutch Air Force, the US Coastguard is asking for sightings of another which left the Canaries mid-December, reported engine trouble soon after, and has not been heard from since.

27

Just Another Day in Paradise

There are squalls overnight. Next morning the water in Falmouth Harbour is still very rough and we decide to forswear our small dinghy in favour of the local water taxi. We have both enjoyed a long and spectacularly sound night's sleep, and I admit that I am not as alert as I should have been when calling up the water taxi on the VHF. As a result I commit the cardinal sin of VHF etiquette: I forget to ask the man who answers my call to nominate a working channel and instead begin giving him the name of our yacht and our location over Channel 16. I am immediately made aware of my error by a fellow countryman – albeit with an accent noticeably winched up a class or two – shouting at me to clear off and ranting about *people* and all the *crap* you get on this channel nowadays.

When we do finally board the water taxi my next cardinal error of the day is to repeat yesterday's. As an inveterate chatterer to strangers I begin a conversation with the water taxi man as we head for the shore. I am barely halfway through my first sentence when he looks into the distance over my right shoulder and says, 'Yes, *Lady*,' with just the same inflection on the second word that the baker used yesterday. Women, it seems, should be seen and not heard. We continue the rest of the journey in silence.

At the marina we spot a bird we have never seen before. We have books on European birdlife aboard but nothing for the Caribbean so we go into the bookshop. A late-middle-aged man is just leaving. Wearing an air of entitlement and a linen suit reminiscent of Somerset Maugham, he sweeps impressively between us as if we don't exist while calling back to someone within that he'll only be an hour or so. It is the voice of the incandescent man on the VHF earlier. He also fancies himself as a broadcaster apparently, and will be heard maundering endlessly on 'Harbour Radio', a channel he monopolises daily with the racing news and weather forecasts as dodgy as his accent.

In a distant corner of the shop a late-middle-aged woman with peroxide hair, and English skin too long exposed to a Caribbean sun, is reclining on a long, low chair with a telephone receiver to one ear. David immediately becomes absorbed in a search for charts of the local waters while I seek out the shelf with the bird books on it. I soon find what I want.

The price sticker is exorbitant, even for a stripped pine and rocking chair place like this one, but it is a very nice book and I am tempted.

David can't find what he's looking for but, still browsing, begins making his way towards me. I turn to look at the woman lying back luxuriantly in the reclining chair on the far side of the shop and wonder if it might be better to call in on the way back to buy the book as we have a lot to do today. She eyes me fixedly while saying down the telephone, with an affected upper-middle-class drawl not heard in England, in public at least, these thirty years, 'It wouldn't be so *baad* if it weren't for these *bladdy castomers*.'

I assume she is making a joke, albeit a clumsy one. Nobody in the real world treats customers like this anymore apart from Harrods. But no, she repeats the sentence even louder, in case I missed it the first time, prefaced with, 'I *said...*'

I still have the book open at the page with this morning's mystery bird on it. I hand it over to David, settle myself into a rocking chair and ponder as he reads. It seems to me that if you aspire to some outdated notion of social elevation then you should encompass all of it, including *noblesse oblige*, not just the snobby bits you fancy. And one of the obligations of rank is being civil to everybody, not just those you consider your equals or above. Alternatively, if being a shopkeeper is beneath you, go and do something else.

As David finishes reading, the woman ends her telephone call, rises from her chair and makes her way with very bad grace to the till by the door to relieve us of money. I take the book from David and put it back on the shelf.

'Don't you want to buy it?' he asks.

Not if my life depended on it.

I nod a gracious good-day in her direction as we leave, empty-handed, with her furious eyes burning into our backs.

Apart from our VHF, all our communication systems have now disappeared. We can no longer access e-mails via our computer. When we try, a message appears telling us that the server has remodelled its system and to get in touch with them by the telephone number provided. One can only assume they gave some sort of notice to their customers but we were crossing the Atlantic at the time and our European mobile phone doesn't work here. The only way to contact family and friends is via the local branch of an American telephone company.

Because of the weekend and holiday Monday, this is the first day since our arrival that it has been open for business so after leaving the bookshop we seek out the phone company. We are the only customers and although there are two women behind the counter it still takes longer than it might to book three phone calls to England because the older woman is making an unseemly fuss to her placatory younger colleague whom she is accusing of making free with her ballpoint pen, despite having been warned *repeatedly* against using it.

We are finally allocated a booth and call David's brother Tony to say that we have arrived safely and give him the address of Falmouth Harbour Marina so that he can forward our mail. We also notify our yacht insurers where we are, and leave a message to be relayed to Ian on the *Spirit of Diana* saying that we are sorry to have missed him in Trinidad.

Our priority now is to find a dentist for David. Given our experiences so far, we approach the Visitors Office with trepidation. The charming young woman inside, little more than a girl really, tells us there isn't a dental practice here and that we shall have to go into the island's capital, St John's.

We ask her if we can consult her Yellow Pages to get an address. She doesn't have one but goes cheerfully across the open area shared with the National Park Office to borrow theirs. An older woman behind the counter there denies having a Yellow Pages, and even when a copy is spotted on the shelf behind her ample figure she shows great reluctance to let any of us look in it. With a lot of coaxing from the Visitors Office clerk, however, it is ultimately yielded up for a couple of minutes. I feel as if we've stumbled onto the film set of a *Carry On* movie, where all the characters are abominably rude to the hapless hero except the *ingénue*.

With the dentist's address written on a piece of paper and the Yellow Pages restored to its glowering owner, the Visitors Office clerk consults her watch and tells us that we can catch a bus into St John's outside her office shortly. Several other yachtsmen arrive and wait for it, too.

Initially there is some confusion about whether the unmarked silver-grey mini-bus that screeches to a halt beside us is in fact a bus or one of the very expensive taxis which the other yachtsmen say they have been warned to avoid. The dreadlocked driver insists his vehicle is a bus, but no-one boards until finally the *ingénue* is fetched from the Visitors Office, nods her assent and we all get in.

28

A Different Antigua

The road out of the harbour has traffic-calming bumps across it but, despite their inherent purpose, our driver clearly sees each bump as a launch pad for some kind of personal land speed record across the spaces in between. The heads of his passengers, meanwhile, maintain a perilous relationship with the vehicle's roof. A sustaining thought throughout the journey is that at least it is a right-hand-drive vehicle in Antigua's left-hand-side road system.

It is a mysterious bus route. For a start, there are no discernible bus stops, and people do not appear to be waiting for a bus, or even wanting to go anywhere especially. But the driver honks his horn, swoops to a stop beside them, they climb in, give him a dollar and off he goes.

It gets pretty crowded, with the later passengers half-sitting on the original ones, and you can't help noticing that the spacious bench seat in the front has been taken up by the driver's non-paying friend. Halfway into town the driver brakes and honks at a somnolent young woman on the opposite side of the street. She has very elaborate hair weaving and is very stylishly dressed.

Another honk of the horn and she undulates very slowly across the road in front of the bus, as if she hasn't actually noticed its being there and is simply passing. When she reaches the pavement, the driver's friend gets out, holds the door open and she slides in between him and the driver. She doesn't pay either, so it's assumed she is the driver's girlfriend. Or the friend's. She doesn't acknowledge either of them at any stage so it is hard to tell. The journey into St John's bus station takes forty minutes.

Compared with the affluence of English and Falmouth Harbours, the people on the streets of St John's do not appear to have very much materially, yet the place throbs with life and good humour. Like the laughing young men in battered old cars, flirting with young women pedestrians who pretend to ignore them, although the men look delighted anyway.

If English Harbour is picture-postcard-perfect with its fresh white paint and beautifully-restored historic buildings, St John's is a sprawling, dusty town with scarcely an architectural gem to call its own. Its dominant building material appears to be concrete and its wide main road is edged with gaping storm drains so big you fear that a turn of the ankle will result in your being swallowed up, never to be seen again.

If the former is touchy and snobbish with a profound sense of grievance, the people of St John's are relaxed, kindly and helpful, giving the place a vibrancy that is positively infectious. You feel energised by it. And it is all about attitude.

Like the slender little assistant in the vast hardware shop, a recent school-leaver by the look of her, sorting cheerfully and unasked through her scattered stock to provide the biggest possible range for us; all the time apologising for the lack of choice although we assure her the first fish slice she puts on the counter is more than adequate. (The handle fell off ours during the crossing.)

Like the 30-something male motorist, trapped in traffic, cheerfully passing the time of day with us as his car crawls alongside; a boon to sociability, the left-hand-drive car in a clogged left-hand-side road system. The policeman who gives us directions to the dentist. The dentist himself, over-stretched, with three patients already supine in three separate rooms and a malfunctioning generator, but sympathetic and determined to fit David in. Bryson's, the big cheerful supermarket. The big cheerful lady in its doorway, with a smile like Mammy in *Gone with the Wind* when Clark Gable gives her that red petticoat, her round face suddenly beaming at our approach as if she has just encountered friends unexpectedly.

'Come into the shade,' she says, moving aside to make room for us, 'it's *hot* today.'

It is a different bus driver on the return journey. He leaps into his seat, slams the door, starts the engine, hurtles forward and is out of the bus station and making a right-hand turn across two opposing lanes of traffic in what seems to be a single fluid movement.

It sets the tone for the entire journey which takes a mere nineteen minutes compared with the outward trip's forty. He never drives at less than full speed even when, to avoid a red light at a T-junction he shoots off to the right, through a service station forecourt, and back out onto the road through oncoming traffic from both directions. My abiding memory is of the resentful eyes of the garage proprietor sitting in a rocking chair between his two petrol pumps observing our bus hurtle past his knees.

David needs a number of visits to the dentist and, along with the opportunity to buy our food from Bryson's, our trips into St John's provide snapshots of Antiguan life. Not least the bus journey itself. For instance, on a near-empty bus the mature ladies in their go-into-town dresses and straw hats could all sit together and gossip if they wanted to. Instead they sit one to a bench seat and converse with each other along the length of the bus without turning their heads. This can only happen on dry days. When it rains the bus is packed, and very hot as everybody with a seat beside a window closes it rather than get wet.

Each bench seat on the bus has a folding jump seat at its aisle end. When the vehicle is full, the people on the jump seats have to get up, raise their seat and hang vulture-like over their neighbours every time someone wants to get off or on. This results in a number of people shuffling about, or bent up double, usually while the bus is moving at speed.

An expatriate with bright green hair complains loudly about over-loading, justifying her right to complain by having lived on Antigua for 27 years. The driver ignores her, but an Antiguan man who has just stood up so that someone else can get on – and thereby prompted the woman's complaint – explains patiently and tactfully that he lived thirty years in Britain and six in the USA and that *'When in Rome...'* Nevertheless she goes on and on and in the end the man tells the driver to stop. He gets off and, head down into the driving rain, finishes his journey on foot rather than continue listening to her. It is something you become very aware of, over time: this intrusion of incomers into small communities, whether as long-term fixtures such as the woman with green hair or continuous waves of temporary interlopers like us.

The school children on the bus are always silent. Neither the voluptuous high school girls with their exotic hair weaving and long curling eyelashes, nor the shy little primary school boys, ever say a word, not even to one another. Perhaps, like women here, children are required to be seen and not heard. Or maybe it has something to do with their workload since they are all weighed down with massive school bags. Nor do I ever hear anyone swear. If they do, it is in patois and passes me by.

On one trip into town we pass two men at the side of the road with the carcass of a cow strung up to a tree. By the time we return it has been cut up into joints and a couple of trestle tables are being used as a makeshift butcher's counter.

We even spot a couple of bus stops eventually, but never see anybody using them. Passengers continue to be scooped up along the way. Nobody says 'please'. Just 'stop here' or 'school house' and the driver complies. On hot, dry days the doors remain open, despite the bus careering around corners, and I try to keep my mind from dwelling on those gaping storm drains.

The capital's book store, The Map Shop, has no stripped pine or rocking chairs or artful table displays. It is cramped and not terribly well lit but its shelves groan with practical bindings at reasonable prices and the man behind the counter smiles as you enter. Among the classics, modern novels and natural history is *A Guide to Karaoke: a complete course to equip you to perform*, and a dog-eared copy of *Gone with the Wind* that looks as if it has been on public loan for many years.

When asked by a customer if he would be seeing him on Sunday, the shopkeeper says thoughtfully, 'With the Lord's good grace'. And later, as he prepares to go out for a while, he says to his colleague, 'Brother Andrew, if I move the car will you put the cones out?' This mystifies us until we leave the shop and see a car-sized stretch of kerb reserved by traffic cones. Each one has 'The Map Shop' neatly handwritten on a white band around it.

The bird book I buy here explains why frigate birds endlessly fight aerial battles over food with other species instead of catching their own. Truth is, they didn't evolve very well. Their feathers aren't waterproof so they dare not dive because they would be unable to take off again. In fact, they are so badly adapted to their environment they even need a consistent wind to take off from their nesting sites. But with a seven-foot wingspan and vicious beak they survive well enough by forcing small terns to drop the fish they have just dived for, and then hurtling spectacularly through the air to catch it before it can fall back into the sea. After my initial interest I find I have no taste for them. I have, in the meantime, encountered the local pelicans and begun what will become an enduring love affair.

On one of our trips into St John's we lunch on fried snapper and lime pudding, at Hemingway's, where the capital's visitors go. On another, we drop in at the Food Centre where local people eat. The choice is Caribbean, Chinese or salad. It has a wonderfully chaotic counter where having paid for your food you have to back away gripping your tray while everyone closes in on your elbows trying to take your place, either to pay themselves or put in their take-away order.

I choose Caribbean and then have to ask the young woman at the next table what I am eating: salt cod in tomato and onion sauce (with lots of small bones), mashed sweet potato (and possibly yams); plantain (the banana variety used extensively as a vegetable) and egg plant. It is bland and very filling. The potato/yam is a neat rectangle. Boiled in the bag, it has managed to retain perfectly its pillow shape and even the impression of the bag's heat-sealed seam at one end. There is also an intriguing item on the menu board over the counter but I don't like to impose on my neighbour again to find out what goat water is.

We visit Antigua's little national museum. Despite operating on a budget that wouldn't qualify for the term 'under-funded' elsewhere it is quite wonderful. Someone, sometime, has put serious thought into how to stimulate a visitor's interest and understanding at virtually no cost and with minimum fuss. The exhibits – from the island's geology to its human origins (the Arawaks) and subsequent development – are imaginatively arranged and labelled; the latter typed on a manual typewriter and cut into strips with scissors.

It has the air of having been assembled by the best teacher you ever had, the one with the natural talent for putting things so well that you absorbed information without noticing. And not more than you could cope with, either. So many exhibitions nowadays assault you with so much data that you feel you'd need to be there several days to do it justice, feel guilty, get tired, give up the struggle and find the coffee shop instead.

Antigua's cathedral is described as 'a building within a building'. It has a beautiful pitch pine inner one and a stone exterior. This double building was intended to withstand hurricanes and other natural disasters, and given that it is currently celebrating its 150th anniversary the plan seems to have worked. Its predecessor succumbed to an earthquake.

On one trip the petrol station at the T-junction has a policewoman on the forecourt. We nudge each other and wait expectantly. There's obviously been a complaint and she is there to put a stop to the iniquitous, not to say potentially life-threatening shortcuts the bus drivers make to avoid the traffic lights. But no. The light turns red, the bus veers across the road as usual, mounts the forecourt, swoops around the policewoman – who doesn't even look up from her conversation with the pump attendant in his rocking chair – and then hurtles out through the oncoming traffic and down the road again.

29

Getting Sorted

Meanwhile, back at Falmouth Harbour life goes on in its own misanthropic way. The woman in the tiny post office bristles with indignation if you dare go inside. The atmosphere in the supermarket is so frosty that you wonder at the need for freezer cabinets and yet it is probably the prettiest supermarket we have ever shopped in. Built in seasoned wood and not unlike an extended ranch house, it is light and airy thanks to the fact that large shutters on its back wall open outwards, providing staff and customers with an idyllic, sunlit view. Although if you say so, the cashier shivers, pulls her cardigan tighter around her shoulders and complains about the draught. It is also the most expensive one we have ever shopped at and you emerge with four basic items and a till receipt that makes your eyes water. You wouldn't mind even that if it weren't for the hostility. Inevitably one asks: 'Is it me?' So I do a straw poll among our fellow yachtsmen.

'Have you *been* in that *bloody bookshop*?' asks one, eyes blazing at the memory.

'A rip off!' says another, fresh from the supermarket.

But the most eloquent describes her experience at Customs and Immigration. *He had three yacht skippers lined up along his counter*, she says hotly. *And walked up and down it like a schoolmaster, criticising everything they wrote down on their forms*: '*Wines and spirits* separately, *I* said!' And he had lambasted her husband's handwriting to such an extent that she was finally moved to rise from her seat in the waiting area to protest. 'He has arthritis. He *can't* write any better than that!'

And it is noticeable that nobody stays around long. All the yachtsmen who arrived around the same time as us have gone except Don and he is recovering from a malarial infection courtesy of a couple of particularly virulent mosquito bites. He lifts his shirt and shows me the two inflamed puncture marks on his back, just above waistband level, like something left behind by a Hammer Horror vampire. And, as if proving the maxim that no good deed goes unpunished, the man who towed a stranger's boat for four days through rough seas and continuous squalls is suffering blood poisoning, fever, joint pain, fatigue and affected nerves. We should have left, too, had it not been for David's dental work and the fact that our mail has still not arrived.

Having decided that something isn't your fault, of course, you begin to look outward. And what you see is a community at war with itself, not just its visitors. We need to make more phone calls and again approach the two receptionists at the phone company, negotiating our bookings through the sniper fire of the older one. And late that same afternoon, on our way back from English Harbour, we happen to pass their building as they are leaving for the day. Their office has a balcony across its front, with a flight of steps down either end. The two women emerge together, the older one still nagging, and as the door clicks shut behind them they turn back-to-back like duellists, stride to opposing ends of the balcony, descend the stairs and stalk off home in opposite directions.

And then there are the Laundry Wars on the dinghy dock. The spoils of these daily skirmishes are the visitors' washing and it is fought over by the representatives of two competing laundries. The traditionally-built Mrs Kinsale, eagle-eyed and with her handheld VHF at the ready, sits astride a stool beside the chandlery. The fine-boned Miss Myrtle defends her pitch outside the cyber café, although both will poach from the other if the competition happens to be absent for a moment. With the line of mega-rich super yachts looming to our right, from which most of their business comes, my plea of, 'I do my own,' shocks them both.

In the end you ask yourself how people can live in such beauty and be so miserable. One young man – the only local apart from the town drunk who actually acknowledges me, except to take my money or lay claim to my laundry – strikes up a conversation one day when a green turtle pops its head up and we both turn to look at it.

It dives immediately and the young man says that an old lady once told him that if you sprinkle flowers and bread on the water at sunrise for a couple of days it pleases the sea goddess, Yamama, or maybe she isn't a goddess but just a god's assistant. Anyway, it's an African belief and it brings marine life to you. 'You can check,' he says. 'She has a website.' But he thinks it's all rubbish. He is tall, healthy, well-dressed, he has a job with prospects and lives in a beautiful landscape with a delightful climate.

A few moments later the green turtle resurfaces and begins swimming lazily on the surface of what is one of the most gorgeous, unspoiled harbours

I have ever seen. 'There you are,' the young man says. 'Didn't need the flowers after all.' And then he adds something that would be incomprehensible to a very large proportion of the world's population. 'I want to travel,' he says wistfully. 'There has to be something better than this.'

We do witness one spontaneous and glorious burst of joy. In the supermarket of all places. A young man, massively built and with a taste in long baggy shorts that make his body appear almost square. What triggers his impromptu dance, from one end of the supermarket to the other and out through the door, we will never know. But with arms raised above his head and his face radiant he boogies down the aisle between the shelves and the freezer cabinets. He does it slowly, rhythmically, in ecstasy, his considerable body fat taking on a momentum independent of his frame. It is awesome but at the same time poetic. It even inspires the perpetually exhausted-looking girl behind the deli counter to applaud.

It rains most days, or sometimes during the night, only briefly but long and heavy enough to freshen up the streets, wash your rigging and decks, fill the odd bucket from the awning to do a bit of laundry, water people's gardens and keep the island green.

We take long walks among the wooded hills above the anchorage, with their lovely vistas of the harbour and the sea. Wild flowers begin to appear and the gardens bloom. Many of the houses are built of wood and very small – a single storey, with just a door, a window or two and a neat fence.

Goats and chickens wander wherever they please. There are lots of butterflies and a not infrequent sight on a quiet road is a mongoose. They are supposed to be furtive creatures, but these just sashay about in the open, turning to look at you over their shoulder in the same insolent way that English foxes do on woodland paths before dismissing you as no threat and sliding away into the brush.

This small Asian mongoose was introduced to the Caribbean from Calcutta by a Jamaican sugar producer called Espeut in 1872 to kill the rats which were destroying the cane fields. Unfortunately he did not research their habits. Mongooses feed by day and do not climb trees, which left the rats free to spend their nights eating sugar cane and retreat up trees if threatened. Not that the newcomers were that interested in eating rats anyway, preferring instead the native wildlife, the islanders' chickens and the small lizards that kept their gardens free of pests.

There are also swimming trips, to Pigeon Beach just inside the harbour entrance and around Black Point to Windward Bay, a beach facing the sea and scattered with coral.

Apart from the handle falling off our fish slice, *Voyager*'s only other equipment failure during the crossing was that the freezer packed up. It at least had the courtesy to wait until it had almost nothing in it, so that wasn't a problem. What is a problem now is that the gas igniter on our small fridge is not working, so the only way to power it at anchor is off the batteries and the drain on them is enormous. Given the cost of even the most basic item here, and with a sense of dread, we get someone out.

Hank is a very tall American, much too tall for the average-sized yacht, but he has found a way to stand fully upright in a confined space by forming his body into a shape which, in the art classes of my youth, was called a Hogarth Lazy S. The back of his head presses against our starboard hull lining while his pelvis is thrust well forward. This curve of his lower back necessarily pushes his stomach to the fore and he rests his hands on top of it the way that women in the later stages of pregnancy sometimes do. In this position he stands conversing comfortably about refrigeration.

Our freezer's plate is leaking gas, he says, and needs to be replaced. Then he makes a suggestion for which we shall be eternally grateful. Basically our situation is this: we have a large freezer although under normal circumstances we keep little or no frozen food on board. In fact, by not chilling it sufficiently we have mostly used it as a refrigerator. Meanwhile our small fridge which, like most of its ilk doesn't hold enough or ever get cold enough, needs replacing. So why, he says, instead of a new freezer plate, don't we install a refrigerator plate in our chest freezer and have a really big fridge we can charge up off the starboard engine, and forget about replacing the little fridge altogether? The suggestion is inspired and he sets off back to his office to get a quote for a new plate. From Italy. Which sounds horribly expensive. But it doesn't cost anything to find out.

In the meantime, *Voyager* is due to have her hull cleaned and anti-fouled, and since we have to stay around anyway for David's dental work to be completed, our mail to arrive and a quote for a refrigerator plate, we might as well get her lifted out here. The obvious choice is the slipway at English Harbour.

On the way there, we see the one-legged man coming towards us, eyes blazing. For a man on crutches he has a surprising turn of speed. We cross and re-cross the road several times to shake him off. Crossing a road seems to slow him down a bit.

The slipway cannot take us, as it is in the process of being repaired after a boat fell over on its side and damaged the tracks. But there is a suitable hoist at a boatyard at Jolly Harbour, further round the island. We telephone its manager, who gives us a quote for the lift-out and his daily boatyard fees, both of which seem reasonable. He says he can take us tomorrow and asks us to check in at his office as soon as we arrive. Before returning to *Voyager* we stop off at the chandlery to buy charts and a copy of a cruising guide to the Leeward Islands by Chris Doyle.

30

Jolly Harbour

We set off mid-morning on the 11-mile journey. As soon as we leave Falmouth Harbour we are within sight of the island of Montserrat. In July 1995 its Soufriere Hills volcano, dormant for centuries, erupted. It buried the island's capital, Plymouth, under 12 metres of mud, destroyed its airport and docking facilities and left the southern half of the island uninhabitable. Nearly five years later its crater is still smoking. Lava continues to flow down its slopes and the wind carries its ash across to neighbouring islands.

We head westward along the coast, passing down Goat Head Channel with the land to starboard and reefs to port. The closest, Middle Reef, is not so easy to see as Cades Reef on the far side of it. This outer reef absorbs the waves so that the water is comparatively calm on its landward side. It would be easy to get fixated by the waves breaking over Cades Reef and forget about Middle Reef – which today has only some coral heads disturbing the surface – and stray too close to it. Then we sail out past Pelican Island and turn north to Jolly Harbour.

Reefs are not the only hazard for us at the moment. As every European yachtsman knows, if you are entering a harbour the green marker buoys will be on the right or starboard side of your boat and the red markers will be on your left or port side, indicating thereby that the waterway in between is a safe channel through any underwater hazards.

In the Caribbean they use the American navigation system, which is the opposite of the European one, so that when entering a harbour you have the *red* markers on your right and green on your left. At least the American system is easily remembered thanks to the mnemonic 'red right returning'. That is to say, if you are returning to harbour, keep red on your right-hand side.

Unfortunately, for a European visitor who has spent a sailing lifetime doing the opposite, it can take only a momentary loss of concentration to put you and your boat in dangerous or very shallow water. And on the subject of shallow water, the second hazard here is the local charts. The only ones we have been able to buy are American and they record all depths in *feet*, as opposed to European charts which give water depth in *metres* and the difference between one foot and three feet of water underneath your hull can be a really expensive repair job.

It is a hot afternoon and leaving David to get *Voyager* ready for lifting I set off on a long, hot walk along the quay and pontoons and up the flight of stairs of the marina office to check in with the manager as requested. The American receptionist takes rather a long while to finish a private telephone conversation but when I do finally get to tell her my errand she says, 'I expect he'll find you,' and turns away to examine something pressing in a filing cabinet. So I trudge back to the boat again. This place wasn't always called Jolly Harbour, apparently.

The local men who operate the hoist are very nice. They lift *Voyager* out and pressure-hose her in the cradle. While this shifts a lot of rubbish, her hulls are nevertheless still sporting a form of marine life which they have never sported before. Each small creature is attached by a 'foot' and has what look like little legs kicking out from a petal-shaped shell. They are probably wondering why they suddenly feel hot and where all their water has gone. We stare at them in fascination.

'Goose barnacles,' says Piet the Dutchman, materialising behind us. He had spotted *Voyager* arriving and has come round to say hello.

We wash *Voyager*'s topsides and are halfway through scraping her hulls when work virtually comes to a stop. We are devoting more time to hopping about, slapping our legs and scratching than we are to the boat. A passing American, recognising the signs, stops to tell us about the local mosquitoes. They are so small as to be barely visible but nonetheless drive you insane. They used to be seasonal, he says, but after the last hurricane they didn't leave. He continues on his way but returns within minutes with a can of insect repellent for each of us. He will accept no payment. Before it became Jolly Harbour, he says, the place was called Mosquito Cove.

Early next morning we begin polishing *Voyager*'s topsides. By the time we have completed all four sides plus the underside of the bridge deck, and applied one can of antifouling paint to the hulls, the day is done. We are pleased with what we have achieved, although we do wonder if the second can of paint will be enough to finish the job. At US$177 a can we are rather hoping not to have to buy a third one.

After dinner I begin reading *The Unbearable Lightness of Being* to David. It is his first exposure to Milan Kundera's critically-acclaimed novel, my second. I had failed to connect with it the first time around and hope a shared experience might bring enlightenment. Too late we realise that our mosquito repellent has worn off and our legs are being chewed unmercifully. But we are in bed and asleep before 8pm, too tired to even scratch.

Next day the paint lasts after all. *Voyager* is now finished. Almost too weary to move by the time we have showered and eaten, I resume reading. By page 46 we are both depressed. Not because of its themes of personal and political betrayal, which are a daily presence in our lives thanks to World Service News, but the bewildering metaphors by which Kundera weaves them into his plot. After falling in love with Tereza, Thomas finds that he has to resort to alcohol to enable him to continue his daily infidelities with other women. We are resorting to alcohol to find the strength to face another chapter. Perhaps it is easier if you are familiar with Czechoslovakia's communist era, or could read in the original Czech, but why *does* their female dog have a male name? We keep plodding on. And on, for several days, because the hoist is being used to hold up a monohull while work is done on its keel and so not available to put *Voyager* back in the water. And then we discover we have a more pressing problem than mosquito bites and literature-induced melancholy.

When we had presented ourselves in a semi-conscious state at the Immigration counter on our arrival at Antigua, and been required to state the length of our intended stay, David had written down a couple of weeks which at the time had seemed more than adequate. We had not expected airmail from England to take this long, or that David's final appointment with his overworked dentist would be scheduled for two days after our official date of departure. Nevertheless, when David fronts up at Immigration today to ask for an extension he is told that to remain at Antigua after Sunday will require a visit to the police station in St John's and the payment of US$150 each.

He manages to get a cancelled appointment at the dentist's for this afternoon. We shall return to Falmouth Harbour first thing in the morning, collect our mail from the marina office and leave on Sunday as required.

Voyager has been lifted back into the water by the time David returns from the dentist. On the way he has stopped off at the marina office to pay our bill which is twice what he was expecting because although all our transactions on the island have so far been in EC dollars, it seems that the price quoted for our lift-out and boatyard fees was in US dollars.

We set off for Falmouth Harbour into a brilliant blue, shining morning and a light wind. We watch a pelican dive for its breakfast – more a splat than a dive, really. The technique seems closer to a wrecking ball than precision fishing and they surface with a great kafuffle of feathers and water. They are not graceful birds, but very appealing. In flight they are almost sedate, while appearing to defy gravity with their top-heaviness and large bodies.

We sail past sandy beaches and palm trees with the misty outline of Montserrat and Nevis in the distance. All we have to do now is dinghy into Falmouth Harbour marina and collect our post, which must have arrived by now, clear out with Immigration and call in on Hank to ask him not to pursue the quote for a refrigerator plate. Then it's off to St Kitts and Nevis tomorrow at dawn.

Unfortunately, when we make what we confidently expect to be our final visit to the marina office our mail has still not arrived. It is rather worrying because it contains some important items including renewals of David's driving licence, our boat registration and VHF radio licence, bank statements and yacht insurance papers. We shall have to think what we do about this on our way to Immigration.

From the marina we walk to English Harbour, part of the way in company with a brown and white nanny goat and two tiny identical kids. In the most isolated stretch of road, where he is usually to be encountered, the one-legged man is lying spread-eagled across the pavement ahead of us, his crutches splayed out on either side of him.

We stop at a safe distance and observe him. He is very still and his eyes are closed. Under any other circumstances we should rush forward and offer assistance. Now we simply look at one another and then back at him. He is young and vigorous with a very strong upper body, and my RYA Competent Crew course didn't prepare me for being brought down by the ankles. Frigate birds hover and occasionally swoop low. We look at one another again.

What we do next is positively biblical: we pass on the other side. As we reach that part of the road where we shall lose sight of him I turn and look back. He is upright and reaching for his second crutch.

At Immigration, the young man behind the counter smiles at us in welcome and is utterly charming. We flinch and glance at each other nervously.

David explains that we need to clear out as our time is up tomorrow, but the official's demeanour is such that I am prompted to add that while we don't want to pay US$300 at the police station in St John's for an extension to our stay, we don't understand why our mail has not arrived by now.

'Oh, well,' he says. 'If you're waiting for mail...' and gives us a generous extension without charge. We are so light-headed on our way back to Falmouth Harbour that we decide to treat ourselves to coffee at the lovely waterside building known as the Engineer's House.

On Monday Hank gives us a quotation for a refrigerator plate. As expected, it is expensive, but affordable even with the installation costs added. And it will solve a growing problem of keeping food fresh and drinks cold in a climate which, already hot, is set to become even hotter. We ask him to order one for us. And since David's dental work is complete there is nothing to keep us here until the new plate arrives from Italy. So we set off to discover a little more about Antigua.

31

A Trip around the Island

We sail clockwise, the same route we took to Jolly Harbour, but as we head down Goat Head Channel this time, between the land and the two reefs, a rain shower passes over us. David is steering and in the short time that it takes him to slip into a jacket we stray very close to Middle Reef, seeing for ourselves just how quickly you can get into trouble.

Five Islands Harbour is a large uninhabited bay almost a mile wide and two miles long. Confusingly there is only one island in the bay, Maiden Island, but the harbour is named after a small cluster of them just outside its south head. With its beaches, mangroves and seabirds it is a place apart, and yet Antigua's bustling capital is only a short distance away. We anchor in a little cove on its south side called Hermitage Bay.

We have no immediate neighbours during our stay. On one day the most distant beach is alive with children for a while, shrieking with excitement as they hurl themselves into the low surf. The next day the sands are deserted but for a young calf taking a break from its field somewhere beyond the mangroves. The only other person we encounter is a man taking his horse swimming and then grooming it in the sunshine.

The weather is as erratic as ever, including a few squalls. So when these have passed through, and a decent bit of wind arrives, we decide to take advantage of it and move on to our next port of call.

Deep Bay has a long and very pretty beach with a lagoon behind it, and just off the north headland a small island joined by a reef. There is an old fort at that end of the bay and the huge Royal Antiguan Hotel at the other. About a mile and a half outside the heads is Sandy Island and Weymouth Reef, named after HMS *Weymouth* which was wrecked there in 1745. It currently has an Antiguan coaster high and dry on it, with its bows stuck up in the air. In the middle of the anchorage lies the wreck of the *Andes*, with its mast stumps sticking a couple of feet above the water. We paddle the dinghy over and peer down at it, but not much of the wreck is distinguishable as the water is not very clear.

Deep Bay is in complete contrast to Five Islands. It is a busy resort and the usual variety of craft competes for space in its waters. Most noticeable are two very noisy jet skiers. Lacking the courage to go out into deeper water they roar about bravely just yards off the beach instead. One of them hurtles past a boy on a sailboard so fast that the latter spins in a circle and capsizes. The other does the same to a small girl in a sailing dinghy with equally disastrous results. We are anchored behind a boat called *Global Surveyor*, which seems a bit ambitious for a family yacht.

Paddle the dinghy ashore and this is a very pleasant place to wander. Fort Barrington offers wonderful views of Deep Bay and St John's Harbour, which it guarded throughout the 18th and 19th centuries. It also served as a signal station to warn the rest of the island of impending attack and was the only fort to see military action in Antigua.

One morning we walk around the lagoon and finish with a stroll through the hotel's grounds with its pink rhododendrons, open-sided dining room and late breakfasters. The road into it has a swing barrier for vehicles. David and I duck under it, the man behind limbos under it, and as the three of us emerge upright on the other side, a smiling woman in uniform rises to her feet and lays her hand on it saying, 'I been watchin' yuh comin' for the last ten minutes,' and apologises for not having raised it in time.

From Deep Bay we set sail for Long Island, past the capital, St John's, then Dickenson Bay with its hotels and holiday makers and into Boon Channel which lies between the mainland and the long coral reef that arcs around Antigua's northern coast.

During our passage up the Boon Channel the wind freshens and gusts for a while, turning over day sailors left, right and centre. A couple on a Hobie Cat spend ages getting their craft upright, standing on the hull which is underwater, and heaving with all their might on the upper one. They look like two actors on a small stage with a low proscenium arch, showing their bottoms contemptuously to their audience. A long way out at sea a motorboat has a parascender aloft, and I find myself wondering what would happen if a squall came up suddenly, and whether he would end up in Puerto Rico.

The wind abates but is followed by torrential rain. Sea and sky become an eerie colour. Not at all the tranquil turquoise of the brochures. We continue down the channel, pass to the south of tiny Prickly Pear Island, with its encircling coral reef, and anchor in Jumby Bay off the west side of Long Island.

Long Island is an expensive resort on a private island. But there are no private beaches in Antigua. It is very pretty here and a pleasant place to swim. There is not a lot of peace though, with planes flying low overhead on the approach to the airfield a mile and a half away on the mainland, and the Brumby ferry which runs every 30 minutes at high speed and produces a large wake. Both offer good reasons for not tarrying too long.

If you sail south between Long Island and Maiden Island you come to Parham, which is on the mainland. Even allowing for anchoring and a brief squall, it takes us barely an hour until we are dinghying ashore and at Parham we feel we have found the Old Carib. Or a bit of it, anyway. There are chickens roaming free and goats tethered at the side of the pot-holed road. There are huge, glorious old trees, sadly with convolvulus devouring them – its multi-coloured flowers pretty but all-pervading as they swallow up the gravestones and vaults in the churchyard and consume abandoned cars whole.

Baby goats graze contentedly, 10 tiny chickens follow their mother while a cockerel and a goose engage in a cackling competition. The rooster struts, eyes blazing, issuing his empty challenge. The slightly grubby white goose, rootling casually in a storm drain the while, matches him utterance for utterance but in an ironic sort of way that drives the cockerel to apoplectic heights.

We meet an elderly, charming man who mourns the decline of his town.

'The church was beautiful,' he says and looks at us hopefully. 'Did you go inside?'

'No,' we say. 'It was locked.'

He nods, sadly. 'The pipe organ was pumped by hand.'

Parham was once the seat of the island's governor and the second most important town after St John's.

'The plantations shipped their crops of muscavado sugar in sacks from Parham's docks,' he says, 'with a hand-cranked crane.'

Doyle's cruising guide recommends a couple of useful places to shop here. Of particular interest to us is Jamy's supermarket offering 'a good stock of basic provisions' and Joyce's snack bar and cake bakery. Unable to find either I go into the small police station and ask for directions. Apart from a desk and a chair there is no other furniture in the room and the shiny white floor tiles are as treacherous as an ice rink after the recent squall. A police woman and a male civilian are at the desk with an instruction book trying to programme a new telephone system. They both stare at me and then, dragging her brain from the complexities of the telephone, the policewoman says, 'Would you repeat what you just said?' I read out the claims in our new local pilot about Jamy's supermarket and the bakery. They both look at me mystified and then give me directions to Parham's only shop.

The woman behind its counter is lovely. Warm and welcoming. Afraid her stock is very limited. We don't mind at all. We're just pathetically grateful these days if somebody behind a counter is nice to us. She laughs when we point to a packet of Garibaldi and say we'll have some squashed fly biscuits and when I buy a selection of sweet potatoes, squash and carrots she adds another item free of charge. To see if we like it. It is a previously unknown root vegetable, like a small hairy potato and it will grace the next batch of ratatouille I make.

Another short journey to the north-east of Parham takes us to Great Bird Island, in reality the exposed part of a reef which rises to 100 feet and has become an island. It is part of a National Park and uninhabited. It is also the last known home of the endangered Antiguan racer snake. For some reason David finds the notion of a racing snake that can't outrun its predators hilarious. There are small white butterflies. A shearwater skims the sea. The bay is an incredible blue, the reefs pea-green and brown.

In the Caribbean, the saying goes, you sail by colour. If the water is dark blue, it's deep; if it's turquoise, it's 15–25 feet; but if it's bright green with a brown bit in the middle you're approaching a reef. That's why, in the days of sailing ships, they kept a lad up in the crow's nest, because they needed height to see the colour changes early enough to give them time to shift all those acres of sail they carried and change course.

I refuse to go higher than the coach house roof. For a start, it's less straightforward than the local sages would have you believe. It only works properly under clear skies with the sun at the right angle. Cloud can turn any depth of sea dark blue and it is unnerving to watch your safe, deep water drift away along with the cloud. A decent pilot book, a chart and an echo sounder is safer.

We go for a swim late afternoon and a man rows over from a 33ft cat, registered in Sydney, Australia – and the only other boat around – to invite us over for drinks later with him and his wife. We have a very pleasant evening and set sail again the following morning.

There are two entrances to Nonsuch Bay and we go in via the southern one, between Green Island and the mainland. We anchor not far from the reef, in glorious aquamarine water surrounded by wooded hills and pale sandy beaches. It is a glorious place to swim, paddle the dinghy and generally wander. Green Island is uninhabited and home to tropicbirds, pelicans, ospreys and white crowned pigeons.

Most extraordinary is the contrast between the tranquil water in which *Voyager* is anchored, and the ocean beyond the reef. The reef lies just below the surface and is almost invisible, but it protects the bay from the turbulence of the sea. And you sit in your cockpit and watch the waves tumbling towards you, but never arriving, Atlantic rollers stretching back for 2,000 miles, all the way to Africa from where we have so recently come.

To complete our circumnavigation of Antigua, we leave Nonsuch the same way as we entered and follow the coast past the large, coral-protected Willoughby Bay, past English Harbour and back into Falmouth.

Back in our old spot, pelicans plunge and feed. They are a source of great frustration for the frigate birds who can only take fish away from another bird by attacking it as it rises into the air with its fish in its beak. By contrast, after diving for its meal, a pelican sits on the water and consumes its catch within its pouch, leaving the frigate birds to rage and fume impotently overhead.

A large catamaran anchors beside *Voyager* and sets about getting some work done. It has two local men on deck, quietly sanding its teak toe rails, and the crew pottering about rubbing at the bright work when suddenly there is a huge bang from the engine bay and great clouds of black smoke and oil belch from the starboard exhaust. Everybody stops what they are doing and stares. There is a second, even louder, explosion and more, even blacker, smoke followed by another oil slick. People begin running about like headless chickens.

In all the chaos, the only coherent words are from the man in the engine bay who bellows, 'Bring me a poly bag!' which in similar circumstances is probably the last thing I should have had on my mind. As the boat is anchored quite close to us I wonder briefly if, in the event of its blowing up, it will take ours with it. Within minutes, though, everybody is back at their original jobs again; sanding the toe rails and cleaning the chrome, all except the man from the engine bay who pants quietly on the foredeck and is rather sooty.

After our first long passage we had created a maintenance and cleaning schedule of our own. Nothing as dramatic as our neighbour's but, as a blue water cruiser, your boat is your home. At the same time – especially if you are almost constantly on the move as we were initially – it is rather like being on an extended holiday. And once the Atlantic crossing has been made you are into a period where there is no pressure on you to do anything. You can island-hop, swim, socialise, sunbathe or spend your days in a languid haze. Sun, sea and pina colada. You have months ahead of you and the cry of *mañana!* can be heard in the land.

What may be good for cruisers, though, is not always good for yachts. The sea is a hostile environment for any vessel. Hot sun, saltwater and high winds all take their toll on its exterior, plus daily wear and tear on a compact living area. It is important, therefore, to strike a balance between that extended holiday and going to seed.

Voyager has also covered 3,000 miles in the last couple of months, quite a lot of it in testing conditions. So, as well as polishing the salty bloom off cockpit and helm, and shampooing the upholstery there is some serious maintenance to be done. Engines, batteries, outboard motor and davits, a complete check of navigation lights and rigging and the mast. And with the bit firmly between David's teeth, we even end up with a couple of usable interior lights that haven't worked since we bought the boat.

He also inspects and cleans our heating system after finding traces of oxidation around a hose and circlip. A little seawater had obviously worked its way into its exhaust system during the Atlantic crossing. Happily the heater still works because, like a house, a cruising yacht is a home for all seasons and we may not be in warm temperatures indefinitely.

Of course, the most crucial reason for getting your boat back into good working order, if you happen to be loitering in a hurricane zone, is the ability to leave at the appropriate time. We have been mulling over our options.

We could sail south to Trinidad, which is below the hurricane zone, or continue on south down to Venezuela or Brazil. Or we could go through the Panama Canal to the Pacific Islands. The problem with all of these is heat.

The temperature here is already quite hot enough for me and it is still only spring. The scorching summer temperatures to be expected much further south is daunting. And while yachtsmen we have met have said what a beautiful cruising ground Venezuela is, they have added that for safety it is best to sail in convoy so that when anchoring in isolated places one person can remain on each of the boats while the others go ashore. They have also said that the people they met there were wonderfully kind, but that the level of poverty was distressing, particularly the effects of malnutrition and the lack of health care.

Rather than going west, to the Pacific Islands, David has a fancy for Alaska, to the north. The distances are immense, however. To get to Alaska would mean a seven-week voyage of 5,000 miles from Panama to Hawaii. We should winter there and then sail a further 2,000 miles to Alaska the following summer.

To do this we should have to be through the Panama Canal by March to avoid the Pacific's tropical storms which blow from June to October. To have done it this year we should have had to leave Antigua after *Voyager* had been antifouled at Jolly Harbour. But we had wanted to see more of the Leeward Islands than just Antigua, and in particular the Virgin Islands beckon.

Our dilemma is solved during a visit to Falmouth Harbour's supermarket one morning. Standing in the queue at the cash desk I get talking with an elderly, somewhat feisty American woman off a little red and white sloop anchored further down the harbour. The conversation turns to future destinations and I mention my reservations about too much heat.

'Why don't you just keep goin' north, to the States?' she asks.

We should love to, I tell her, but our budget requires that we anchor wherever possible and we couldn't afford American marina rates.

'How tall's your mast?' she asks.

Unsure as to what that has to do with the price of marinas, I tell her.

'And what's your draught?'

I wonder if I have just joined her in something Americans call 'a senior moment', but I tell her anyway.

'Go up the ICW,' she says, and proceeds to tell me about the thousand miles of inland waterway between Florida and Virginia where you can anchor pretty much all the way, and even tie up for free once in a while. Its disadvantages are that it is very shallow in places and there are also some fixed bridges, so for yachts with a tall mast and a deep keel it is out of the question. For *Voyager* there would be no problem at all.

'And it's all different,' she adds. 'Rivers, lakes, marsh, grassland...'

I blink at her. It sounds too good to be true, like the sort of thing people sometimes talk about but haven't actually done themselves. My thought must be evident in my face because she says a little huffily, 'Bin doing it ten years!'

32

Moving On

The new plate arrives and we arrange a berth on a pontoon at the top end of Falmouth Harbour. This area is known as Catamaran Marina although ours is the only cat we have ever seen in it. The reason we are here is that Hank needs electricity so that he can fit a dryer to our refrigeration system which needs to run all night to ensure that all the moisture has been removed. In the meantime we acquire, hunt down and remove a cockroach and Hank introduces us to Roach Hotels: little boxes available from the supermarket that you put in dark corners and cupboards, which lure the wretched things inside and from which they never leave.

While on the pontoon we are conveniently placed to visit a nearby bar recommended in Chris Doyle's cruising guide as offering probably the cheapest lobster dishes in Antigua. We decide to treat ourselves to dinner there. After a long walk in the dark and a fruitless search we ask a couple of passing policemen. They purse their lips, think very hard and stare at one another in puzzlement until the older one remembers that there used to be such a place but it went out of business a long time ago.

Back out at anchor we decide to remain over the weekend to ensure the refrigerator plate works. On Saturday the Australian couple we met at Great Bird Island arrives on an overnight stop in the harbour and we spend another sociable evening together. On Sunday we get a taxi up to Shirley Heights, a former military lookout, now a bar and restaurant which puts on a barbecue Sunday evenings with a steel band and rum punch from 4pm and Reggie from 6.30.

There is a big round table with a big friendly atmosphere around it, much of it courtesy of a tall Trinidadian – who introduces himself as Carl Wilcox, stage name Stretch, 'the original limbo dancer' who performed at the London Palladium in its televised heyday – and his Canadian wife who was once employed by the fashion designer, Norman Hartnell, to write out his clients' bills 'because of her lovely handwriting.' Ah, those gentle, blue remembered days! Shirley Heights also has a spectacular view of English and Falmouth Harbours and is a wonderful place to watch the sun set.

We walk back down through extensive military ruins – officers' quarters, artillery barracks (subsequently an asylum) and Clarence House also a ruin but with a terrace lined with oleander and a terrific view over English Harbour. Night is well fallen by the time we get back to our dinghy and the sky is overcast. We have forgotten to bring a torch with us and dinghy back to *Voyager* in darkness.

Our new fridge plate is working wonderfully, with just fifty minutes on tick-over from the starboard engine daily being more than enough to charge it up. Unlike the little standard fridge, there is a lot of room, it gets really cold and I don't have to get on my knees to stock it or retrieve something from the back. The only slight disadvantage with our new arrangement is that if what I want is at the very bottom, my feet leave the floor. The answer is to line it with two trays of Caribbean beer so there will always be something cold to offer guests.

We have only one last thing to do now and then we are ready to leave.

Monday morning we dinghy into the marina to enquire after our mail. The receptionist in the marina office is someone we have not encountered before. Her name is Layla and she says her father posted a parcel to her from England at the beginning of December but she has still not received it. She also does something none of her colleagues, nor the local postmistress, has done: she explains Antigua's postal system to us.

Individual letters or postcards, she says, are delivered direct to the addressee but anything larger – packages, parcels or large manila envelopes such as ours – remain at the sorting office in St John's and a blue postcard is sent to the addressee – in our case to Falmouth Harbour marina office – advising that our mail is available at the sorting office for collection.

Before receiving it, however, it has to be opened in front of a post office official and the contents inspected and assessed for taxation against the various scales of tax which are levied on different categories of goods. When we tell her that our two envelopes will contain only paperwork she says that is taxed, too. So much for an invoice, so much for a letter and so on. We take the next bus into St John's and make our way to Antigua's cavernous sorting office.

The island's postal service is operated via school exercise books and biros. The two women behind the massive counter consult their exercise books for a long time before declaring no knowledge of our two manila envelopes. In between times they have made several visits to a room behind them, through the swing doors of which can be glimpsed a vast floor space covered with parcels and packages.

Finally one of the women suggests we check at the marina office again when we get back, to see if a blue card has been received in the meantime. This defies logic, because if there is no record of our mail having arrived at this sorting office, how can a blue card have arrived at the marina since we left there this morning? We are being given the run-around. But the scene which has been playing out to our right convinces us that it is nothing personal. This is just good old-fashioned bureaucracy at work.

Along the counter stands a local couple with two very small, obedient children close beside them. You know just by looking at them that they are nice, decent people who keep a loving home. Everything about them reminds me of an immediate post-war childhood in an economically-devastated England. Their leanness. Their worn but clean and well-pressed clothes. Their quiet endurance.

While the family stands passively before him the official tears open the cardboard box addressed to them. It is soon apparent that it is from a friend or family member overseas. Someone earning better money and with easier access to goods than those back home. Also obvious is that it contains Christmas presents because each small parcel that emerges is neatly wrapped in festive paper, tied and labelled. A Christmas morning treat for loved ones far away, on the Christian calendar's most joyful day. Except that it is now February.

The man in uniform behind the large counter slowly and methodi-cally strips the cheerful wrapping from every item in turn and holding it up to the light inspects minutely the little bright-red Santa stocking, the child's toy or the small adult luxury, notes down the amount the family will have to pay for it and then tosses it onto the growing pile of gifts and torn wrapping paper beside him. All to be scooped up and shoved back willy nilly into the cardboard box afterwards and pushed across the counter to the couple when the tax has been paid. The mother, meanwhile, has subtly used her body to shield the children's view of the entire proceedings, so that at home, restored in some measure to their wrappings, the little packages can still be a treat for them.

After getting off the return bus we book a call to Tony who says that he will start applying for replacements or copies of the essential items in the two envelopes he airmailed to us six weeks ago. Given that Layla is still waiting for the Christmas parcel her father posted from England eleven weeks ago, plus our experience at the sorting office today, there seems no point in waiting around for our mail any longer.

Meanwhile, at Falmouth Harbour a sea change has been taking place in recent days. It is almost as if we have passed through some sort of minimum residency period or perhaps it is simply that we have become a familiar presence. Both Mrs Kinsale and Miss Myrtle greet us cheerfully on our arrival at the dinghy dock now, without any interest in our laundry. While the young woman at the supermarket has become positively cordial, engaging us in conversation yesterday, and putting our purchases in double poly bags today before dispatching us with a 'Take care now' that is almost affectionate.

When we check in one last time with Layla at the marina office and tell her that we have decided to abandon our mail, she very kindly offers to have it re-directed when the blue card arrives if we will telephone her with an address. And last, but by no means least, when we go and clear out at Immigration the officer on duty wishes us a happy return.

NEVIS

33

Charlestown Harbour

Before setting out on the 55-mile passage to Nevis we listen to Harbour Radio's weather forecast. The promised 10 to 15 knot wind turns out to be weak and fluky and in order to arrive before dark we need both engines on.

Once out at sea, however, we enjoy again the sight of the islands in a shimmering sunlit sea; Nevis and St Kitts, the tiny Redonde where nobody goes because there is no anchorage, and Montserrat breathing ash from its crater.

We also have our first-ever sighting of brown boobies, large, beautiful, graceful birds, intent upon the flying fish they are feeding on. It is a pity that human traits are ascribed to birds. As a result the gannet is condemned as greedy, the albatross doom-laden, and the boobie stupid, possibly from the Spanish slang *bubie*, or dunce, because they were so tame they would stand about on sailing ships and the sailors simply scooped them up and ate them.

According to a local newspaper, some fishermen on Tortuga, an island off Haiti, have found another use for boobies. Apparently their fluffy white chicks make excellent bait for catching langosta, a species of lobster, for the restaurant trade.

The top of Nevis's dormant volcano has been wreathed in cloud ever since we first spotted it ahead of us. We arrive off the island just as it is getting dark, find a suitable depth of water near to the beach and drop our anchor.

We dine on corned beef, vegetables and a glass of red wine. Corned beef makes a quick and nourishing meal after a long day although its tins are said to be responsible for more visits to Accident & Emergency wards than any other single cause. The ones we have on board are the sort where you turn a very small key round and round so that it peels the tin into a long, very narrow strip of thin metal until it forms a large, unstable coil around the tiny key and which springs suddenly, leaving you with the unpeeled part of the can containing the exposed meat in one hand and the lid and the key in the other, joined together by the domestic equivalent of razor wire.

We both sleep like logs.

We get up into a morning that seems to be made of shimmering silver. It is the effect of a low, bright sun on water set aquiver by a sea swell. When a large, four-masted yacht passes between us and the sun, the brightness through its sails and rigging turns the whole vessel into filigree. And there are brown pelicans everywhere.

Some of them are bobbing on the water. Some have made other arrangements, for moored close inshore there are a number of open, wooden fishing boats, about 12ft long. They have names like *The Ark*, *Noah* and *One Day At A Time* and all of them have been commandeered by pelicans. In a bid to keep them off, given the inevitable mess seabirds leave behind them, one of these small painted boats has a wind-driven bird-scarer revolving on its bow and a spinning anchor ball at its stern. The pelicans have simply arranged themselves around these obstacles and one recumbent body and massive beak is even draped around the boat's name – *Sea Bird*. There are also a lot of flies.

After breakfast we dinghy into the island's capital, Charlestown, which is only a short trip away. The dinghy dock is unusually high. There is a more accessible one but it belongs to the local fishermen and our cruising guide advises yachtsmen not to tie up to it but to use this public one.

Since taking up sailing, somewhat late in life, I have acquired a number of new skills. Among the more picturesque has been: leaping onto a slimy pontoon into a 25-knot offshore wind clutching a mooring line; hanging by my feet from a pulpit to hook up a mooring buoy; and balancing on one leg on *Voyager*'s cabin roof in an Atlantic swell to hold the radio aerial as far up the backstay as possible because it's the only way David can hear the weather forecast.

I now add something more usually encountered on an Army training assault course. The part where new recruits attempt to scale a high wall but, on failing to clear it, either slide back down or end up dangling from the top of it by their finger ends.

Charlestown's dinghy dock is effectively a narrow pier leading from a high bank. It is over six feet high, built of rough timber and the only way to reach the top is to haul yourself up. The solitary toehold is the V provided by two slats nailed between the uprights although this is as likely to trap your foot as provide a platform from which to launch yourself upward. And that poses the other problem. Too little vigour and you risk falling back into your dinghy. Too much, and you go right over the top and into the water on the other side.

The best I can manage is to get my upper body lying across the top with my legs still hanging over the edge. Notwithstanding the splinters, the raw planks are actually a benefit in that they provide the necessary bit of purchase that enables you to hold on long enough to drag one knee upward onto the planks, haul the rest of yourself up after it into a kneeling position and then stand upright. When both of us are firmly on land we make our way into town.

The island of Nevis is seven miles long by five wide and sombrero-shaped, thanks to the volcano at its centre which rises to a peak 985 metres high. It is the smaller of the two islands which make up this small country whose formal title is the Federation of St Kitts & Nevis. Once British, it became independent in 1983. The name Nevis derives from its one-time Spanish name, *Our Lady of the Snows*, and may have been derived by linking the white cloud around Nevis Peak with a 4th century Catholic miracle story about snow falling on one of the seven hills during a hot Roman summer.

It was here that the young naval captain Horatio Nelson, on his tour of duty in the Caribbean, met and fell in love with Fanny Nisbet, the young widow of a plantation owner. They married on the island in March 1787 and set up home in England a few months later.

This is only the third Caribbean island we have ever visited (the first being a week's package tour in the late '80s), but it will soon become apparent that each one has an identity all its own. On some there is a tangible apartheid between the local culture and the foreign environment created by tourism. At the other extreme, the benefit to the island's standard of living from tourism is embraced so wholeheartedly that it's like holidaying in a shopping mall.

To our delight, Nevis has been slower to develop than some. Here the islanders, on this brief acquaintance at least, appear to treat visitors as they do each other, which is in a kindly, courteous, God-fearing way. Sadly, this may be about to change. The construction of a neat little shopping complex for luxury goods is well advanced and has already set itself apart, not just spatially but by its modern design and building materials. In contrast the town centre, where real life is lived, though very neat and tidy is a little worn.

Indeed, some of Nevis's public buildings belong to another century, earlier even than the one we have just left behind, and it is in one of them that we find a neatly dressed, polite young official from the Harbour Authority. She carries out her duties in a battered, wooden lean-to, built against an inside wall of a very old and disreputable-looking warehouse. Her office resembles an open-fronted garden shed, with just a counter and a high shelf on the wall behind her containing dusty boxes of paperwork.

As well as housing the Harbour Authority, the warehouse doubles as the Customs shed and incongruous among the cardboard boxes and parcels that litter its dirt floor is a new, gleaming white, vitreous enamel toilet that someone somewhere on the island is waiting to have installed. We pay EC$20 to the Customs man and EC$12 in harbour dues.

Since we are so close, we pop into the tourist office for local information, provided by a very friendly and helpful young woman, and then make our way to the police station which doubles as the Immigration Office. On our way there, a middle-aged woman with a welcoming smile stops to pass the time of day with us.

The public area of the police station is a small room with a counter and a couple of chairs against one wall. Behind the chairs is a notice board which contains a sheet of A4 paper bearing Nevis Constabulary's Mission Statement: to answer calls, reduce crime and be honest and efficient.

While David stands at the counter and fills in a form with our details and the duration of our visit (after first checking if there are any financial penalties for overstaying) I sit in one of the two chairs and observe the large blackboard opposite. In permanent lettering across the top it has *Life Has No Spare* and *Jesus Saves*. Below, written neatly in white chalk, are the island's traffic statistics – one accident in February (today is the 22nd) – followed by the names of current disqualified drivers. There are four men and one woman, along with the dates on which they will get their driving licences back. When a door opens behind the counter there is a glimpse of a cell with its tenant leaning in the open doorway chatting to an officer. Nevis boasts 'virtually no crime'.

A woman comes in to ask if her nephew has finished giving his statement yet. Told no, she asks the officer behind the counter to tell him to meet her at the supermarket when he has. This request is called out to another officer, behind the thin wall, who calls back the nephew's query as to which supermarket she means; and the officer behind the counter and the one behind the wall relay data back and forth until the meeting place of the woman and her nephew has been established.

When our paperwork has been completed we go into the bank to withdraw some money and feel reassured by quite a long tract in the bank teller's window about trust, honesty and keeping faith with the Lord. Then we go and spend the money in the nearby supermarket on essentials which include a fly swatter, of which we are much in need.

By the time we get back to *Voyager* there is quite a sea swell. The owner of one of the small wooden fishing boats paddles out to it on a surf board, leaves it tied to his mooring buoy and goes off in his boat to fish. We have lunch, put up our feet and read the literature from the tourist office. There are two things in particular that we should like to see. One is the former home of Alexander Hamilton which is now a museum. The other is the island's famous African green or vervet monkeys which are most likely to be spotted from Golden Rock, formerly a sugar plantation and now a hotel. The Hamilton house is nearby and we shall visit it tomorrow. Golden Rock is some distance away and will make an ideal outing another day, once we find a way to get there.

Meanwhile, our new fly swatter works a treat. After all, why destroy the ozone layer with aerosols when you can bring the little critters down manually and get exercise at the same time. David is recording his tally with little silhouettes in biro on the plastic handle.

34

A Little Local History

After breakfast, and before we shower, I give us both haircuts out in the cockpit while we watch the pelicans. Not far from us is a wrecked freighter which a hurricane drove onto the rocks some years ago. The pelicans use it as an observation platform.

Brown pelicans are related to gannets and they fly with the same languid, flap-and-glide as their gannet cousins. They also acquire their food in a similar way, at least initially. Firstly, they seek out their quarry. Then they soar above it to an appropriate height, lower their heads and plunge onto it with the most terrific force. But where the gannet rises gracefully from the depths to swallow a single fish, the pelican bursts forth with its pouch bulging with fish and water.

The pouch, which extends underwater, holds far more than the stomach can, so all the water has to be disposed of before the fish can be swallowed. This is achieved by an undignified and rather comic performance involving much head-shaking and large quantities of seawater flying from the sides of the beak.

When they have breakfasted, the pelicans settle themselves on the fishermen's boats and begin their grooming regime which involves a thorough investigation of their feathers and much drying of wings. A particular favourite among the small boats seems to be one with the words *Let Them Talk* painted on its side in shaky writing. Twelve pelicans complete their grooming here before settling down to sun themselves. They really are the most affable of birds. They don't fret or complain if, after arranging themselves comfortably in the limited space, another pelican decides to join them. Far from screeching in protest or physically attacking the intruder as another species might, the present incumbents merely budge up a bit to make room for the newcomer. It is all very civilised.

With our own feeding and grooming completed we take the dinghy into Charlestown Harbour and brave the assault course again. These things are always less challenging the second time you do them and I lose hardly any skin off my knees and elbows at all today.

The Hamilton house sits at a fork in the road. It is substantial and built of stone. The actual year of Alexander's birth is a bit vague, but somewhere between 1755 and 1757. He was the fourth son of a Scottish laird and a local woman of Huguenot descent married to, but separated from, somebody else at the time. Born and raised in Nevis, Alexander was sent to be educated in New York, at what would become Columbia University. He later became the first US Secretary of the Treasury and a Founding Father of the US Constitution. He died in 1804 following a duel with a political opponent.

I found it a fascinating house, not just in its style and solidity, but also because despite being a museum now, in an odd sort of way it still seems almost lived in. Its rooms haven't been buffed and neatened into a parody of themselves, as the former homes of the famous often are. In the kitchen you can imagine cooking being done over the open fire amid the thump and clatter of its pans, big stone jars and kitchen utensils, not to mention the rush and noise of children running across its stone floors. In fact, one very appealing exhibit is a determined attempt to preserve children's games from the old days before they are lost forever.

We visit a church and a bookshop, buy a book about whales and dolphins in the Caribbean and before heading home make enquiries about getting a taxi to take us to Golden Rock tomorrow. We are quickly accosted by a man who says he is a walking-tour guide. We know the hotel is some distance away on the other side of the island and, wondering if we should still need a taxi or whether he has a car, we ask him how we would get there and he says on the bus.

We try to establish how much he will charge for his services but he is very vague, saying it depends how much we want to do, how far we want to go into the rainforest, and so on. What we are asking for is something as basic as how much an hour, but we don't get an answer. It also hadn't occurred to us until this moment to go into the rainforest. With something of an aversion to wet clammy places and snakes and spiders and other biting things that run up your legs it is something I had intended to leave to more adventurous souls. A glimpse of the monkeys and lunch was as much as we'd planned for. We tell the man we'll think about it.

As we lower ourselves down the precipitous wooden dinghy dock we notice a small local boat tied up behind our dinghy. Its owner has put a series of nail boards and wire across the top of its cuddy, the little boat's tiny cabin, to keep seabirds off. Heaven help him if he ever stumbles getting on or off his boat. He'll need to have his tetanus injections up to date. A bit of guano must surely be preferable to stepping onto a bed of rusty nails. On the other hand, they do make a mess.

Talking over tomorrow's outing during the dinghy ride back to *Voyager* we ask ourselves: if you can get to Golden Rock by bus, why go to the expense of a taxi? And why not postpone any decision about a guide until we get there?

After lunch, and a squall, I do some laundry with the water gathered from the awning while David swabs the decks. Blue water cruising means using whatever opportunities offer themselves, and fresh water at anchor is not something to be ignored.

Another squall is imminent which will provide a final freshwater rinse for the laundry now pegged out on the rails, as well as plenty of water for baths tomorrow. By the time the second squall has passed through, the atmosphere is so fresh it feels as if the whole planet has been washed clean. We are even able to look up and see the top of Mount Nevis without its cloud for the first time. There is also a rainbow, which somehow makes it all picture perfect. High cloud provides a cool, restful evening. At bedtime a narrow strip of sky on the western horizon clears and a blazing peach-gold sun slips into the sea.

When you leave a chilly, appliance-based environment for something as basic as a yacht at anchor, especially in a tropical climate, you become part of the natural world and your life takes on its rhythms. Accordingly you wake as it begins to get light and what with the mornings being so warm, and the sunrises so captivating, it takes no effort at all to rise at daybreak. Similarly, you begin to yawn as night falls. Everything becomes more simple and spontaneous.

Meals are not pre-planned; you buy what is available. Laundry and personal hygiene is not a problem given the brief but heavy shower virtually every afternoon. Bathing, in secluded places, is most pleasant in the cockpit in collected rainwater heated by the sun. Communication with the outside world tends to be brief – at anchor there are more important things for your batteries to do – but the desire to maintain that link with your homeland remains strong.

Much as our parents' generation clustered around their Bush radios for news from war-torn London, we hunch over our SSB for World Service's *Britain Today* between 6.30 and 6.45am Eastern Caribbean Time. Hunching is necessary because reception is not as good here as it was in Antigua, with the radio announcer fighting a losing the battle with what appears to be variously a bagpipe player, a male drunk and a woman wailing some unintelligible but heartfelt lament.

The FM version of World Service, also broadcast from London but relayed locally, is easier to hear but makes only a brief mention of UK news, concentrating instead on international events. It has an American presenter with the most wonderfully reassuring voice backed by soaring, heart-warming music that makes you feel all is well with the world – both utterly inappropriate given the unrelieved human misery from flood, famine, human trafficking and ethnic cleansing being reported on the channel every morning.

35

A Bus Called *Babylon*

At 10.30 this morning we seek out the place where the local buses gather – Memorial Square, opposite Happy Hill Alley – and ask which one of them goes to Golden Rock. They have names instead of numbers and the one we need is called *Babylon*.

All these vehicles, we will discover, carry a printed injunction to the effect: *No eating or drinking – 14 passengers max*. It is one of the few areas of conformity they share because Nevis's buses are as individual as their owner/drivers, each one reflecting his particular tastes, in music especially, which is played *very* loud.

I've always had a well-developed sense of survival and it was reinforced many years ago when David and I took an activity holiday in rural France. A member of the group, an aviator and mechanical engineer with a melancholy side to his nature, was convinced that while the white-water canoeing and potholing were of no great risk to us, the transportation between sites definitely was. And as we clattered daily around steep hairpin bends in geriatric French vehicles he could be heard intoning gloomily, 'Have you noticed how much he's using his gearbox on the corners? That's because his brakes are shot.' Or, 'Hear that? That's the...' and pinpoint to a nicety the actual bit of this particular vehicle's gearbox, steering or braking system currently announcing its own imminent demise. And possibly ours. Ever since that time I have always tried to travel in newer vehicles rather than old ones, wherever possible, on the premise that their essential parts are likely to outlast my journey.

We approach the bus with *Babylon* painted across the front in vibrant graffiti-style letters and I am gratified to see that it is a very recent model. Although the whole vehicle, including the half-dozen other passengers already waiting in their seats, is vibrating to a reggae beat.

There is only one road around the island and it is a winding, pot-holed switchback. Combined with the Caribbean bus driver's commitment to unrestrained speed, it is a wild ride. At one point we come to a narrow bridge over a river. The banks slope steeply down to it and as we breast the top of the slope we can see that a car has stopped on the bridge and a man is standing beside it, chatting with the driver. *Babylon* is already being driven flat out but, as it descends the slope, gravity lends an added momentum and it positively hurtles down onto the narrow bridge.

There is a communal intake of breath from the passengers, almost as if by doing so we can somehow make the bus narrower. The horrified pedestrian, luckily a very slender young man, presses his pelvis against the parked car, and raises his hands high in the air to make himself as flat as possible. We zoom past him, with only inches to spare. As one, everybody on the bus – apart from the driver – turns to see if he has survived and observe his sickly smile of disbelief as he stares after our disappearing bus. I let out an involuntary, 'Jesus!' and a second quiver of shock runs through my immediate neighbour at my blasphemy. Fortunately, only she has heard it above the pulsating reggae which is making all the metal on the bus hum.

Our driver does seem to have a gentler side, though, for the bus makes a detour down a narrow dirt track to drop off a very small, very elderly lady at her door. But in case anyone should suspect him of going soft, this is immediately followed by a wheel spinning, gravel spitting reverse up someone's steep drive and a head-banging, pot-holing lunge back up the dirt track and onto the road again.

Babylon finally lurches to a stop and lets us off. The moment we close its door the bus roars away. There is an immediate sense of relief as the ear-shattering reggae disappears into the distance.

It is a long, steep, winding trek up to Golden Rock. We are, after all, climbing the foothills of a volcano. There are thickly wooded slopes on both sides of us with the addition of a deep gully to our right, culminating in a dry river bed. Halfway up we are given a wondrous display of the very thing we have come to see. From the far side of the gully on our right, across a small wooden bridge, comes a troop of African vervet monkeys. It is a family group, descending in size, age and gender from a surprisingly large patriarch, through a variety of smaller adults and even smaller adolescents to springy little youngsters less than a foot high. They are slender and graceful, with black faces, long tails and a green tinge to the fur, most noticeably on the youngest. And despite their numbers on the island – estimated at around 45,000, or five times the human population – they are apparently elusive.

Following the lead of the patriarch, the troop leaves the bridge, climbs the river bank, assembles onto the track and then makes its way across it in single file. We stand quite still and they pass a few yards in front of us, without haste, effortlessly vaulting the steep bank to the left of us and disappearing one at a time into the trees. All except one. Among the first to reach the trees, he perches negligently on a branch and gazes back at us until the whole troop has gone and then he also turns and vanishes into the foliage.

By the time we reach the hotel we are hot so we have a beer in the bar. Its refrigerator produces tall narrow glasses so cold that when the beer is poured into them the condensation that forms on the outside freezes instead of dripping onto your lap. Golden Rock is run by friendly, middle-aged American women and the one serving our beer tells us that the bar is in what was originally the long house where 300 people were fed daily. It must have been hellish with heat and noise but is now a very pleasant place with large windows overlooking dining tables on a flagged terrace bright with exotic flowers.

One of the hotel's features is the rainforest, which begins at its back door. An American couple return from it, dripping with perspiration, order cold beers and ask if they can join us. Having established that they are wet for entirely personal reasons, and that the rainforest itself is bone dry, we say we should like to visit it, too, and they give us their 'thirty minute' trail map with its thirty numbers relating to flora of interest. They had got lost at number 10, they say, and been gone so long that the hotel's elderly black Labrador had been despatched to find them and bring them back. We pass the Labrador on our way out. She is soaking her feet in a small fish pond and observes us with a professional eye as if assessing whether another search and rescue mission is going to be required this morning.

Leave the long house, cross a stretch of lawn with a foot-weary Labrador in it, turn right and you enter the rainforest. Although even with a competent navigator along, it isn't easy. The map itself is a model of obfuscation. Down its left-hand side is a column of numbers each with the name of a tree or plant beside it. On its right side is another column of numbers with a description or 'legend'.

Confusion begins early, because there are 30 numbers and names on the left-hand side but only 24 'legends' on the right. None of the numbers relate to one another so that, for instance, you crane your neck to stare up into the branches of an enormous tree with the number 3 on it, while the legend of the same number on the map describes a small, delicate plant. It is compounded by the fact that a quantity of the weather-beaten numbers, painted onto small pieces of wood and nailed to specimen trees or small posts, have disappeared.

We reach number 10, where the American couple got lost, and never do find another number. But forewarned is forearmed, and we simply roam at will along narrow paths among huge trees and low scrub with a sense of delight. For we are not only making our first ever foray into a rainforest, but climbing higher up the volcano as well. Its peak, which dominates the whole of this small island, is wreathed in cloud again today. In fact, apart from the day of the squalls, we never do see its peak again, giving the impression that it is permanently steaming gently.

When the paths disappear we follow dry stream and river beds and it is magical. There are hummingbirds, large black butterflies, tiny lizards with tails no thicker than a darning needle and, although we never see them, we can hear the monkeys way above our heads in the forest canopy. Technically we are lost, but happily so, until finally we stumble onto a path whose shape David recognises from the map and we return to the hotel. Lying on her side in the grass now, the Labrador raises her head, acknowledges us politely as we pass, and then flops gratefully back down on the lawn again.

We lunch on the terrace, among the exotic blooms, on lobster sandwiches three inches thick, full of tail meat and with the crusts cut off. A flaky white couple across the way is lunching with a black couple from the neighbouring island of St Kitts. The flaky woman says, 'Hey, wouldn't it be *great* to go back in time to when this was *real*?' Her fellow diners do not express an opinion.

There are tiny lizards stalking slowly among the table legs and diners' feet, a tongue darting out now and then to snatch an insect out of the air. Then, behind a large flower pot, two of them embark on an unseen but noisy squabble until the winner chases the loser under our table at incredible speed, across the terrace and out of sight.

After lunch we stand on a promontory of dense spongy turf looking down onto an incredibly blue sea and up the steep forest slopes to the white cloud wreathing Nevis Peak. A small guest bungalow nestling in trees nearby bears the sign *Paradise*.

Instead of waiting for a bus to come along we decide to walk back towards Charlestown so that we can stop by the Hermitage, said to be the Caribbean's oldest inhabited building. It is a most pleasant walk, mostly downhill, with neat painted houses and gardens with the kind of colours and lushness you'd expect in this climate.

When we pass the school, girls in immaculate uniforms are running a race along the street, barefoot, although they exhibit a distinct lack of enthusiasm when their route takes them under the wall of the boys' playground where the boys leer down on them and shout abuse. Even in Paradise, it seems, some things don't change.

After about two miles we notice that a very tall, thin man, wearing only shorts and wellington boots, is striding along behind us. He is swinging a machete in his right hand and talking very loudly to himself. A couple more furtive backward glances establish that he is also gaining on us. Apart from this man, and us, the road is deserted.

We are discussing various unlikely scenarios for escape when another glance behind reveals a bus hurtling down the road. Abandoning all interest in the Caribbean's oldest inhabited building, we leap to the edge of the pavement and flag it down. It has *Prodigal Son* in a beautiful cursive script above the windscreen and screeches to a halt just far enough ahead of us for us to read the word *Jehovah* across its rear.

We wrench open its door and scramble in. As we slam the door shut the man overtakes us and from my seat I can now see what was hidden before. Behind a very high hedge there is a garden gate with a middle-aged woman leaning on it, taking the air. The man pauses level with her, and while David pays the driver I stare back in horror fearing some terrible bloodbath. The two of them merely exchange a cordial greeting, however, and then the man with the machete resumes his long stride and his monologue. It is not until we are some distance down the hill that something occurs to me. We are, after all, riding in a bus with *Prodigal Son* on the front and *Jehovah* on the back. Given the religious propensities of this little island, might the man simply have been conversing with his god?

In the meantime, the afternoon has become very hot and I'm not at all sorry to be seated and in the shade; quite a lot of shade, in fact, as the side and rear windows of this bus are heavily tinted. They also have engraved scrolls in the corners reminiscent of the kind you used to see on very old hearses and travellers' caravans. The statutory sign says *14 passengers max* as usual but in place of *No eating or drinking* it has *No indecent language* although how anyone could possibly hear any I can't imagine. The pulsating music making the interior throb is gospel and while the man behind the wheel drives flat out for Jesus a small, scrubbed schoolgirl at the front sings along to every hymn, accompanied intermittently by several of the matrons sitting behind her.

Back in town we find the *other* supermarket, the source of confusion between the woman and her nephew in the police station when we cleared in. It is new and heavily air-conditioned, and we emerge with a bargain purchase pack of fifteen chicken drumsticks at a ridiculously-low price. They will stay at a safe temperature against our new and wonderful refrigerator plate, although fifteen large drumsticks is still a lot to get through. I figure chicken in thyme, honey and lemon juice with fresh vegetables for one meal; cacciatore with spaghetti for another; fried with ratatouille and potatoes and then the odd three cooked in curry sauce with the meat then sliced from the bone and served with rice. Very versatile, chicken.

36

Pinney's Beach

A few more days and we begin to think about a change of scenery. Our water tanks are also running low so we decide to combine firing up the water maker a few miles offshore with a trip up the coast to the northern end of the island. When we reach Tamarind Bay, its anchorage turns out to be very small and already full of local boats. Oualie Beach is very shallow – only 1.6 metres even some way out – and it has buoys everywhere. So we settle on Pinney's Beach, just along the coast from our previous anchorage. I make ratatouille for later in the week and what turns out to be a very tasty chicken cacciatore for dinner tonight. We have it with a glass of red as the sun goes down with Gladys Knight & the Pips singing *Midnight Train to Georgia*. Not a spectacular day in terms of activity or achievement, and yet we feel we've had a really lovely one.

We have a number of lovely days on Nevis. This island is the closest we come to our Caribbean idyll: a solitary boat anchored off coral sand fringed by tall, spindly palm trees. Three glorious miles of it, in fact, running past our door and with nobody here but us. Warmth. Sunrises and sunsets. The daily arrival of fresh water, the company of pelicans and civil people when the need for supplies drives you ashore.

Although I admit to being a little intimidated, the first time we take the dinghy onto Pinney's Beach, by the sheer power of the surf. It is beautiful to watch from *Voyager*'s cockpit, crashing and fuming against the land, but something else entirely when you come to thrust a small aluminium dinghy into it. But we land in good order and walk along the beach to have a look at the abandoned Four Seasons Hotel, a victim of Hurricane Lenny.

Its jetty hangs in tatters. The beach has been driven upwards and thrust into the buildings closest to the sea. Along with the sand it has lifted the large concrete blocks containing the beach showers and thrust these at the seafront buildings, too. Further back, what has escaped the sea, the wind has destroyed. Large numbers of local people, someone in town tells us, have lost their jobs.

Not long ago we spent some weeks in the Canaries, waiting out the hurricane season. While we did so, Hurricane Lenny was causing this kind of havoc through the Caribbean, at times reaching 155mph. The eighth hurricane of the season and a category 4, it took everyone by surprise: not only by arriving after the season was supposed to be over but by travelling west to east, instead of the other way around as hurricanes normally do. Since most development in East Caribbean islands occurs on their usually more protected western shores, Lenny's effect on homes, jobs and tourism was devastating. And it added even more rain to the severe flooding in the Leeward Islands already caused by Hurricane José less than a month earlier.

Although Lenny, the strongest Atlantic hurricane ever recorded in November, had caused some damage on Antigua, we did not see it. This is our first experience of the kind of devastation a hurricane can leave in its wake. Thanks to the Luftwaffe there were quite a few bombsites littering our early childhood but once the areas were rebuilt that was it. I simply can't imagine what it must be like to have one's home and livelihood under threat annually by an irresistible force of nature. And not just once a year either. The 1999 Atlantic hurricane season, June to November, produced 16 tropical storms, half of which developed into hurricanes. We retrace our steps along the lovely coral beach and paddle our dinghy back through the surf to *Voyager*.

Tired of being the junior member of this little two-island country, and dominated by the larger St Kitts, Nevis had at one time considered seceding, concluding ultimately that a population of 9,000 was a bit small for a nation state. Gazing about me at the blissful isolation of our present location I ask David if *Voyager* might constitute a nation state of two and what we needed to do to legitimise our sovereignty.

He says print some stamps. I ask if we'd need an army but he says he would simply tank me up and send me out. He reckons two small beers and half a bottle of red and we would be in nuclear deployment mode. I remind him that he would need to deploy me *before* the inevitable migraine set in and made me ineffective for two days and slightly muted for a third. He says that would be a national secret we could never divulge as the enemy would then know it only had to wait 24 hours for us to be defenceless. I wander off to the galley to contemplate UDI and make a chicken curry for tomorrow from our bargain purchase at the new supermarket. Like casseroles and chilli, curry is always tastier a day or two after cooking.

The vulnerability of the small and defenceless recurs, in a different form, just before sunset when we find ourselves in the centre of a life and death struggle. Alerted by a loud splash, followed by an agitated rustle, we find the water around us filled with millions of tiny, bluish almost transparent fish with shoals of large snapper- and trout-shaped fish leaping (the splash) and feeding on them. With every attack, the little fish turn en masse (the rustle) and rush away, but with nowhere safe to go.

'Get into smaller groups and spread out,' I yell at the little fish, appalled. 'You're too big a target!' But they don't listen. They simply leap sporadically in small groups but remain part of the great mass which changes direction endlessly only to be attacked again. The carnage goes on all night.

In our less dramatic moments we are re-reading Jerome K Jerome's *Three Men in a Boat* together. Reading aloud is not much done nowadays, I imagine. But on a boat, devoid of talk radio and television, it is a shared experience, a source of mutual enjoyment and quite often a subject for discussion. And as can be observed in cinema audiences, comedy is also keener when it is shared. Along with making us laugh, parts of this humorous and witty book are particularly pertinent: the uncluttered, un-materialistic lifestyle to which its three young oarsmen aspire, despite filling their boat to the gunnels with clutter they will never need; the changing conditions on the water from delightfully solitary to maddeningly overcrowded; and the occasional fretful behaviour of even the fondest people when pressed up close on a small boat.

Nevis has been a delight, but it is time to move on. We sail back to our original anchorage, which is handy for the dinghy dock, and clear out with the authorities. Then we have a last trawl around the new supermarket. *Never miss an opportunity* has become a motto of ours because you never know what you are going to.

When we get back to the waterfront with our shopping, the dinghy dock is being dismantled. I don't think it is anything personal. It had always had a rather temporary look about it, the original undoubtedly a victim of Hurricane Lenny at the same time it devastated the Four Seasons Hotel along the coast. And presumably they are now preparing to build a more permanent structure. One can only hope that it will also be a bit more user-friendly.

If disembarking has been difficult, getting back down into our dinghy has been more so. *Leap of faith* are words that come to mind, requiring as it does hanging by my fingers from a wooden plank while David holds the dinghy steady with one hand and uses the other to guide my outstretched foot to where my weight, when I finally let go of the plank, won't sink us.

As if this were not challenge enough, the dinghy dock is now partially-dismembered strips of timber, exposed nails and that fluttering tape that workmen use to stop people entering their workspace but which is simply another hazard because our little dinghy, down there among the wood fragments and sawdust, is our only means of getting home.

I put so much concentration into getting into the dinghy, without either falling backwards into it or capsizing it, that I am seated and ready to go before discovering that I forgot to undo the painter before making my descent. I'm just considering the best way to clamber back up again, now that my original foothold has been removed, when a workman appears from nowhere and very kindly unties us.

As we pull away I wonder briefly why we are so law-abiding; why we didn't just tie up on the fishermen's dock which is much more accessible, since despite being warned not to in the cruising guide other yachtsmen do. It is only later that we hear that one of them returned to find his dinghy trashed.

Back on *Voyager*, we set about raising our anchor. The water is so clear that even six metres down you can see it dug into the coral sand, and its chain snaking out along the seabed behind it. Then we set off for St Kitts.

ST KITTS

37

Brimstone Hill Fort

The capital of St Kitts is Basseterre. We anchor in its harbour and dinghy into the marina to clear in, as advised in the cruising guide. Hurricanes José and Lenny have given this area of the harbour a thorough drubbing and, with only some wooden piles and a small shed remaining, it resembles a demolition site. The cruise ship wharf is completely wrecked and part of the wall that protects the marina has been destroyed. The marina itself seems to be undamaged although there is not a boat, not even another dinghy, in it.

We are greeted by two large cheerful men who say we must pay a US$5 security charge to leave our dinghy here. There is little alternative, any other access to land being through large areas of mud. The two men hover above us on a concrete dock around five feet high. I look around for a ladder of some kind. The two men drop to a crouch and extend a hand each. Foolishly, I grasp them. Within moments my arms feel as if they have left their sockets. By the time my feet touch the dock my rib cage seems to be a greater distance from my pelvis than it used to be.

We are directed into a very fancy marina building, with several very fancy secretaries, to pay. Although what they have to do all day I can't imagine as the marina has no boats in it. We should like to see the island and visit Brimstone Hill Fort, but since getting ashore by dinghy is such a pain David asks one of the secretaries what the marina's rate would be to berth *Voyager*. She quotes him their standard rate, which is expensive, but then adds that it would be triple that for a catamaran. The amount makes his eyes water. No wonder there are no boats in the marina.

In the meantime I hand over a five dollar bill to the other secretary. 'What shall I put on the receipt?' she says. 'Under protest,' I suggest. 'Five dollars to tie up a dinghy while you clear in *and* get unloaded like a sack of coal is a *disgrace*!' She looks upset. But not as upset as I am.

Customs and Immigration is at the commercial dock. To get there we traipse the length of the seafront, about a mile and a half. It is not an inspiring walk. The area is industrial and litter-strewn and traffic hurtles past us at frenetic speed. All except the lorries. They travel slowly because they are so overloaded. They also have men draped over them, who appear to be there in place of ropes, to hold the load on, although they can barely cope when the vehicles take the road's corners. If men really are cheaper than ropes, I wonder if when the trucks reach the place where they are unloaded, these men will be used in place of forklift trucks as well.

A cane train runs parallel with the road, a diesel pulling two grubby tanks on two wagons, with men draped over them. I find myself wondering what services they will be required to perform when the train reaches its destination.

At Customs and Immigration there are two men at neighbouring desks, each one with just a stapler on it, and a conversation going on between them which we have to wait for some time to end before one of them addresses us. We decide we have seen enough of St Kitts and will clear out at the same time as clearing in so as to save another long, dispiriting walk here. We will thus be due to leave the island the day after tomorrow.

We set off on the long trek back to the marina, eyed balefully by two young bulls chained up in a cane field. On the way, we take a walk through the town. Independence Square and the Circus are filled with competing election speeches. There are loudspeaker vans marked *Labour* and *Political Action Movement* and posters everywhere, some of them claiming, 'One good term deserves another'.

In town we buy bread from a bakery which radiates an overpoweringly sweet smell of boiled sugar, and then head for the supermarket. In front of it a hen, with two tiny chicks in tow, grazes among the parked cars and generally behaves as if the street is entirely her own territory.

The most dominant creature in all these islands has to be the chicken: the cockerels strutting their stuff and chivvying the hens; the hens scratching for delicacies for their tiny following offspring. They are everywhere – in gardens, on pavements, trolling across in front of the supermarket's sliding doors, browsing under parked cars then, as the cars are driven away from the kerb, stepping out from among the wheels in a slightly ruffled huff. And you can forget about roosters heralding the dawn. They herald every minute of the day and sometimes the night as well, in endless competition with one another. Across harbours, hills and valleys their boastful crowing must make life very easy for any passing mongoose.

We are at the supermarket checkout and the first of our few items are rolling down the conveyor belt towards the middle-aged woman standing ready to bag them when the street door opens and a boy of eight or nine comes and stands quietly beside her. It seems that *he* should be bagging our groceries not her and she snaps at him that he is late. He lowers his head deferentially and offers his apology. With the speed of a lizard's tongue her hand shoots out and lands an almighty slap across his small face. He slowly raises his head and, by virtue of our relative positions at the checkout, for a moment his eyes look straight into mine before he turns them towards the woman. They sparkle with a mixture of pain, humiliation and something else. A look which says *that wasn't fair and I'll* never *forgive you.* I turn my head towards the woman, too. She glares at me defiantly for a second and then turns away.

By the time we get back to the marina the Security Team has gone home for the day. My ribs are not ungrateful and I manage perfectly well without them. After all, I did train for this type of manoeuvre at Nevis's dinghy dock. In the anchorage we have been joined by *Europa*, a four-masted cruise ship. During the evening it entertains its clients with a steel band that periodically loses the battle with the loud speaker vans still blazing out their political messages on the coast road. In the rare moments of quiet the local dogs bark. Yet I sleep so soundly that I miss the 6.30am news.

Over breakfast we watch six local fishermen in an open boat cast a large circular, weighted net of very fine mesh out across the water. They raise it slowly while drawing it closed, to trap as many fish as possible inside. As the circle becomes smaller the surface water becomes agitated as frantic fish of all sizes make a desperate bid for freedom.

Faced with the prospect of heaving ourselves up and down the marina's concrete dock again, we ponder whether we can be bothered to make our planned trip to Brimstone Hill Fort. In the end we make the effort. Without the two men on the marina wharf to help me I scale it with my ribs, and even the skin on my knees intact. We pay another US$5 at the marina office to tie up our dinghy and go in search of the newest-looking bus we can find that goes to Brimstone Hill Fort.

'Top of the hill or the bottom?' asks the driver.

'What's the difference?' we ask.

'Ten EC dollars up the hill.'

We pay it.

The laidback, sultry rhythms booming through the bus speakers are strangely at odds with what turns out to be another white knuckle ride, although we do slow down a bit going through the villages. This seems to be so that the driver can engage in meaningful eye contact with nubile young women on verandas and balconies or shout greetings to pretty young mothers with tiny infants in tow. The island, meanwhile, turns out to be far more attractive than its capital suggests.

The driver finally stops his bus on a steep incline saying, 'It's just ahead now,' but when we turn the bend in the road below which he dropped us off we find that we still have a long walk to the top. Nevertheless, it is cool and shady under the tall trees, the sides of the road are lush with a very attractive type of tradescantia that is green on top and deep purple underneath, while the newly-mown grass all around us smells absolutely divine.

Brimstone Hill is the result of a tumultuous upheaval in the landscape caused by volcanic eruption. It thrust an enormous shaft of volcanic rock – known then as brimstone, a word meaning burned stone – up from the bowels of the earth to a height of nearly 800 feet.

It was upon this massive and atypical promontory that the British began building Brimstone Hill Fort in the 1690s. Or, more accurately, British military engineers designed it but like so much else in the Caribbean the fort was built and maintained by African slaves. It is a dreadful irony that the hell-on-earth created for Africans by the dominant European nations of the time should take place on idyllic islands named for Christian saints dedicated to love and self-sacrifice.

St Christopher, the original name of St Kitts, was the first Caribbean island to be settled by the English and the French together, and they shared it between 1627 and 1713. In its heyday the fort was known as the Gibraltar of the West Indies, a reference to its dominating height and the belief that it was impregnable. When the British and the French fell out, however, the impregnability proved to be a fallacy.

From our elevated position we can see crops for the first time. There is also a sugar plantation on the island and a narrow gauge train passes along the shoreline below us, its wire cages full of cut cane. This island originally grew tobacco, but in 1640, unable any longer to compete with the colony of Virginia, it switched to sugar cane.

From the fort's walls you can also see the islands of Nevis and Montserrat, Saba, St Barts and St Martin, all of them spread out before you in a sparkling blue sea. It is breathtaking. So is the woman in the gift shop, although for a different reason, and who bears more than a passing resemblance, physical and otherwise, to the woman who struck the little boy across the face in the supermarket yesterday.

David is buying a roll of film for his camera and politely querying the not inconsiderable difference in the amount she has taken from the note he gave her compared to the price on the film itself. '*Jesus!*' she snarls, scrabbling a few more dollars from the till, slamming them onto the counter and looking ready to throttle him. I am across the way, considering a rather nice piece of pottery, but decide not to risk enraging her further by attempting to buy it. Instead, we go outside and wander among the ruins of where so many of our countrymen, and hers, lived and died. It is early and we are the only visitors.

Neglected for over a century, the site has been restored over the past couple of decades. It is beautifully kept and we roam around the citadel, the magazine, the bastion and the ruined quarters of the Royal Engineers and the Artillery Officers. Then we have lunch above the Infantry Officers' quarters.

Like any archaeological site, time and restoration have left little that is recognisably human. Until, that is, you get to a tiny graveyard down a slope below the foundations of what was once the hospital. Somehow, in death, the place comes alive. Everywhere else has been cleansed of people, spit and polish, the smell of wood smoke and gunpowder, human sweat and animal ordure, of leather and tobacco, the sounds of cannon fire and laughter, of pots and pans and the jingle of horses' harnesses. What remain are the dark, square building blocks of volcanic stone with their lime mortar and white archways.

But beneath the few surviving headstones lie the bones of men who once lived here. Some of them not for very long. One was only 19 when he departed this life. Another, aged 38, rests below an inscription that brings a sting to the eyes. It is from his wife. This stone, she says, is her last duty to him, and all that is left for her to do for him now.

We walk back down the hill to the main road, making a detour to the kiln where the limestone clinging to the lower parts of the hill was converted into mortar to build the fort. At the bottom we cross the railway line that carries the cane trains, past a tin shed with a young woman sitting outside it in the shade, reading a book. Beside her lie two long poles, each with a red flag tied to one end. She is the level crossing keeper.

We catch a bus immediately and embark on the ride home. Every time I get on a Caribbean bus, or more particularly when I stagger off one, I vow that *next* time we will pay the extra and take a taxi. On the way to the marina we approach three large trees that initially appear to have been decorated all over with white plastic medallions of some kind. When we pass them, they turn out to be dozens of little egrets perched on the branches, their backs turned to the sun and a blistering white in the afternoon's brightness.

When we get back to the harbour *Europa* has gone and been replaced with an enormous motor yacht complete with a small helicopter and revolving radar scanner, although why you would have a radar scanner operating at anchor we have no idea. Its large RIB mills about importantly, driven by a crewman in livery with a handheld VHF clamped to his ear. He looks so pompous that I start emulating him – like mad Michael mimicking the major in *Ryan's Daughter* – with one hand to my ear and the other on an imaginary steering wheel, only to find a man leaning on the rail of the motor yacht watching me. I slink below.

The motor yacht leaves shortly afterwards and is replaced by a two-masted 140-foot sailing ship, named after a famous Briton, and offering people tuition in sailing and diving. They could also do with a bit of training in how to use a RIB in an anchorage. They roar theirs round and round at high speed, heeling it over onto one side before hurtling into the marina past a sign saying, '5 knot maximum speed – This is a no wake zone'. Then they do the same thing coming back.

Voyager is presently covered with tiny rectangular black specks of a surprisingly consistent size and shape but which quickly spread into sooty smudges. We are not sure if they are fallout from a large chimney in the direction of the cane processing plant which pumps out black smoke continuously, or ash from Montserrat's most recent eruption. We are also being driven demented by flies but have stopped bothering to notch the handle of our swatter as there are just too many of them.

At 1.30 next morning the dogs on shore have reached a crescendo, as have the revellers on the sailing ship bearing the famous name. He wouldn't have approved. He was a man of modest habits, strict discipline and a profound belief in individual responsibility. I sleep soundly, regardless, thanks to ear plugs, and wake at dawn dreamily to see from the cabin window a fuzzy whiteness behind the sailing ship. I get up, find my glasses and discover *Ocean Queen*, a massive cruise ship five decks high. The sailing ship's RIB is roaring round and round it.

Ocean Queen begins lowering her own jolly boats just as *Ocean King*, a matching five-decker, arrives and begins to anchor. After several more roars around the anchorage the people under sailing instruction pull up their RIB and begin to raise their anchor. It seems to take a long time and they end up rather close to the nearest cruise ship. All this activity in the anchorage is occurring, of course, because Hurricane Lenny destroyed the cruise ship dock.

I sometimes feel sorry for people on cruise ships. It's not just the gleam they bring to the eye of local traders, as if they were walking wallets. It's the advertisements. They give the impression that there will only be you on the ship, and that you will become young and beautiful in the process, but when you board you find four thousand similarly deluded people. Then horror of horrors, you find you are travelling in tandem with a doppelganger, identical except for half the name on the ship's bow, and filled with four thousand more deluded people. And everywhere you visit the queues are terrible. We are glad we did Brimstone Hill fort yesterday. It will be standing room only up there today.

As we are making our preparations to leave, two small local boats roar either side of us leaving David, currently perched on *Voyager*'s back steps and securing the outboard, clinging on for dear life. The size and power of cruise ships, not to mention their audience potential, tends to bring out the worst in virile young men in small boats. When we set about lifting the anchor, after raising only a small amount of chain the anchor winch dies and David raises the rest by hand.

As we set out along the coast he points to two small local boats bobbing in the distance.

'Shall I blast between them?' he says with rare malice. 'D'you recognise 'em?'

'Er...' I say. I've always found that my own petty acts of retaliation go badly astray and the colours of these two boats look wrong. There had been some orange paint on one of the offending boats and green on the other, with a bare-chested stud in micro shorts at either tiller. The boats ahead of us look grey but that might simply be the effect of the sunlight on the water. And anyway, we don't create enough wash even at speed to affect anything much.

We decide to take the nobler course which is just as well as the boats do, in fact, turn out to be grey. The one on the left contains two dignified, elderly men in shirts and trousers, and the one on the right three people in scuba gear receiving an orderly lesson from a fourth. All of them give us a friendly wave.

We have the most wonderful sail along the coast of this fish-shaped island. Our route follows the direction of our bus ride yesterday, past fields of cane being harvested, the cane trains tooting their presence and the fort towering above us. Beyond Brimstone Hill lies one of the three mountain ranges that make the centre of this island too steep for habitation. This one is the highest and contains the volcano's crater. Originally called Mount Misery, the name was changed in 1983, when St Kitts and Nevis gained independence, to Liamuiga, the name the Caribs gave to the whole island and which means fertile, which it surely is.

It is a stunning sail. The sun sparkles on a gentle sea. The cane leaves shimmer bright green in the sunlight. And although received wisdom says flying fish manage a maximum of 30 feet we witness a flypast from one of them that continues for so long we initially think it is a bird.

SINT EUSTATIUS

38

Such Friendly People

We arrive at Sint Eustatius, known simply as Statia, at lunchtime. At Oranje Stad in Oranje Baai. This island is Dutch and both the town and the bay are named for the House of Orange, the Netherlands' royal family.

In the harbour of Orange Bay, contrary to our Caribbean cruising guide, we have to pick up a buoy as they no longer allow anchoring here. After lunch we paddle ashore to the place where it recommends that visitors land their dinghies. It isn't easy as there is a strong swell, rocks to be avoided and as you clamber up a metal ladder the dinghy surges upwards and drops so violently away beneath your feet you feel it must surely overturn at any moment. We pay US$10 at the customs shed on the harbour and then make our way up into the town to the police station, to clear in with Immigration.

The island is lovely. Saddle-shaped, it has a large dormant volcano at one end and two small ones at the other, with a flat bit in the middle where most of the population lives and there was room to build an airport.

It is a world out of time. The little town has a stone-walls-and-flowers neatness to it. There is no litter. The residents greet you warmly and genuinely as you pass and the motorists wave – or, where appropriate, stop to offer you a lift.

They don't lock their cars when they park them, or even wind up the windows. Mobile phones and handheld VHFs lie on passenger seats. Ask for directions and instead of telling you they drive you there. There are only around 2,000 inhabitants and too few visitors to be a threat, whether of unwanted change or anything else.

We visit the tiny museum, formerly the family home of the Dutch merchant Simon Docker and also for a time the HQ of Britain's Admiral George Rodney after he captured the island from the Dutch in 1781 in the aftermath of an historic salute.

We have already noticed how, so often in these islands, the small local museums turn out to be little gems. Here, the history of the island is presented on a number of levels: the house itself, showing how a Dutch merchant lived; the mercantile environment in which he operated; and in the basement – underground as it were, to where the colonial invaders consigned the native populations they gradually supplanted – is a large model of Amerindian society.

The house itself is on high ground, light and airy, and would have been a delight to live in. Some of its rooms contain contemporary furniture and furnishings, although probably not the original ones given the rapacious habits of Admiral Rodney.

One of the museum's informative displays shows how the prosperity of these islands was based on the transatlantic slave trade. From the late 16th century to the early 19th the major European powers operated a triangular trading system. For example sugar, in the form of molasses, produced by slaves on the plantations of the Caribbean or American colonies, was exported to Europe to be distilled into rum. The profits from the molasses would be used to buy goods there which were then shipped to West Africa where they were bartered for slaves who were taken to the Caribbean or the colonies and sold to the planters. In this way, no ship need ever sail empty. The result was enormous profits and 250 years of unspeakable human misery.

When filled with the horrors of man's inhumanity to man it is comforting to think of simpler societies who got their living from what the land and water immediately around them provided in abundance. If I had ever harboured illusions of an Elysium, however, some Nirvana, or Eden before the Fall, I am soon disabused. Around the painstaking model of Amerindian village life filling the basement are descriptions of the religious rituals, tribal customs and stifling superstitions that circumscribed and encumbered daily life. Like the Polynesian islanders – around whom the artist Gauguin wove a blissful state of innocence and freedom from guilt that was later recognised as a myth of his own making – Man has an inordinate capacity for tormenting himself and everybody else.

We wander around the fort. There was once a small militia here and every able-bodied man from 16 to 60 was on reserve, although it does not appear to have been a serious deterrent to anybody. For as the British parliamentarian Edmund Burke said of the island in 1781, 'Its utility was its defence,' its commercial abilities making it 'an emporium for all the world.'

Back on board *Voyager* we consult Doyle's cruising guide about things to see and consider climbing one of the volcanoes tomorrow, the big one called Quill, and exploring its crater and rainforest.

On waking next morning we decide against a walking tour to the volcano's crater even though we feel we ought to. It would undoubtedly be tremendous once we got there, but it is going to be a long uphill hike in heat and humidity and from our experience of the cruising guide so far we are a bit concerned about just how long it is actually going to take.

As if to prove the point, when we dinghy into the harbour this morning we discover another place to disembark with less swell and a set of concrete steps to get off onto that isn't mentioned in the guide. The only reason we've found it is that the place it said to use is unapproachable today because the increased swell in the harbour is making it untenable.

This growing swell convinces us to abandon any guilt about not spending the day up a volcano. We decide instead to take a wander around the waterfront and the remains of that 'emporium' described by Edmund Burke.

From 1756 Statia had been a freeport, an early version of a duty-free shopping complex, and it had become very rich. As a journal of the early 1800s in its little museum testifies, buyers could promenade through one warehouse after another bursting with silks, cottons, silver plate, tapestries, jewellery, pewter, fine furniture and virtually anything else they desired.

Erosion and hurricanes have reduced these waterfront buildings of the lower town to ruins. But it is still an evocative experience to stand among what remains of their thick stone walls with the sea lapping at your feet. In the 18th and 19th centuries, when all those bold but impoverished young men set off to the West Indies to make their fortunes, and lay the foundation of an elevated lifestyle back home, this would have been one of the places they came. Not just the fictitious Mr Rochester in Charlotte Bronte's *Jane Eyre*, or Sir Thomas Bertram in Jane Austen's *Mansfield Park*, but many a real-life aristocratic family throughout Europe and America owes its present-day magnificence to these islands and their trade.

Something else that Statia's merchants supplied in abundance was weapons, to anyone with the money to pay for them. This made it one of the few places where the thirteen rebellious American colonies could get hold of the guns and ammunition they needed to fight the British. And although accounts of how it actually happened vary, what is undisputed is that on 16th November 1776 Statia was the first place in the world to salute an American naval vessel, thereby acknowledging the American colonies as an independent nation.

One account says that when the *Andrew Doria*, an American brig, came into Statia's harbour of Oranje Baai and fired a salute, the island's Governor Johannes de Graaff returned the salute not realising that, although the *Andrew Doria* was a merchant ship, she was under the command of an American rebel navy captain.

Another version claims that Commander de Graaff's return salute from the canons of Fort Oranje was a conscious decision resulting from the profitable relationship between Statia and the rebel colonies. Whichever is true, it was the first international acknowledgement of what would henceforward be known as the United States of America.

Such was the animosity felt in London that in 1778 the parliamentarian Lord Stormont claimed that, 'If Sint Eustatius had sunk into the sea three years before, the United Kingdom would already have dealt with George Washington.' No small achievement for an island measuring only 8 square miles, quite a lot of it taken up by volcanoes.

What with continued arms dealing to the American rebels and giving them what became known as 'the first salute', the subsequent capture of a British ship was the final straw. Britain declared war on the Netherlands and Admiral Rodney invaded Sint Eustatius. It was the fourth of the Anglo-Dutch wars and proved disastrous for the Dutch economy.

The people here are extraordinarily friendly. We have only just begun our walk up to the town when a man offers us a lift. He is a German and has a restaurant and guesthouse and he goes out of his way to drop us at the shop where we can buy a Netherlands Antilles courtesy flag which is the one our cruising guide says we should be flying. The shop owner says no-one ever flies it, they don't have one anyway, and sells us a Dutch courtesy flag instead. We also buy a walking map and set off up a long hill to find the Jewish cemetery marked on it.

After a long climb we reach a fork in the road which isn't on our map and ask a passing motorist – for a very small island everybody seems to travel by car – which fork will take us to the Jewish cemetery.

She is very sweet and says we are on the wrong road and to hop in. She takes us all the way back to where we had started, to the gates of the Dutch Reform Church. So we give up our search for the elusive Jewish cemetery and decide to look around this one instead. We visit the church and climb up its tower, which gives wonderful views out to sea while below us a small herd of goats play I'm-the-King-of-the-Castle on the family vaults, leaping up and standing on top of one until amiably dislodged by one or more of its fellows. Very sociable, goats.

These tombs are unlike any we have ever seen before. Some resemble half-submerged wartime Anderson shelters with square ends, one of which has to be broken open to inter subsequent family members. Some are standing wide open so heaven knows what has happened to the incumbents. The largest ones are so tall that you would have to haul yourself up and straddle it if you wanted to read the tiny inscription panel on the top.

When Admiral Rodney took control of this island he developed an interest in graveyards, too. In particular he noticed that for a relatively small community of wealthy merchants there were a surprising number of funerals. He had one inspected and the 'corpse' turned out to be a large haul of valuables. After mounting a search he found a great deal more treasure interred in the various burying grounds, which he confiscated as personal booty.

What upset the British government about this was that while Rodney was busy lining his coffers with Dutch spoils on Statia – equal to millions in today's currency – he was supposed to be defending the east coast of America. In his absence the French, with 23 naval ships and 150 merchant ships, reinforced the American rebel army which resulted in Britain's loss of the American colonies. Only a subsequent naval triumph elsewhere saved him.

We lunch at the town's bakery on freshly-made steak pie and shop at Duggin's supermarket. They don't deal in Eastern Caribbean dollars here. They use guilders and US dollars. We buy a $5 phone card and telephone Layla on Antigua. We have no mail.

America is dominant in all these islands, supplying everything from food to manufactured goods, which is hardly surprising given its proximity. Kit Kat is made by Hershey and the metal mailboxes outside Statia's homes and businesses all have the words 'Approved by the US Postmaster' embossed on their sides.

On the way back down to the harbour yet another motorist stops to offer us a lift. The steep, wide road that we are on is the old slave road, he tells us. Noting our lack of enthusiasm he wrinkles his nose and says with distaste that it isn't really. The real one, where they brought the captives up from the ships, is further round the island but was considered too insignificant. 'So they decided to claim this was it instead.' His sigh says it is a sad day for humanity when the horrors of slavery become a tourist attraction.

We return to the boat, put up our new courtesy flag and flop. After a very roly night, on Saturday morning we get the 8.30 weather forecast and leave our mooring in Orange Bay soon after. We should have liked to remain longer but the swell is increasing and there is no protection from it here. We put up the genoa and follow the coast northwards. Once past the tip of the island we sail north-easterly for some distance towards St Martin, with the small island of Saba on our port side.

We should have liked to visit Saba, despite the 800 steps up to the town. Sadly, despite a forecast swell from the north, the wind is actually coming from the south-east and a swell from this direction will make Saba's anchorages uncomfortable and getting ashore difficult. We gaze across at the little island from our cockpit as we pass. It is only five square miles and very tall, its potentially-active volcano, Mount Scenery, at 877 metres making it the highest point in the Netherlands. But the thing you notice particularly about its green, almost perpendicular rise is the distinctive road that zigzags crazily up it.

ST MARTIN

39

A Schizophrenic Island

The first three Caribbean islands we have visited – Antigua, Nevis and St Kitts – all share their recent history with Britain. Statia and the elusive Saba are Dutch. The island where we are currently headed, and which is named for St Martin, is divided in two. The southern half is Dutch, the north is French.

St Martin's history inevitably follows the pattern of its neighbours in the Lesser Antilles: that is to say, Amerindian crop cultivation, interspersed with tribal raiding parties. From around 800AD St Martin was settled by Arawaks from South America. They were subsequently joined by Caribs who called the island *Soualiga* after its salt deposits. One imagines they rubbed along pretty well for nearly seven centuries – give or take the odd cannibalistic war ritual – until attracting the attention of Europe's major powers.

In 1493 Columbus, an Italian, claimed it for Spain and named it after a 4th century French saint famed for dividing his cloak and giving half to a beggar. One version of the story has it that during the night St Martin's cloak miraculously became whole again. By 1631 a small Dutch colony was collecting salt at Groot Baai (Great Bay) while the French quarter produced a little tobacco.

From 1633 onwards the island was continuously fought over by Spain, France, the Netherlands and Great Britain and changed hands at least fifteen times. By 1816 the Dutch and the French were the only ones still circling the remaining chair when the music stopped and they decided to revive an earlier agreement whereby, like Martin's cloak, the island had been divided into two parts.

This previous division of the island had occurred in 1648 when, according to folklore, the Dutch and French communities had chosen a walker each, stood them back to back at one extreme of the island and told them to walk – *not run* – in opposite directions along the shoreline until they met at the other extreme of the island.

A line was then drawn between their start and finish points with the French ending up with around 60% of the island. This, the French claimed, was because their walker had chosen wine for his refreshment whereas the

Dutchman had opted for gin. The Dutch accused the French walker of running.

We arrive in Sint Maarten, the Dutch half, at Philipsburg in Groot Baai – where the Caribs and those early Dutch settlers had gathered salt – at around 4pm at the end of the day's racing. It is Heineken Race Week and very crowded but with a very amiable atmosphere and we find a nice space to anchor behind an old black-hulled ketch called *Lady Carola* that turns out to be a floating bar. So it's all rather jolly and companionable and also rather pretty, because if Nevis has a constant accompaniment of brown pelicans, Sint Maarten has yellow butterflies. Not exotic ones, just your basic flying cornflakes, but so many of them. From a lack of pesticides, presumably, as little is grown here due to a lack of fresh water.

Few of these islands, even the ones with water, grow crops commercially. Most import virtually all foodstuffs, including fruit and vegetables. The import duties, combined with transport costs, make for a high cost of living. When you ask the obvious question, the answer that comes back is that there have been attempts at home production.

A typical venture mentioned is growing bananas. Although once the new plantations began to produce fruit, it is said, the importer dropped its own prices below anything which the local growers could match. Prices would stay low for several years until the local businesses went under and then the price of imported bananas went up again.

On Sunday morning we go into Philipsburg, Sint Maarten's major town. This is a duty-free port so there are no Customs formalities to be completed, but we do need to clear in with Immigration. According to Chris Doyle's cruising guide we should do this at the police station. So we dinghy into Bobby's Marina, tie up and set off into town.

On the way we pass through a wonderful jumble of decking, small jetties and cobbled terraces. The variety of textures and building styles is delightful and very Dutch. We stop at a tourist information booth and ask the woman there if she can give us directions to the police station so that we can clear in with Immigration. 'To the courthouse,' she says, 'and second right.'

There is a vibrant street market in the square near the courthouse while the congregation in the Baptist church to our right sing their hearts out. The rhythms and enthusiasm are so infectious that I long to go inside, but looking at the young man on the door – with his neat black trousers and shirt, patterned waistcoat and white tie – I fear our rumpled, straight-off-the-boat look might indicate a lack of respect, so we continue on to the police station, swaying along to the singing as we go.

The policeman behind the counter says Immigration is on the other side of Bobby's Marina, where we left our dinghy. At Bobby's Marina the security staff there says it is at the big pier, out by the entrance to the bay, and best to take the dinghy.

It is a long ride, about three-quarters of a mile, to a very large pier intended for large commercial vessels but with nowhere to tie up a small boat nor any clear means of climbing up onto the top of it so that we can walk ashore. There is also a *really* big swell out here. We rise and fall alarmingly as we try to work out how to climb up from our very small dinghy onto this very high pier, until glancing around us we realise that there is no sign of a Port Authority or Immigration Office anyway. Nothing at all, in fact, except a very high pier and us, in a very small dinghy, surging up and down, the way seabirds sometimes do, only they always fly off pretty quickly to somewhere more congenial. I feel *extremely* vulnerable. If one of these huge surges of water breaks, we're done for.

We dinghy back to the marina complex and after a long walk down a wooden pier end up in a dive shop and ask there. 'Where you were,' says a diver. 'There's a place in the corner to get off.' It must have been pretty well hidden because we didn't see it, and I am not willing to embark on another test of nerve to find out if this landing place really does exist. Especially since, so far, nothing else has.

Instead we take a long, hot walk down a busy, dusty road without a pavement and with the grit from passing cars intermittently peppering our faces and bare limbs. The Port Authority is in a small shed, tucked away among containers and silos on an industrial estate which is just across the road from the long, high pier but not visible from as low in the water as we were. When we ask *where* exactly we should have disembarked from our dinghy the Immigration Officer, a kindly man, shakes his head. 'Nobody's supposed to land there,' he says.

Mindful of our experience in Antigua, and as we have done at each new island ever since, before filling in the length of our stay we enquire as to the penalty for overstaying. As British subjects, he says, we automatically get three months. He is bewildered as to why Antigua, formerly British, should be so perverse and says that if *he* fined everybody who overstayed, Sint Maarten would be rich.

We have spent an entire morning simply clearing in and by the time we get back to our dinghy we are into the hottest part of the day. Not a time when I am at my best. We go into the cool of a shady bar for a pina colada and remain for lunch. It is heavenly. But then it usually is when you don't have to cook it.

On the way home we stop off again at one of the tourist information booths to pick up a free local publication of Sint Maarten events. A very engaging woman tries to sign me up for a visit, *right now*, by taxi, to a 5-star hotel complex with scuba diving and $60 off dining as long as I tell the people back home how good it is.

By now it is apparent that these booths are not official Tourist Information at all. They are hustling for business, which becomes glaringly obvious when I open the expensively printed, full-colour brochure of local events that I have just been given. It doesn't actually contain any events, not even Heineken Race Week, only advertisements for jewellery and restaurants. The publication's French founder, whose svelte lines grace the contents page, is described as a 'pioneer in the field of tourist publications'.

It is 37°C in the saloon when we get back to *Voyager*.

40

Philipsburg

Next day we begin to discover our environment. It is nicer to do this in the early mornings when it is pleasantly warm, leaving the hot afternoons for stretching out on board, in the shade of our awning, with cool air blowing through the front windows as *Voyager* noses into the breeze.

The tourist boats zipping around us are called *Pinta*, *La Niña* and *Santa Maria*. Like the slave road on Statia, there is often a profound irony to tourism, the events being used to attract or entertain visitors concealing very painful periods in history. The names of these tour boats are those of the three ships Columbus took on his first voyage towards the Indies in 1492 and which would make such a major contribution to Spanish expansionism in the following century. This included the colonisation of the Netherlands, beginning in 1568 and the 80-year war the Dutch waged to free their country from Spanish domination. It was a fight that would define their nation, their religion and their art.

There are five America's Cup 12-metre yachts anchored here. Each has a professional skipper and a crewman and they take people out for a race daily. There are two of Denis Connors' boats, *Stars and Stripes 86* and *Stars and Stripes 87*, and three Canadian boats, *Canada II*, *True North I* and *True North IV*. These sleek racing yachts look particularly beautiful heeled well over, beating into the wind.

In their prime they were the epitome of racing technology and cost an absolute fortune. Yet all such yachts have only one season of glory before the new contenders with their new designs make them as out of date as last year's smartphone. Built for one race series, by the next they will have been superseded. But at a cost of millions they are definitely a sport for the seriously rich.

Also gracing the bay is the SS *Norway*. She began life as the SS *France* and, at something over 1,000ft, was the longest passenger ship ever built at her launch in 1960. She was designed as a luxury ocean liner for the trans-Atlantic run after the Second World War, to compete with the original *Queen Mary* and *Queen Elizabeth*. Ultimately, sea passages gave way to air travel and in 1979 the *France* was bought by a Norwegian cruise line, modified for cruising duties and renamed the SS *Norway*.

We go shopping and discover Sangs supermarket. It is *huge*, Chinese, and currently being extended, or having its roof fixed – it is not clear which but Hurricane Lenny did do enormous damage to this island. The mayhem of having the builders in whilst still open for business is made manifest by the unexpected appearance of items from areas that have been hastily cleared, including a towering stack of woks, red with rust from water damage, trolleys full of tinned tomato juice with their labels peeling and mud spatters on the ice-cream cabinet.

For the rest it becomes a culinary mystery tour. Like the fascinating little fancy parcels in a glass-fronted cupboard, wrapped in cream paper and tied with a bow. Their labels have the words 'sell-by date' in English but everything else – including the date itself, the ingredients and the cooking instructions – in Chinese characters.

The freezer cabinets are full of things like pork stomach, tripe, beef kidneys, salted mackerel and chicken's feet, none of which I have recipes for. And, given these staples, there has to be a question mark over what exactly goes into the sausage they sell here. So we end up with chicken. Again. And a tray of Carib beer, to keep the fridge lined and ourselves cool in the afternoons.

On another morning ashore, David has a futile time trying to get an e-mail connection at the cyber shop, and when he telephones Layla on Antigua there is still no sign of the two airmail packages posted to us on 6th January. She is still waiting for the Christmas parcel her father sent from England in early December. It is now the second week of March. While he wrestles with the internet, I set off for the town's pharmacy. In these islands, items readily available in European supermarkets such as vitamin pills, aspirin or first-aid supplies – and sometimes even toiletries – are often available only from a chemist's shop which, like here, may be some way out of town.

At Philipsburg's pharmacy anyone with a prescription takes a ticket and discreetly waits their turn. But there is a distinct lack of privacy at the counter because the local men are lounging against it and chatting companionably. So when a woman wants to discuss her intimate needs with the pharmacist she has to do so over or between these men, who put their own conversation on hold while they listen intently to hers.

Three cruise ships and a clipper ship have made for *a lot* of visitors suddenly. The atmosphere is quite jolly, however, thanks to the throbbing

Caribbean rhythms inviting the newcomers to step inside the World's HQ of Guavaberry or succumb to the allurements of Last Mango in Paradise.

As for the hordes of vendors that the cruise ship passengers bring out onto the streets, they don't bother a solitary woman striding purposefully past them on the assumption that she has been around long enough to be satiated with solar-powered T-shirts whose black and white motifs convert to colour in the sunlight. So why bother with me when there are endless undecided groups and browsing couples milling about?

The tension among the taxi drivers is palpable as they try to separate those intending to visit the surrounding shops from those wanting a tour of the island or a restaurant further afield, and each tries to be first to secure a fare. But although there is occasional shouting from these men, mostly at one another, the body language is not aggressive.

What is aggressive is the swarm of women blocking the road with wads of 3-for-$10 Caribbean T-shirts over one arm. As I slide between them and go on my way I pass two American couples trying to decide at which restaurant to have lunch. But the T-shirt vendors are determined to get their own needs settled first. So when the four Americans, intent on their guidebook, fail to respond immediately to the shouting directed at them, the largest and loudest of the women moves up very close to them and bawls.

'Hey, *you*! I'm talking to *you*!'

Not so much the promised trip of a lifetime as a glitch in the merchandising process.

If the town is busy, so too is the harbour but there can be little hope of anyone conforming to moderate speeds when the Port Authority's own vessel roars across your bows at 20 knots to get to an anchored cruise ship. It returns almost before its own wash has subsided, at similar speed but adding a wheelie this time and causing a small tidal wave that sends all the dinghies crashing against the concrete dinghy dock.

There is also a dive boat that hurtles about bearing the name *Still Waters*; an irony not lost on anyone in the anchorage left clinging for support to a stove or shower fitting in its wash. Add to that the shuttle service taking the cruise ship passengers to and from town, the tour boats, assorted tenders, dinghies, fishing boats and day boats all frantically rushing about, and since we are getting low on water anyway, we decide to look for somewhere a bit quieter.

Next morning we set out for the island of Tintamarre off the French half of the island, a passage which also gives us the opportunity to turn on the water maker and fill up our tanks. We decide not to stay the night, however, as there is a considerable chop to the water and no protection from the prevailing wind. And as the wind looks set to increase, at best we should have a very bumpy night while at worst we could end up on the rocks.

So we return to the shelter of Groot Baai for the night and set off again next morning for Simpson Bay which has a couple of major attractions for us. One is that it gives access to a large sheltered lagoon and the other is an electrical repair company where we can get our anchor winch repaired.

41

Simpson Bay Lagoon

It is only a short sail along the southern coast to Simpson Bay where we anchor and wait for the bridge to open. The lagoon occupies a large part of the western side of the island and is divided almost equally between the Dutch and French halves of the island, although for yachtsmen the Dutch half is the more popular because the French side has shoals.

The Dutch have built a short canal to give access to their half of the lagoon. Crossing it is a lifting road bridge which is raised twice a day, once in the morning and once in the late afternoon, to allow access for boats. Before going through you have to dinghy into the canal to the bridge control tower and sign a waiver against any damage to your boat while passing through the lifting bridge.

While we wait in line, a man from Michigan tells us about his recent visit to Saba and the hospitality of the man from the island's diving school, who had hung around for three hours waiting to help him get his yacht onto the commercial dock because of the heavy swell. When a freighter was still unloading there at 7pm the man told him to leave his yacht at anchor where it was and come ashore. The man then put him up in his own home for the night.

The lagoon itself, when we get inside, is very crowded with anchored boats as well as RIBs and dinghies whizzing past notices saying, '3-knot-max – no-wake zone'. To the buzz and fumes of outboard engines is added the roar and fumes of planes taking off or landing a few yards away. Very low and very loud.

The island is served by the world's major airlines but Princess Juliana Airport's short runway, with the beach on the seaward end and the lagoon at the other, is a favourite photo-opportunity for those eager to capture spectacular shots of a KLM747 only a few metres above beachgoers' heads and who are periodically blown over by the jet engines' blast.

We have two attempts to anchor in the soft mud but, hopefully for David's back, we will have an anchor winch working before we have to raise it again. Leaving me on board in case we drag, David goes ashore to find the repair company's landing stage and arrange for an inspection. The landing stage has been virtually demolished by Hurricane Lenny and David finds himself accosted by dogs.

Stray dogs are a feature of all the islands but we have never encountered aggressive ones before. Normally they stay well away from humans and have a hard time of it, especially the females who are always either pregnant or trying to protect and feed themselves and their pups.

However, someone from the repair company will come and look at our anchor winch on Friday if they have a cancellation, otherwise on Monday. The weather forecast is for increasing winds by the weekend.

The early morning airwaves are pretty busy here. We listen as usual to *Britain Today* on World Service at 6.30am, but then tune into the VHF for the Big Fish Net at 7am; the Radio Net at 7.30 with weather, goods for sale and AA meetings; then the Security Net at 8.15 followed by another weather forecast at 8.30.

One of the items, which will become something of a *cause celebre* in coming days, concerns a Swede who accidentally rammed an unattended American boat while leaving an anchorage under sail and then fled the scene. A hue and cry is out for him, not least among his fellow Swedes, who ask darkly over the VHF network how they can capture this man who is giving them all a bad name.

Something else we learn from the Security Net is the regularity with which yachtsmen's dinghies go missing here. Even more worrying are reports of burglaries on yachts with people not only losing money, valuables and passports while they are ashore but on occasion waking in the night to find a thief at work inside their boat. So today we make a tour of the chandleries.

Going ashore at the designated dinghy dock, another victim of Hurricane Lenny, is a test of agility. Its temporary replacement is constructed of large sheets of plywood fixed to several pallets, which do not have sufficient buoyancy to keep it properly afloat when you put your weight on its outermost edge. To have any hope of keeping your feet dry, therefore, the instant you step from your dinghy you need to sprint landward as fast as possible. If two of you make the mistake of standing on the edge at the same time, it sinks.

The assistant in the first chandlery is very pleasant but gives the impression that he wouldn't shop here himself. And he doesn't have what we need anyway. The staff in the second give the impression that everything is possible if you will just hang on a minute while they find it although, like the previous shop, they are out of stock of most things. A fellow yachtswoman, making a futile trawl of the depleted shelves alongside us, sighs and says it probably has something to do with the regatta.

We do finally get our hands on a security cable and padlock for the dinghy and a battery-operated motion detector for *Voyager*'s cockpit, along with a variety of other things such as charts and a pilot book for the British Virgin Islands and various electrical bits and pieces. In the Caribbean, getting your hands on what you need is rarely the end of it, however. There is then the vexed matter of price. In these islands the price at the till is rarely the same as the one in the catalogue, on the shelf or on the item's own price sticker. Shelves and individual items don't have prices on them much of the time anyway, which is why catalogues are available as you go in.

The prices at the present checkout are considerably higher than those in the catalogue David is holding but, when he mentions this, the cashier points to a printed disclaimer above the till about prices being subject to change without notice. When David looks resigned and starts fishing in his pockets for more money the cashier says that actually they're using last year's catalogues.

While ashore we encounter the skipper off the damaged American yacht and accept some of his posters – identifying the Swedish boat which damaged his own – to put up for him at our next port of call, Anguilla.

Crossing the bridge on our way home, gliding effortlessly below us just under the surface of the water, is a large, flat, brown creature shaped like a stealth bomber but with pale spots on its back and a very long thin tail. It is the first stingray we have ever seen.

Before bed we place the motion sensor above *Voyager*'s companionway doors but have forgotten all about it by morning and when I step out into the cockpit to greet the new day I am met with an ear-piercing scream. As, indeed, are our neighbours. So, every morning now, whichever one of us is up first has to limbo backwards through the doorway to get under its beam and snake up an arm to turn it off.

Sean from Dublin comes out to inspect our anchor winch as promised but having removed it finds it is not their type of work and takes it to a local company which repairs it very quickly. Sean comes back and replaces it. It is quite costly but will save David a lot of future back strain.

We now enter a period of high winds that are too strong to encourage anyone to go anywhere, even ashore unless essential, and like everybody else we are simply grateful for the shelter of the lagoon. And we have everything we need: food, drinking water, propane for cooking, excellent refrigeration, books, music, videos, sunshine, shade, brief bursts of rainwater for baths and – to keep us in contact with the outside world – World Service and our VHF. And given the present conditions our wind generator is producing plenty of power.

While the Security Net reports on safety advice and items that have been stolen, on the 7.30am Radio Net yachtsmen call in about items they have found and their owners are welcome to come and collect them from the caller's boat. These are normally small, lightweight items such as binocular cases and cockpit cushions, that tend to slip overboard but, given the current strength of the wind, today's list includes two 30ft racing yachts which have dragged during the night.

Today is my birthday. We had planned to visit the northern half of the island to sample some of its French cuisine in celebration, but abandon the trip because it is so windy. Instead David produces a delicious candlelit dinner on board although we have to eat it indoors to prevent the candles from blowing out. Or, indeed, even some of the lighter items of food from leaving our plates.

Next day the Security Net reports that theft from the anchorage has now escalated from dinghies and outboards to a whole yacht. A steel one called *Diablo*.

There are more items of interest on the Security Net in coming days. One of them is that Montserrat's volcano has blown again and there is talk of a 'dome collapse' caused by the heavy rain. There has been an explosion, followed by flows of mud and fire, and light ash is falling on boats at Antigua. It seems that when a lava dome that has formed over a volcano's crater collapses, the explosions within become more dangerous due to a combination of the dome's debris, the type of lava produced and the build-up of gas pressure.

Also on the Security Net is a report from a meeting between cruisers, boat boys and tour guides with the Prime Minister of Dominica following break-ins on leisure craft. He is new to the job, he says, but eager to tackle the situation. Nor does his status exclude him from the tribulations of the people he represents. Apparently a robber arrested last week had recently turned over the Prime Minister's own house. There is a very high unemployment rate, he says, 60% among young men, who refuse to take the few agricultural jobs available to them. Unfortunately, he says, Dominica is exporting crime to neighbouring islands and there are, for instance, 160 young Dominican men currently in Guadeloupe jails. He is trying to get inward investment from the Japanese and also asking the French for help as this would be cheaper than keeping people in jail.

And last but not least, during a lull in the high winds the owner of *Diablo* hired a small plane and has discovered his stolen yacht anchored in a secluded bay. The weather forecaster who follows begins his report with, 'Very unusual weather patterns for this time of the year,' as he does most mornings.

David, meanwhile, is captivated by some of the names of the yachts around us calling one another on the VHF. A particular favourite is: '*Resolute... Resolute...* this is *W C Fields.*' It even sounds like the man. It gets us started on some of our favourites from the past.

Over time we have gathered a list of boats with inappropriate names, the most recent addition being that life-denying couple Gene and Erica on *Carpe Diem*, with its imperative to seize each day and live it to the full. But still clinging to the top of our list is the man at a yacht club where we once stayed. Each morning he would call up the club's jolly boat for a lift ashore and in a voice from the crypt would intone with a dying fall, '*Ode to Joy*, this is *Ode to Joy*. Come in please.'

One of the things about high winds and an anchored boat is that it keeps you focused on your cleaning and maintenance schedule because you can't escape by finding something more interesting to do ashore or sailing off somewhere. But the wind does finally begin to subside and we begin to make plans to move on.

We collect our first mail in three months. Among the items is a renewal of our VHF radio licence which we are pleased to have before we visit the French half of the island.

'They fine you if it's out of date,' a fellow yachtsman had warned us when we'd mentioned going there. 'The French fine you for everything. It's an easy form of income generation.'

We buy a new snubbing line from one of the chandleries, the existing one having broken from the constant tugging of the recent relentless wind. We also join the great rush to the fuel dock. Because the weather has kept people at anchor so long, now everybody wants to buy fuel and move on.

The fuel operator moves at the speed of a glacier. The American couple in front of us, on a Grand Banks 46-footer, proceed with a similar lack of urgency as they negotiate their bulk discount. In the meantime, an increasingly bitter Frenchman circles for 45 minutes before reaching some sort of emotional crisis and hurtling away, while the skipper of another American motoryacht radios in every 15 minutes for an hour and a half to ask when he can expect to take on fuel.

42

Marigot

With our fuel tank finally filled we check out of Sint Maarten, motor out to sea and turn on the water maker. We are heading for Saint-Martin, the French half of the island, and in just over two hours are anchoring off its capital, Marigot.

We go ashore – there is an excellent dinghy dock – clear in and have a look around. The town is much more European than any we have so far visited. We refresh ourselves in La Belle Époque overlooking the marina, which is very pleasant, and then go for a big shop-up in Match, quite the best supermarket encountered in the Caribbean so far. It is so good that we intend to dinghy in again for more tomorrow, as our stores have been depleted and we do not know what opportunities we shall find at our next port of call. After that we intend to clear out with the French authorities, stow our shopping and set off for Anguilla. A swell develops during the night which is big enough to interrupt our sleep.

The following day begins well enough. Despite the swell we have another decent trip into Marigot's dinghy dock. It is a generous length and, unlike the temporary plywood one with a tendency to sink under your feet that we've been using lately, it is a substantial one.

Unfortunately, as we shall discover, its length and strength is also its weakness for those wanting to leave a dinghy safely while they go ashore. Since yesterday larger boats have been allowed to tie up alongside, reducing the space left for dinghies to only a few metres. But there is only one other dinghy here and we tie up alongside it.

We set off to the Match supermarket and fill our rucksacks – not least from its wine shelves where the prices, unusually for the Caribbean, are very reasonable. At Immigration we wait in line to clear out, behind an anxious woman enquiring about a yacht well overdue from South America, and then return to the dinghy dock.

At first we think our dinghy has been stolen. Then among all the others, butting and grinding into each other on the swell, we spot what appears to be the propeller of our outboard sticking up and realise that it is still there, only upside down. Shortening the dinghy dock has put unreasonable pressure on space. Dinghies are now three or four deep and to get ashore from their own dinghy people have to climb over other people's.

An aluminium dinghy does not behave like a rubber one. Someone has stepped onto its edge and flipped it over. What is unforgivable is that they have simply left it that way, with our outboard under water. We drop our rucksacks onto the dock and rush forward in the hope that we are not too late to save our outboard. A crowd begins to gather.

A tall young American steps out of it and takes my place in the struggle to turn over and empty our dinghy. I am very grateful to him, not least because an aluminium dinghy full of water, with a heavy outboard attached, takes a lot of very awkward lifting; but also because the gathering crowd has cut us off completely from the two rucksacks we abandoned when we first spotted our tender under water.

Given the amount of theft being reported over the airwaves here, I suddenly become panic-stricken that, shielded behind the growing crowd observing the resurrection of our dinghy, someone may be walking off with them. The loss of our ship's papers, insurance documents and passports – all the things you have to present to officialdom when clearing in or out – not to mention things such as cheque book and credit cards that we no longer feel confident about leaving on board *Voyager* when we go ashore – would cause enormous problems, time and expense. And with the companionway door key gone we should have to break into *Voyager*. Thankfully the rucksacks are still where we left them but I drag them to where I can keep an eye on them.

As soon as the dinghy is upright our first priority is to see if the engine will start but it has been too long under water. The problem now is to get it somewhere fast before the salt ruins it completely. The obvious solution would be to take it to someone here at Marigot. Unfortunately, because of all the reports of outboard thefts, we have chained it to the dinghy. The key to the padlock is on *Voyager*. And no-one can tell us if there actually *is* anyone in this very small town who can service it. Although the French half of the island has the largest land mass, thanks to its 17th century wine-bibbing walker, it has by far the smallest population and the island's service facilities all appear to be located on the Dutch side. Which was one of the reasons we went to Simpson Bay Lagoon in the first place, to get our anchor winch repaired.

We have another problem, too. There has been a forecast for a severe swell here by Sunday, which is why we had been planning to leave for

Anguilla today and be settled there before it arrived. But the swell appears to be arriving earlier than predicted and the exposed anchorage at Marigot Bay is not a place to be when it does.

When you live close to the elements in a constantly changing environment your mental processes settle into an ongoing equation that involves not simply wind speed and direction, weather and sea state but also limited supplies, erratic services and the time it takes to get anything done. Into the present equation has to be added the fact that neither our present anchorage, nor paddling back and forth in a dinghy is tenable. If we are going to save the outboard we have to act quickly, but we also need to do it safely. We decide to return to Simpson Bay Lagoon. Apart from being sheltered, we also know where we can get our outboard fixed.

Naturally, our baler and all those useful things you keep in a dinghy have floated away and initially we fear our paddles will have gone too, leaving us no way of getting back to *Voyager*. Fortunately they are still wedged under the seat. Nevertheless I rain curses on whoever did this to our dinghy because it takes a feverish amount of paddling to get back to *Voyager*, not just in what has become a greatly increased swell but also the rapidly rising wind and sour grey clouds of what appears to be an approaching squall.

On the one hand our decision turns out to be justified, since the lowering cloud and rising wind turns out not to be a passing squall but the beginning of prolonged stormy weather. On the other hand, it involves us in one of our nastiest sailing experiences ever.

43
Back at Simpson Bay Lagoon

It is a rough passage back to Simpson Bay. We have hours to wait for the 5.30pm bridge opening and even at anchor the swell is disturbing. So I find it horrifying watching David preparing to paddle his way through it. We are the only people in the anchorage but during our stay earlier there had been so many people roaring about in large RIBs with powerful engines that with a lot of nagging I persuade him to make a call on the VHF and ask if one of them would be willing to collect him and our outboard and take them into the repairer. Shortly afterwards an American called Will, off a ketch called *Lucky Strike*, comes through huge waves in a little grey rubber dinghy and takes David and our outboard into the lagoon.

Will is extremely kind and waits with David at the repair shop for several hours so that he can bring him back. He drops David and the outboard off around 4.30 and, much thanked, sets off back for his own yacht. By this time a lot of boats have arrived for the bridge opening and as the time gets closer a melee ensues as they begin jockeying for pole position to go through the canal into the lagoon. The behaviour is appalling, to the point of recklessness.

Most of them are much bigger than we are but despite being the first boat there we decide to go through last rather than have *Voyager* damaged. But even by simply remaining where we have been for the last umpteen hours there is no escape when the dead-eyed man on the flying bridge of a 90-foot Argyll motoryacht sporting a red ensign begins remorselessly bearing down on us.

Assuming that like him and almost everybody else we are milling about he clearly expects us to get out of his way, but had he bothered to look over his huge bow he would have noticed David on the foredeck struggling to get our anchor up. Before he rams us I leave the steering position and waive the fool off with some choice words while the lady of the house waves decorously back at me as she tiptoes about in an abstracted sort of way with a fender with a knitted sock on it. Fishermen and rich people!

The sea swell is even bigger than before and combined with the wash from so many large boats constantly circling in a confined area, as they keep pushing relentlessly to get closer to the front of the queue, the result is pandemonium.

The time arrives and there is a surge of boats towards the opening. We gravitate to the rear. An American yacht falls in behind us so that we are the last but one. Our turn finally approaches. Immediately in front of us two fishing boats and a large yacht fight for who will go through first, and for a time it looks as if, with none of them willing to give way, they are going to charge the narrow channel's entrance three-abreast. We anticipate one of the fishermen at least having to go into reverse, to avoid a collision, for which David allows room.

Throughout this unseemly exercise, a man in a dinghy has been roaring about among the boats frantically waving them ever faster into the channel. He now appears beside *Voyager*, waving us furiously on. David accelerates to maximum speed.

You need to concentrate when going through a narrow opening in heaving water. He is going flat out straight for it when a man in blue overalls appears on the platform beside the bridge waving his arms and shouting. David has two engines roaring behind him, a doghouse roof over his head and a man in a dinghy beside him yelling at him while revving his outboard engine to a high-pitched whine.

I look at David and realise that he can neither see nor hear the man on the bridge platform. I can't hear what the man is saying either. I assume it's to go faster but I climb up onto the side deck anyway. When I get there I can see that the bridge is no longer fully upright and that the man is waving at us to go back.

'They're closing the bridge!' I shout down to David in disbelief. 'What?' he shouts back, all his attention on the entrance to the lagoon.

I begin again, 'They're...' but I go no further.

In retrospect, there is always a fascination at the working of the brain in times of crisis. How it receives data, assesses it, forms a conclusion and initiates action, all in the blink of an eye. There is no possible way, at this distance and at this speed, that *Voyager* can be brought to a stop before she hits the bridge.

Our mast is right beside the helm. Fixed around it is our sturdy doghouse roof. When the mast comes down and brings everything else with it, David is going to be underneath it all. Even worse, he won't know it is coming and will have no chance to dive for cover.

The bridge is coming down slowly. There should be just enough room. I am unaware of actually making a decision. I simply react. And standing on the side deck, eyeing the man above me, I yell, 'Keep going!' and like the man in the dinghy beside us I wave David furiously on.

The man in the blue overalls is now screaming at me in rage but the bridge begins to go up again and we pass through. David has to go into reverse the moment he has us the other side because the two squabbling fishing boats and the yacht are milling about in front of him. And it suddenly becomes obvious why they make you sign a waiver before letting you enter.

The man on the bridge is dancing about apoplectically.

'I'm going to see you get the maximum fine going!' he roars. 'I'm going to report you to the coastguard! You're gonna get *fined*...' David, bewildered by the shouting behind him, looks up and sees the man on the bridge for the first time. But only briefly, as he now has to shuffle *Voyager* between the bridge and the three boats in front of him which are still engaged in some sort of scuffle and leaving him nowhere to go.

Meanwhile, the man in the dinghy is still roaring his outboard engine and yelling at the top of his voice behind us, the ultimate absurdity being that although the man on the bridge and the man in the dinghy appear to be working together they do not communicate with one another. From his position on *Voyager*'s port side, the one in the dinghy was just as incapable of seeing the bridge coming down, or its yelling operator, as David.

Given that middle-aged laundry ladies can maintain effective ship-to-shore communication via a handheld VHF, one feels it should not be beyond the wit of a bridge operator and his colleague in a dinghy to do as much. If they *had* communicated with one another, what happens next would not have occurred.

I look up at the hysterical madman above me at the bridge's controls, still dancing about and waving his arms like something from a pantomime. But if he is angry, I am *furious*. This is the most outrageous, dangerous behaviour I have ever experienced.

'You can't stop a boat *there*!' I roar back at him, jabbing my finger behind us, at the other side of the bridge opening. But to my horror I realise that he has. The American yachtsman behind us, the last man in line and the only person polite enough to wait his turn, is still being urged hysterically forward by the whipper-in in the dinghy just as we had been – while having the bridge dropped right in front of him.

As he wrenches the wheel violently, to avoid hitting the bridge at full speed with his mast, the only thing that prevents him smashing his boat onto the rocks beside him is the quick thinking of the only other decent man on the water that day. He drives his RIB between the yacht and the rocks to cushion the impact and then uses the full force of his engine to push the yacht off them.

We find a place to anchor and I insist on going with David to clear in. He has no first-hand knowledge of what just happened and there is no way any fine in my name is going to be paid for the actions of a homicidal maniac in blue overalls.

Sint Maarten's motto is *The Friendly Island*.

Next morning, on the 7.30 VHF broadcast, a rather shaky-voiced American says he would like to warn yachtsmen of a navigational hazard in the form of a marina employee who drops bridges on people without proper warning for the saving of approximately 12 seconds. The marina says it would like his complaint in writing. He still sounds angry from the previous evening. Which is not surprising, really, since on top of everything else he's had to ride at anchor all night in a vicious swell until the bridge opened again this morning.

He is followed by a pastor of the Sint Maarten International Baptist Church which runs this 7.30am network who says the bridge is only supposed to be open for fifteen minutes (I don't recall seeing that anywhere on the waiver we signed but it might go some way to explain that unseemly stampede of yesterday evening) and that when there is an ambulance waiting they drop it at a moment's notice. (I didn't read that anywhere either.) He also says that a few years ago they did the same thing to another yachtsman who had a heart attack and died.

We go ashore to post some letters and send some e-mails. We also learn that the fugitive Swede, appalled at seeing his and his boat's identity on posters everywhere, has given himself up and that he and the American whose boat he damaged are sorting out the matter of restitution amicably.

When we return to *Voyager*, the boat beside us has the same music blaring out of it as when we left although it has been unoccupied since early morning. As before, people are driving RIBs and dinghies at enormous speed and setting all the yachts heaving, while planes roar overhead every fifteen minutes. So we move further down the lagoon where it is uncrowded and very pleasant.

We invite Will and his wife over on Sunday afternoon, as a quite inadequate thank-you for Will's kindness – and courage – in making the journey through that huge swell four times on our behalf in his small dinghy. On Monday we leave the lagoon. I take up my position on the side deck and eyeball the operator for any sign of revenge on his part but the bridge stays up.

There is a forecast for a swell from the north and our intention is to make another attempt on Saba. But the swell turns out to be coming from the south-east, the same as before, so we abandon Saba a second time.

Given the passage of time and the unpredictability of the weather we also abandon our plans to visit Anguilla and head directly for the British Virgin Islands instead. Apart from a brief period with an engine on, just to charge the batteries, we sail all the way. All through the warm Caribbean night.

THE BRITISH VIRGIN ISLANDS

44

Paradise to Purgatory

I have begun to think that this entire venture had its origins in the mid-sixties. It was then that David read an article about the Mamas & the Papas singing for their supper in the American Virgin Islands. The group that was destined to become so rich and famous was unknown and penniless at the time and its four members had gone to the islands because living there was cheap. But accompanying the article were pictures of golden beaches, palm trees and a yacht anchored in a beautiful, secluded bay. For someone born and raised in England's industrial heartland it was the stuff of dreams.

He had mentioned it to me once, years ago, but until I heard him chatting to a fellow yachtsman recently I had forgotten all about it. And by the way he spoke of it to the yachtsman I think so had he. However, I suspect that unconsciously the Virgin Islands have become for David a highpoint because whenever the name arises for any reason, he presses his lips together in a sort of half-smile as if savouring a future delight. And it will, after all, be the culmination of our trip in the sense that it will be our last Caribbean location before we have to leave the region ahead of the hurricane season.

The 90-mile journey there certainly does not disappoint. It is one of those magical night passages of warm light winds, billions of stars and a breathtaking dawn. The winds are relatively light, but not wanting to arrive in the dark anyway we have been more than content to enjoy the sail and simply ghost along.

Our destination is Road Town, Tortola, the capital of the BVI. Shortly after dawn we enter Sir Francis Drake Channel via Round Rock Passage to the east of Ginger Island. This channel is a long, broad seaway surrounded by tropical islands. It is so early that there are no other boats about, just us on a gentle blue sea and everywhere you look there seems to be an endless series of rocky islands, with their golden sandy beaches and palm trees, and names like Lost Jerusalem, Cockroach Island, Fat Hogs Bay, Nanny Cay and the Blinders. It is Paradise. Barely nine miles further on we enter Purgatory.

At 11am on a Tuesday we drop anchor off Road Town. Our thermometer says the temperature is currently 35°C in the shade but we are not in the shade and by the time we have finished anchoring we are *very* hot. Then David goes off in the dinghy to clear in.

The Customs counter is manned by a very nice young man who warns David to be careful because it is expensive here. Downstairs the woman in Immigration appears to have graduated from the same school of deliberate offensiveness as her opposite number in Antigua, only with honours. In the supermarket the truth of the Customs officer's words is revealed, if the price of the few basic food items purchased today is anything to go by.

Our plan now is to be lazy for the rest of the day, have a look at Road Town tomorrow morning, and then leave for a drift around the islands. The weather forecast is for light winds.

Mid-afternoon we see a man in a dinghy bringing in a yacht. *Reckless* has engine trouble and the people on board look very resentful. After taking them ashore in his dinghy, the man returns and brings *Reckless* a short distance from our starboard side in an easy-going, leisurely sort of way, climbs aboard her, throws out her anchor, pays out some rope, drops back into his dinghy and chugs back to land in that kind of slow, laid-back attitude you associate with the Caribbean lifestyle.

Too laid back, as it turns out. Like so many yachts out here the anchor is on rope, which is cheaper than chain but being so much lighter it doesn't lie on the seabed and help the anchor to stay dug in the way that chain does. Also, the recommended ratio of rope to water depth is 6:1. The water in this part of the anchorage is around 40 feet. Nothing like 240 feet of rope has been let out. Nor has the dinghy been used to reverse the yacht and test the anchor. But what the hell? This is the Caribbean! And there's not a breath of wind to ripple the surface anyway, which bodes well for a restful night.

A little after 2am we are woken by heavy rain. We get up and close all the hatches, left open on what had been a very hot night. We go out on deck to collect rainwater in buckets from the awning, filling four in no time, and then we take down the awning. With the arrival of the rain the wind has increased, and we are now facing inshore, to the south-west. It has become an unpleasant night but we are happy that we are comfortably at anchor and about 3am we return to bed. Before we do, David removes the bung from the dinghy to let out the water that has gathered in it, and prevent it filling overnight.

An hour later I am woken by David leaping out of bed. There are noises outside. By the time I reach the companionway doors he is already on the afterdeck, although barely visible. It is difficult to comprehend what is happening, as it so often is with sudden, chaotic events, because so much is in motion; so many things hit you all at the same time.

The rain in my face so that I can barely see.

The noise of the wind howling in the rigging and the sky roaring.

And the darkness. After so many night passages I am used to functioning in the dark, but now I am disorientated. I don't recognise anywhere. Neither a light nor a brooding landmark that I left an hour ago is there any more.

The wind has shifted again and increased dramatically in strength. We appear to be in the grip of a very nasty squall and *Reckless*, the yacht anchored yesterday afternoon with such gay abandon, is lying across our stern. David is frantically trying to push it off. When I join him, slipping and sliding on the streaming, plunging deck, with the rain slapping my sodden nightclothes against my body, I can see that the yacht is bending our heavy duty stainless steel davits sideways and our dinghy is about to be crushed. But even with both of us pushing against the yacht we have no effect on it whatsoever.

The noise is overwhelming. Even side-by-side we have to shout to make ourselves heard. And along with the howling wind is the clatter of the most ferocious rain I have ever experienced. It is most agonising on the face, making you close your eyes involuntarily when you most need to see. Turn your face from the wind, however, and the rain simply streams down from your hair and blinds you anyway.

What is confusing us utterly is why the boat on our stern is immovable. David yells to me to go and start the starboard engine, to pull *Voyager* forward, away from the intruder, but as soon as I put it into gear the engine stalls. My attempt to move forward on the port engine also fails. The yacht's anchor rope appears to be wrapped around our propellers.

The port davit rope snaps and our dinghy's bow falls to the water. The aluminium boat is now dangling by its stern from our mutilated starboard davit and being crushed against our transom. Its outboard is still attached and, with so much weight hanging on a davit that is also bending sideways, it can be only moments before the second rope snaps too.

We get the outboard engine off the dinghy and David lets down its stern. It is only when it begins filling with seawater that we remember taking out the bung earlier to prevent it from filling with rain. I run to the chart table for the bung. David drops down into the dinghy, and struggles to screw in the bung with the dinghy tossing on the waves and rapidly filling with seawater under him. I am horrified. Holding onto the dinghy's painter I look down on his crouching back with this damned yacht grinding remorselessly above him and I am sure he is going to die.

Finally he clambers out of the dinghy onto the back steps. Never an easy operation at the best of times, even worse barefoot, in driving rain with the wind tearing at your clothing. From the back steps he pushes with all his might against the yacht while I drag the dinghy free and tie it up to a cleat on the beam.

In all the chaos it takes us some minutes to realise that *Voyager* is lying with her port beam into the wind instead of her bow. And with *Reckless*'s bow held fast to our port quarter, its stern is being pushed towards our starboard quarter by the wind, which is ferocious. Just how ferocious we will not know until later in the day when a local broadcast reports that it was in the mid-forties, or Severe Gale 9. Nor does it pass over in the time it takes for the average squall. It just goes on and on.

Having flattened our davits, the yacht is now beginning to grind into our pushpit and gallows which are in danger of going the same way as our davits, only faster as they are nowhere near as sturdy. After it has demolished them it will be grinding into *Voyager*'s actual stern. While I fend off as best I can, David attaches a rope to *Voyager*'s stern cleat and the other end to *Reckless*'s bow roller. Then he climbs aboard and pays out a metre or so of the yacht's anchor rope. Once slack it floats free of our underwater gear, the boat falls back from us and *Voyager* swings into the wind. David climbs back aboard *Voyager* and pays out more of our own rope so that *Reckless* falls well behind us.

The wind gradually dies away completely and we are left in an almost unnatural quiet after the frenzy and confusion of the night. By now it is nearly dawn and wearily we are able at last to draw breath, make a cup of tea and in the light from the coming dawn reflect on what happened.

Reckless we knew had dragged her anchor, but only now do we realise that she had drifted about with every wind change, circled us, and not only wrapped her anchor rope around *Voyager,* but also a nearby marker buoy which is currently being dragged below the surface every time *Reckless* plunges. We have no way of knowing if the yacht is being held by its anchor, or the marker buoy or whether, if we let it go, it will drift away and damage other boats in the anchorage, not least the little sloop directly behind us. So we keep it tied to us.

Around 7.30 we manage to raise someone on the VHF who contacts the yacht's owner, a charter company, and one of its partners, Jerry – the man who had anchored *Reckless* yesterday afternoon – comes out at 8am to take it away. He is regretful, accepts responsibility for the damage to our boat and thanks us for not leaving his to drift. He tows it away saying that he will be back shortly to see about our davits.

Soon after he has gone, the owner of the little sloop behind us comes over. He says he had been watching from his saloon – we had seen his lights glimmering in the worst of the gale – and that it had been 'a wild night'. He gives us his name and address, and says he is willing to be a witness if necessary. Like us he had watched *Reckless* being brought in by dinghy the previous afternoon, and the negligent way it had been anchored.

He is just about to leave as the charter company's boat returns. It is not Jerry this time, but his partner, an altogether different sort of fish. Simon is offhand to the point of rudeness and glares at our departing visitor. He is clearly angry that his partner has accepted responsibility for the damage, although it is difficult to see how he could claim otherwise.

Resentfully, Simon talks about repairs. We suggest new davits. Simon snorts. Our point is that given the degree of damage, how can the present ones ever be expected to be as strong as they were, and what on earth are they going to look like? His response is simple. We can accept the offer of repairs or make a claim through his insurance company. That will take months – through the hurricane season – or we can have our own repaired and back in place in a couple of days. And he will get the welder to put strengtheners in them. If David removes the davits, he will take them, and us, to the welder. We don't appear to have much choice. David fetches his toolbox.

On the drive to the welder Simon starts complaining to us about his own problems saying that his secretary has just caused $3,000-worth of damage to one of the company's cars. He seems to be expecting sympathy but having spent part of last night watching my husband only inches from being crushed or drowned I find myself wondering if she damaged anybody else in the process, and whether the unhappy family removed from the malfunctioning *Reckless* were reimbursed. Or whether negligence is a company byword and with this sort of track record if it even *has* any insurance.

Failing to get the sympathy he feels due to him we travel in sullen silence until he receives a call on his mobile. He listens briefly, eyes us resentfully in the rear view mirror, says, 'I think it's got past that now, Jim,' and hangs up. I assume that he has just received legal advice about not accepting liability but that in between seeking it and receiving it he has discovered that we have a witness and a case. Looking at his spiteful face I regret not having cut his boat loose to smash itself to pieces after all. But the welder seems friendly enough and promises a quick job so that we can be on our way as soon as possible. He says to telephone him Monday.

45

Tortola

Next morning our backs ache from the strain of yesterday. My arms hurt as well, and I have a large bruise between my left wrist and thumb where *Reckless* squashed it as I tried to protect our gallows and stern light. On the other hand, we are relieved, and not a little surprised, to be still alive and unharmed, that *Voyager* is otherwise undamaged and we still have our dinghy – a bit dented but intact. We take it ashore and have a wander round the town, observing as we walk down Main Street its major landmark, Cockroach Hall, a doctor's premises throughout the previous century but currently a real estate office.

Late Friday afternoon a small group of boys form a line in front of a large yellow and white striped marquee and drum – for *hours*. It isn't particularly loud at this distance, but so insistent that you can understand the effect it has traditionally had on infantrymen. After the first hour or so even I am marching about the boat as I carry out my domestic duties.

When the drumming stops, a hot gospeller holds a meeting inside the marquee. Unfortunately for his congregation he begins in the top register so has nowhere to go and the result is an endless harangue with only the words, '...the Kingdom of Gard...' discernible at regular intervals. It is difficult to gauge the effect on the congregation because there is no audible response from it.

But you do wonder about the collision of cultures in a place like this when the wet T-shirt competition gets underway at the pub just a few yards away and the weekly all-the-mussels-you-can-eat night costs more than an islander will probably earn in a week. And far more than these two blue water cruisers can afford. The waterfront meanwhile is overrun with young men in pressed shorts and polo shirts carrying clipboards and you realise that daydreams take a long time to reach fruition and places change dramatically in forty years. As if to reinforce the message, today is the first day of April. All Fools Day.

On Sunday there is another gospel meeting in the marquee, only this time the preacher begins lower down the scale and builds up gradually to a climax, which is far more satisfying. It is all part of a Millennium Crusade apparently.

On Monday BBC World Service's new schedules come into play which is important because World Service is our contact with the outside world. The announcers have been talking about 'the changes' for a month now, without ever actually saying what they are. They are mentioned repeatedly during the course of today, but specific times are not confided. And programmes are trailed repeatedly without anyone saying when they will actually be broadcast.

This morning, at the time when we traditionally listen to our home news programme, *Britain Today*, someone talks endlessly instead about how much better the new schedules – 'now on two interlinked channels' – will be for us. *But they don't tell us what they've done with the programme we've just tuned in for!*

Like us, quite a large proportion of World Service listeners probably don't have easy access to the internet and thus the BBC's invitation to consult its website and discover its elusive new schedules is maddening. I don't know how the Third World does it but for us it means a long dinghy ride across the bay and round the cruise ship dock, going ashore, booking a slot at the cyber cafe and waiting for a computer to come free.

At least David can check our e-mails while he's there and telephone his brother, the welder and Layla for any sign of our mail turning up at Antigua. I spend the time in Freeman's Laundrette and get chatting to an American there who tells me about a marina at Washington DC that lets you anchor for $25 a week. It is apparently only a hop and a jump from there to the US capital's major landmarks, galleries and museums including the Smithsonian.

After she leaves and my washing is installed in a couple of machines, the laundrette's manager very kindly offers me a chair to take outside in the shade where it is cooler. There I read through the BVI tourist booklet, although even the tourist office can't find anything more to offer us on Tortola as we've already experienced Cockroach Hall.

There is, however, a nice article on a repaired pelican. The impressive plummet executed by a brown pelican can result in serious injuries if refuse has been dumped at sea. This one had such a large tear in its pouch that it was unable to retain any of the fish it caught and was doomed to starve. Happily the bird had been rescued and a local surgeon persuaded to use his skills in sewing up the hole in its pouch.

The biggest difficulty had been confining the bird on land so that it could be fed by hand while its wound healed because if allowed to return to its normal habits it would burst the stitches. A pelican in captivity, like any large bird living on a diet of fish, is a problem because it excretes so much mess that if kept in a cage it becomes a health hazard to itself. The solution was to tether it by one of its legs and keep moving it to new locations until it was successfully released back into the wild.

I have become inordinately fond of pelicans. Apart from being comical, beautiful, graceful in flight and unbelievably amiable, they make no sound except *Ha* – loudly when threatened, softly when contented. So you can sail past a large colony of them and instead of the harsh squabbling you often hear with large groups of birds the most you get from pelicans is a sort of communal sigh.

Thanks to a combination of wind direction and the wash from the large number of RIBs roaring about we return to the dinghy dock to find our little aluminium one squashed underneath the pontoon with just the air release valve on the fuel cap of the outboard sticking out. We rescue it and sit in the shade under a palm tree for a few minutes to review our individual sorties and decide if we need to do anything further before making the trip back to *Voyager*.

I can report that our washing is *immaculately* clean – not something you can say for every laundrette we have ever used and I have, in addition, the location of a future US anchorage that sounds delightful. David says there is still no sign of our missing mail in Antigua, that he has failed to get a telephone connection to his brother in England and the welder will not have our davits ready for us today as promised yesterday because his polisher is off sick. They will definitely be ready tomorrow. 'But phone first.'

David has also learned that Tortola's Regatta is imminent and we should prefer not to be here when it takes place. In fact, but for the damage to our davits, we should have left here the morning after we cleared in. The holding is poor, the town has been given over to yacht charter companies and its cost of living puts even Antigua's finest in the shade.

Another day, another dinghy ride and another telephone call to the welder. He says, 'Phone tomorrow.' At least one of these trips is made worthwhile when a passing yachtsman, carrying a large cardboard outer of Fosters lager cans, tells David where they are selling it off cheap. American brewers put a six-month time limit on their products and the Fosters is past its sell-by date, which rather chimes with our feelings about this whole place.

Each day, morning and afternoon, a large tourist catamaran sails past us. On board, an American woman, with a voice that could seriously damage concrete and enough synthetic enthusiasm to power a battleship, generates good feeling among her day-trippers before they head for home by encouraging them to take it in turns to get a note out of a large conch shell.

The finale is always the same: 'You guys are *great*!! Yeahhhhhhh!!!! And you've had a great day and made a lotta new friends! Yeahhhhhhh!!!!' It all seems a bit juvenile given that her clientele is mostly pushing fifty, but every day they dutifully blow into the conch shell for her.

Late afternoons the drummer boys arrive and drum into the evening, ahead of another preacher.

Finally the welder says the davits are ready and describes where to go to collect them. There won't be room in the dinghy for both of us and two large davits so David goes alone. When he finally finds the place, there is no dinghy dock and he has to carry our extremely heavy davits one at a time across a building site and down a rocky bank. Getting them into the dinghy is quite a struggle, too. So is getting them out of the dinghy, lifting them up onto *Voyager*'s stern and then bolting them into place. Our backs ache terribly afterwards.

It is also very hot. Even the heavy rain during the afternoon fails to cool the air. And Tortola's regatta begins tomorrow. The anchorage is already overcrowded. We leave it early the following morning. To add insult to injury, our anchor winch, so expensively repaired at Sint Maarten, grinds to a stop and refuses to move again.

46

Paradise Resumed

For a little while there is just enough wind to get some help from the genoa, but when we change course to go up Thatch Island Cut we have to take it down and motor the rest of the way into a head wind.

We pass some classic little beaches, including one with a hammock slung between two leaning palm trees, and anchor off Little Jost Van Dyke Island. It is rumoured to be named after a Dutch privateer, but nobody knows for sure. There is a lot of fakelore about.

What is undeniably true is that in 1744 it was the birthplace of John Lettsome who was born into one of the early Quaker settlements in this area. Sent to England to be educated at the tender age of six, he grew up to be an ardent reformer and a famous doctor with more than a touch of whimsy, writing:

I, John Lettsome,
Blisters, bleeds and sweats 'em.
If, after that, they please to die
I, John Lettsome.

It was doubtless an ironic commentary on the medical practices of the time for in 1773 he used his radical ideas to found the London Medical Society and a year later became a founder-member of the Royal Humane Society. Both continue to this day. He was also an abolitionist and when he returned to this island on the death of his father he freed all the slaves he had inherited under his father's will.

Voyager lies only yards off a rocky shoreline broken by two tiny beaches which are alive with pelicans. They are perched on trees and rocks, diving, swimming and even thinking contented thoughts if the soft 'Ha' that the nearest one utters is anything to go by.

To starboard of us is the truly wonderful Sandy Spit, attached by a reef to Green Cay but to all intents and purposes a tiny desert island complete with golden sand and a leaning palm tree. From where we are anchored one softly-contoured wooded island overlaps another. You can't even see the ocean. It is as if you are sequestered in a large lagoon.

Halfway up the nearest hillside a line of brown goats treks resolutely towards its summit. A young one, tentative, falling behind, unsure of a foothold and craving reassurance from its disappearing flock, cries like a baby. The water here has the most amazing variety of colours from dark blue through cerulean, aquamarine and turquoise. Small shoals of fish leap out of it sending silver shivers across its surface.

We finish *Our Mutual Friend* during the afternoon, Dickens' novel about personal identity and social class, and are temporarily bereft because we've enjoyed it so much. We dig out *Framley Parsonage* to cheer ourselves up with some Trollope. I think it is fair to say that for the present at least we have given up the sombre and significant in our reading habits and decided to be happy instead.

I always used to make myself finish a book, or at least put it to one side for a future attempt, because received wisdom said it was a classic and if I didn't relate to it then I must have failed to read it properly. I now concede that one size does not fit all. That even acclaimed literature suits some people but not others. It is a reflection on neither the writer nor the reader. For art, as somebody once said, is what a dominant group of people says it is. Why else do artists go in and out of fashion?

David made it to the end of *Moby Dick*. I didn't despite an introduction from a Harvard professor saying it is the greatest work in English literature, and scholarly exegesis claiming that the *Pequod* and its crew are a metaphor for America. For me the moral and spiritual heart of the book – conveyed through Ahab's hatred of the great white whale and his soul-destroying obsession with revenge – is negated by Melville's own obsession with killing whales; right down to the minutia of the best kind of knives, scrapers and diverse cutting tools with which to slice, dice and skin them. Having spent a sociable afternoon with a Minke I take immense satisfaction in stuffing *Moby Dick* in among the egg shells and potato peelings. There will be no further attempts on my part.

I did finish *The Brothers Karamazov*, but after being dragged through so many pages of moral depravity, delirium tremens and the kid putting a pin in the dog's food so that it dies horribly – and then dying miserably himself from guilt – the denouement wasn't worth the journey and Dostoyevsky went into the gash bag, too. Since I knew before I started it that greed, murder, larceny, fornication, cruelty, gambling and alcoholism do not lead to a happy, fulfilling life, and with the book's literary subtleties lost in translation, there didn't seem any benefit to be had from another reading.

Our present philosophy is: if you are happy, why spoil it by reading books that make you miserable? And we are happy here. We wake most mornings as it begins to get light and watch the sun rise over Sandy Spit. This morning a heron stands motionless for ten minutes as a great red orb begins to form a stunning background and turn the striking lines of the bird into a spectacular silhouette. Only as the composition achieves perfection and I finally persuade the camera to focus does the wretched bird stalk away.

We breakfast in a pale golden sunrise among the pelicans. The trees are full of them and in so many variations. Some are small and brown. Some large and brown; some are large and grey; some have a white under-belly and underwings, some white heads and necks. One, with its great webbed feet wrapped around a tree branch, has a huge white chest and on top of its light brown head is a perfect fez of dark brown feathers. One, completely brown and sitting motionless on a rock, has large flat eyes like two sets of tiddlywinks.

Some days they are joined by a flock of boobies. With their sleek brown bodies, long beaks and long pointed wings they are beautiful in flight. When the sunlight catches their backs they glow like warm brown velvet.

They are related to the brown pelican, and also the gannet which they resemble physically, and like both these species the boobies are ener-getic divers. When a shoal of fish passes through, they rise into the air one after the other, arc, and hit the water like tracer bullets, even pursuing their prey under water. One of them is even bold enough to dive-bomb a large elderly pelican who takes it with characteristic patience, giving it an old-fashioned look as if to say that standards have fallen considerably since he was a lad.

Seabirds are diminished by large numbers of us humans and our refuse. Their natural habits are corrupted and some become habitués of rubbish tips. Others are forced to swim and feed in untreated sewage or a vile scum of diesel, industrial effluent, poly bags, plastic bottles and nappy liners. But here they are in their element. Clean and perfect. The untainted water is a glistening aquamarine at present and the white bellies and under-wings of the pelicans and boobies reflect it, turning their undersides in flight into pale green.

It is like being allowed to anchor in a bird sanctuary and watch undisturbed without even being asked for an entrance fee.

After breakfast each morning we take the dinghy over to Sandy Spit and swim. It shoals here quite steeply so you can sit on the sand to put on your mask, snorkel and flippers and then simply push yourselves out into deep water. There are hundreds of thousands of tiny fluorescent almost transparent green fish, angel fish, blue tangs, parrot fish and squirrel fish while the seabed offers a cornucopia of coral and sea fans. The water is so warm and so clear that it is a joy to simply float on the surface and let the current take you gently along while you gaze down upon the fish and coral. And lying there, with arms and legs spread out like a starfish and making no movement, apart from the occasional glance upwards the fish ignore you and go on their way in their brilliant, multi-coloured shoals.

47

Treasure Island

With time passing we feel that we should discover some of the other islands, but before we make a move we have to wait for the latest squall to pass through. Everywhere becomes grey with a rain so furious it bounces off the water like hail off a tin roof. When it stops and the clouds begin to pass, all the different shades of blue and green in the water begin to merge together and a large hawksbill turtle pops up through the kaleidoscope of colour for air. We haul up the anchor and head back into the Sir Francis Drake Channel and towards the southernmost island.

By lunchtime we are tied to a mooring buoy in a large bay called the Bight at Norman Island. It is known locally as *Treasure Island* and over the years has been dug up repeatedly by Tortolians thanks to rumours of buried treasure. In its present-day incarnation it is a sailing ghetto. What should have been the anchorage has been buoyed within an inch of its life, leaving just enough swinging room for the average yacht. Like Road Town, the bay has become absorbed into the charter boat industry.

On a dinghy that someone has left tied to the buoy beside us, to reserve it like a beach towel on a deck chair, we have our first view of Laughing Gulls. They are the only gull we have seen here and not until now as they winter in Venezuela and do not arrive until April for the start of the breeding season. They have very white bodies, grey backs and wings, and heads that look like they've been dipped in dark chocolate. Two of them stand on the neighbouring dinghy's bow, leaning forward into what is becoming an increasingly strong wind, for hours. The one stares ahead without moving. The other repeatedly shuffles its feet, staring first at the buoy and then turning anxiously to its partner, whose eyelids gradually droop. And as you watch them the dialogue of the novice sailor's first experience of anchoring begins to form in your head.

I think we're too close/No we're fine.

That rope doesn't look very strong to me/It is really.

I'm sure we're closer to it than we were/I don't think so.

I could see the whole of that ring when we landed and now I can only see half of it.

It is heart-rending.

In between times other Laughing Gulls land on our own bow. The American habit of using rope to anchor being widespread here, the birds are not prepared for the sheer weight of chain. Nevertheless they try valiantly to lift ours in the hope of finding something tasty lurking underneath. When it proves too heavy for them they give up and stand around looking thoughtful instead.

By 4pm all the buoys are taken and the latecomers begin circling and looking anxious. Early evening a man in a dinghy and a Hawaiian shirt comes to relieve us of an unseemly amount of money for a night on the buoy. The back of our receipt says that mooring is at our own risk and if the wind speed gets up over 40 knots (the very time you need a secure mooring) we must vacate the buoy immediately.

Just the thought of 50-odd holiday sailors all abandoning their moorings together in a Force 9 is enough to make you give up sailing. And unfortunately this sort of wind strength is not an unlikely possibility. It is what we experienced on our first night at Road Town and will be repeated over and over.

The forecast is for strong winds throughout the coming week so next day David decides to head for Gorda Sound which is a large, protected area. Because it is almost circular you will always be able to find a sheltered anchorage and hopefully one that is less crowded. We also plan to make an overnight stop at one of the anchorages en route to do a little sightseeing.

On the way we pass the small island of Dead Chest, off Deadman's Bay, said to be the origin of the song:

Sixteen men on the dead man's chest,
Yo ho ho and a bottle of rum!

It is associated with the pirate Blackbeard (c.1680–1718) who is said to have marooned some of his crew there, although the song's first appearance is in Robert Louis Stevenson's *Treasure Island*, not published until 1883.

We head for Trellis Bay on the north side of Beef Island but it is very crowded and has no room left to anchor. We cross the short expanse of water to the anchorage between Marina Cay and Great Camanoe Island. That too is very crowded. Like Trellis Bay it has been heavily buoyed and has only very deep water left in which to anchor. So we continue on, past the Dog Islands to Gorda Sound.

We enter the Sound an hour before sunset, via the northern channel between two islands with uninviting names: Prickly Pear and Mosquito. Coral reefs stretch into the channel from both of them but there are marker buoys to give a safe passage. We skirt round Colquhoun Reef and head for Drake's Anchorage, which is sheltered by the reef and Mosquito Island, but that too is full. This turns out to be the pattern. There are so many boats afloat that you have to find an anchorage much earlier than you really want to stop for the day; in some places by lunchtime at the latest. We cross to the more exposed Great Ghut Bay at Virgin Gorda and drop our anchor there. Happily it bites first time.

Gorda means fat. The name Virgin Gorda was bestowed upon the island by Columbus because of its resemblance, he claimed, to a fat woman lying on her back. It is surprising how much of the world's surface reminded Columbus of a woman lying on her back. It probably had something to do with the length of time that sailors spent at sea.

The back of my left hand meanwhile has become swollen, hot and rather sore. I assume a bite of some kind but can see no puncture mark.

Strong winds and a nasty chop in Great Ghut Bay keep us awake much of the night. Next morning we decide to seek somewhere quieter and follow the coast around, past all the resorts: Leverick Bay, Biras Creek, the Bitter End and Saba Rock. All of them are filled with buoys so we head for Prickly Pear Island which should give us some protection.

48

Prickly Pear Island

Since the failure of our anchor winch we have been using the lighter Danforth anchor but we cannot get it to bite here and in view of the expected high winds decide to use the much heavier CQR. Even then it takes two attempts. The wind is coming in strong gusts making *Voyager* swing and snatch at her anchor. It is far from peaceful and we keep an anchor watch throughout the night.

High winds continue for days, gusting up to 40 knots, with reports over the VHF of 50 knots being recorded on the hilltop at Tortola. But it is an ill wind that blows nobody any good. There is plenty of time for reading and some necessary housekeeping. David washes away the leavings on our bow from the Laughing Gulls at Norman Island and the muck off the fenders from the fuel dock at Sint Maarten. And there is no shortage of battery power for the laptop.

We also dig out our small television and videos for the evenings and wallow in old favourites such as *Groundhog Day* and *Kind Hearts and Coronets* which seem to get better every time you watch them. David recorded a lot of films from our home TV before we set off, and the tail ends of the videos he filled up with a variety of half-hour programmes, so you never know what you are going to get after the credits roll from the main feature. One of the nights it turns out to be an episode of *The Simpsons* that we don't remember ever watching.

Sideshow Bob (Kelsey Grammer) has been released from jail, put there by Bart who with the rest of his family is now in a Witness Relocation Program – it says so on their T-shirts. When Bob arrives on the family's boat to kill him, Bart delays him long enough to get police assistance by persuading him to sing the entire score of *HMS Pinafore*, complete with full costume changes and popcorn. It is *glorious*!

We have a double snubbing line on the anchor chain to absorb the snatching and keep pressure off the winch but it is so rough during these few days that the rope shreds three times. My left hand is now a shapeless, bloated thing, my wrist has expanded and the swelling is currently creeping towards my elbow. I can remain on board and risk being really ill or I can take my chances in a small tossing dinghy trying to find a doctor. Procrastination has served me pretty well so far.

More days pass and we start to get low on a few things so during a brief lull in the weather David takes the dinghy to the Bitter End to shop. The open-fronted English Pub has a small grocery in one corner but a very limited range. He returns with probably the most expensive loaf and packet of crisps in the history of the world.

I'm just relieved to see him come back at all as it was quite a long way in a small dinghy in such a strong wind and with quite a chop on the water, especially going past Saba Road. Getting back on board *Voyager* is also some-thing of a feat, since once he lets go of the controls to reach for *Voyager*, the wind sweeps him away from her and ultimately the only way to get him back on board is for me to snag the dinghy's painter with the boathook as soon as he gets close enough.

Something else he has brought back with him is a copy of the April issue of *Nautical News*. Its headline on page 6 strikes terror: 'Virgin Gorda to hold Fishermen's Jamboree'. We have visions of them getting drunk, having wet trawler competitions and throwing fishing pots and discarded nets everywhere but it turns out to be a competition for visiting anglers. So that's alright. We used to get a lot of those around the reservoir at home. They sat on little stools for hours in all weathers without moving and were no trouble at all.

An advertisement in the same newspaper gives a fascinating insight into the process whereby the meanings of words change over time. *Boutique* has traditionally meant a small shop selling stylish clothes and accessories. Here an American chandlery chain reports that its 'new store's marine-orientated boutique will stock foul weather gear and crew uniforms.'

We continue to do anchor watches through the nights, not so much from fear of our own boat dragging as the possibility of being hit by somebody else's. Notwithstanding what a supposedly experienced charter boat owner at Tortola did to us, we are surrounded by boats chartered by people with little or no experience of anchoring, especially in wind condi-tions like these. Simply hurling an anchor over the bow and strolling back to the cockpit to raise a glass fails to keep a number of them in place.

You don't get the usual sunrise or sunset here because of the surrounding hills. This morning the sunrise looks like a huge fire burning behind one of them. Not long afterwards there is torrential rain and every-where becomes grey with the rain bouncing off the water. When it stops, a large hawksbill turtle pops up for air – like the one at Little Jost Van Dyke

Island did. Apart from that, and the occasional gull, I don't remember ever seeing so little wildlife. But at least my hand is back to normal. I assume the culprit was a spider although I've never had a reaction so extreme before. They set up home under ropes and side rails and get very resentful when they are evicted, however unwittingly.

Ultimately the wind does begin to abate but there is still an uncomfortable sea, especially for the 1,000-mile voyage ahead of us, so we dinghy into the Bitter End Yacht Club for an outing and a look around. It's gorgeous. Twee, but if you're that rich... It has a super dinghy dock with a fish-feeding area in the middle and the individual species identified around the rails.

Contestants begin arriving for the fishermen's jamboree and I abandon any notion about anglers as people who sit on soggy British river banks with a rod and line and become acquainted instead with what Americans call 'the sport fishing boat'. These are high powered and typically 35–40 ft long with a very high central superstructure so that a lookout can spot prey, rather like a crow's nest on a whaler.

The sport fisherman himself is strapped into a chair on the afterdeck facing astern like the shark hunter, Quint, in *Jaws*, while behind him are spare rods so that replacements are always to hand in the event of the one being used getting damaged. These spare rods are fastened to the cabin's sides, but being so long they stick up above the superstructure and make the boat look as if it is bristling with antennae.

When you've bought yourself something like this there is no way you are going to putter through anchorages and marina entrances at 5 knots so they roar about as if the 3-minute warning has just sounded, sometimes in packs, with their massive wake sending kayaks, canoes, dinghies and even some of the smaller anchored yachts several feet into the air.

49

Clearing Out

To prepare for our voyage to Florida we need fuel, food and other supplies, e-mail and telephone services and somewhere to clear out. There is only one place to do all this and we leave Prickly Pear Island around 10am for Tortola.

When we reach there, the *Elysium* is berthed in Road Harbour. It is obviously a non-smoking cruise ship because it has huge 'No Smoking' stickers on its bows and stern, which is all very well except that its elegant red and white funnel pumps noxious slate-grey smoke over the residents of Road Town all afternoon. They have had quite a bit of smoke to contend with lately. Since we were last here the restaurant at the Moorings marina burnt down.

Next morning we get up early, shop for food and revisit the place that's currently selling the cheapest beer in town (the out-of-date Fosters). Honestly! It'll be meths in a brown paper bag for the crew next.

David drops me and the supplies aboard *Voyager* and then, with gritted teeth, sets off for Immigration and the world's most offensive official. David is one of the most even-tempered people I have ever met but even he has his limits and he is gone a long time. I hear a police siren in the town and when he still fails to return I begin to worry that he might have confided his views on her people skills a little too frankly and be sharing a windowless cell with cockroaches.

The long delay, it turns out, is caused by two things. One is that there is a very long queue as the office will close this afternoon for three days over Easter. The other is that with the improvement in the weather a large number of yachtsmen are getting ready to leave.

During the long wait there is regular reference by newcomers to the queue about the woman behind the Immigration counter in terms which, thanks to political correctness, have ceased to be common currency in recent years. Respect, however, is a two-way street, and having been taken unawares by her offensiveness clearing in, they are more than ready for her clearing out. But the officer on duty today turns out to be an utterly charming young man who makes every effort to move the queue along as fast as he can, notwithstanding a new arrival with an out-of-date passport.

Another cause for the delay in David's return gradually becomes visible from some distance away. He is rowing laboriously through a strong swell and a brisk headwind. Road Harbour has so much refuse floating in it that one of its numerous poly bags has wrapped itself round our outboard engine's propeller.

Then it is off to the fuel dock at Moorings marina. It is pandemonium. There is the outside fuel dock, where we are, and another inside the marina which is deluged in day boats and has dozens of dinghy fuel cans lined up waiting to be filled for the charter boats. The pump attendant today is the marina manager and the poor man is on the run between the two but very good-humoured and apologetic about the delay.

We leave his dock at 2pm. The traffic in and out of the bay is as bad mannered as everywhere else, roaring at full throttle. Two sports fishing boats roar down our port side, sending *Voyager* thrashing, cut across our bows, roar up our starboard side and then come to a halt leaving us struggling to regain our feet. They could easily have passed behind our stern or – heaven forfend – travelled at moderate speed because it turns out that all they are off to do is anchor, and after their frenzied arrival spend ages pottering about seeking the best spot. But if you own a sport fishing boat, it seems, you have to behave as if you are off on some vital mission, possibly with lives at stake.

At least *Voyager* has the weight to withstand them. Two of them send one poor couple entering the marina in a small yacht rolling toe rail to toe rail. These are closely followed by another two roaring towards them from their bow and then a commercial boat at full throttle from the stern – and the yacht actually spins around.

Sports fishermen always look terribly pleased with themselves as they hurtle past at 20 knots addressing each other as 'Captain' over the VHF. And there's clearly a bit of psyching-up going on since the angling competition begins tomorrow with 'a $2,000 prize for the biggest Wahoo!' although the biggest wahoo will in all likelihood be at the controls.

What we want now is a peaceful anchorage and a good night's sleep before setting out on another long passage. We know just the place.

NEXT STOP, AMERICA

50

At Sea Once More

We wake before dawn, get *Voyager* ready to go to sea again and then breakfast with the pelicans. Today is Good Friday. It is time to go. Not simply to make a timely exit from the hurricane zone but because it is too hot and, even here at Little Jost Van Dyke Island, it is getting very crowded. Already there are nine boats clustered around Sandy Spit. There had been ten but the skipper of the very grand motoryacht who dropped his anchor over there last night – in anticipation of a Caribbean idyll for himself and his guests today – got so indignant about this morning's arrivals that he took off in a huff. It is likely to get even more crowded everywhere shortly as in addition to the angling competition there are two days of racing planned. Although lack of wind may be a problem as there currently isn't any.

We motor out past Sandy Spit and then head north, following the coasts of Green Cay and Little Jost Van Dyke until we are able to set a course of 325° and head back into the Atlantic again. Because there is almost no wind we have on both engines to get us clear of the islands and then, to conserve fuel, we use just the one.

Our last view of the Virgin Islands is through a diffused morning light that turns the hills into soft shades of grey and the sea to sparkling silver. After a while there is just enough wind to put out the main and genoa. And then it becomes one of those days where everything is a delight, even a simple lunch, a glass of red wine and an afternoon with Anthony Trollope.

For dinner we have pasta and the Italian meatballs that have been fragrancing the fridge since yesterday morning's shopping trip. I don't think they can be meat. They don't produce fat, fall to pieces, change shape, shrink or stick to the pan. And they give you indigestion for 24 hours afterwards. But they *are* delicious. And we see flying fish again for the first time since our arrival at the BVI, apart from in the supermarket. Either they avoid coastal waters or they all end up in little polystyrene trays covered with cling film.

We haven't eaten fish since arriving in the Leeward Islands, not after reading a letter from a visiting doctor in a free local paper. She had warned of the dangers caused by poisoned reef fish. Toxins in the tropical and subtropical waters of the Caribbean and Pacific adhere to coral, seaweed and algae. These are nibbled by herbivorous reef fish which are then eaten by carnivorous fish and so the toxins gradually work their way along the food chain. The doctor said that her twin sister had died after eating locally-caught fish.

The condition is called ciguatera and symptoms include nausea and diarrhoea followed by headaches, muscle pain and even hallucinations. They can last weeks or even years, leading to permanent disability. Ciguatoxin is particularly heat-resistant so conventional cooking methods have no effect on its toxicity.

In a separate article in the same paper a yachtsman described having succumbed twice. Once with six other crewmen from mackerel caught on board their ketch, and once at a barbecue ashore where he and another cruiser had taken adjacent pieces of fish from the grill. By morning the other man was dead and he himself was ill for two months. It is not a new illness, having been recorded aboard HMS *Resolution* in 1774.

There is a glorious sunset in scarlet and gold. It is lovely to see one again after being anchored on the eastern side of one hill or another for so long and with the sun going down behind it, out of sight.

We are back to night watches again, although they are very pleasant in these climes. Even at midnight it is 26°C so there is no foul-weather gear attacking your kneecaps or giving you a crick in the neck. Tonight is just warm air, the smell of the islands and a huge russet moon behind our stern.

When the wind moves behind us we take in the main to stop it shading the genoa. The main was difficult to pull out today and it gets stuck now as we try to haul it back in again. So we have to turn into the wind, which means the genoa has to be taken in to prevent it flogging against the mast while we mess about. We do finally release the main but the knot tying the outhaul to the sail's clew unravels and the end of the rope disappears inside the boom. The only solution is to pull it out completely and then re-thread it. This is not easy because the inside of the boom is quite complex and the task requires daylight so it is better left until tomorrow.

Sometime later two huge sets of lights appear behind us. One is recognisably a cruise ship, albeit lit up like a Christmas tree with fairy lights from stem to stern; whichever is which, since with light-strung cruise ships it can be impossible to tell their front from their rear at night except by the direction in which they are travelling. This is because their navigation lights are hard to see at the best of times but with a full set of fairy lights it is impossible.

Its companion is not so much a Christmas tree as a gigantic version of one of those novelty fibre optic lamps that people used to put on top of their television sets. The ship is a nervy mass of vibrating gold in the darkness, a multitude of tiny, dancing pinpricks of light. There are no discernible navigation lights among them to give a clue as to its route, until the great blazing monster locks onto our stern and comes writhing towards us. Then alternately a red light and a green light do finally become visible but with so much gold flaring into the night sky it resembles nothing so much as some vast Chinese dragon with odd-coloured eyes. Very small eyes.

That's the extraordinary thing about cruise ships; despite being very large they have incredibly small navigation lights. In fact, having failed to see any at all during my first few encounters with cruise ships at night I once visited a berth to inspect a couple, just to convince myself that they did actually have some. They do, but so small you can barely detect them in anything less than really good visibility or up very close. And this one is getting *very* close. In fact, it is on a collision course with us. Since it seems impervious to our navigation lights I put on our deck lights, to reinforce our presence, then go below and wake David.

'Is it 1 o'clock already?' he mutters amiably. It is 10.45pm and he has been in bed for only forty-five minutes, but I'm afraid we're about to be run down and, asleep in a stern cabin, he will be first in line for annihilation. By the time he reaches the cockpit, however, the vessel has begun making a leisurely turn after which it mooches off behind its friend.

The two of them are wasting away the night, possibly on a passage from St Thomas in the US Virgins to Road Town in the British Virgin Islands, and they don't want to get there before morning. By loitering out at sea overnight a ship can save on berthing fees. But because they are not following a predictable course, and since their navigation lights are invisible, their erratic movements are very confusing not to say worrying because when they do suddenly decide to go they can really shift. And the last place you want to be is in their path. Which also raises the question, on tonight's experience, as to whether *your* navigation lights are actually visible from inside their blaze of glory.

Or maybe in this case a bored ship's officer thought it would be fun to scare the living daylights out of a yachtie. Either way, I am irritable. I do so hate waking David before time because he doesn't easily go back to sleep again. I feel so bad about it I give him an extra hour before getting him up for his next watch.

Ruminations

On Saturday morning the moon remains with us until well after dawn. Sunrise is yellow gold. Several transmissions crackle out of the VHF from Puerto Rico, very broken, one of them about a missing boat with two people on board and asking for all ships to look out for them.

Not long after, something comes floating towards our port bow with two white patches on it. Are they hands, clinging on to wreckage? Too white by far for hands, but given the anxious broadcast I've just heard I'm already running forward under the sail to get a closer look.

Two black-headed gulls, riding on a wooden plank, look back at me and laugh uproariously. I am so startled that I trip on a cleat and nearly fall overboard. Oh, how they laugh as they fly away. When we have sailed a safe distance from the plank, they return to it and resume their joyride.

It is a lovely bright blue day. I listen to World Service News. Ticket holders arriving at Silverstone for the British Grand Prix practice day have been turned away because the public car parks are waterlogged due to heavy rain. $5m losses are expected. Formula One boss Bernie Ecclestone is asked why the date of the event has been moved from July, given England's reputation for wet Aprils, but I do not hear his reply.

Today is also Brazil's 500th anniversary, it being 500 years since Portuguese sailors landed on South America's east coast. Trade unions and minority groups are protesting about 500 years of genocide by an elite against indigenous peoples and the downtrodden. There will be sailing ship regattas and fireworks to celebrate. With the money spent on these and the recent Millennium celebrations, someone asks, might they not have rid the country of leprosy and housed the street children instead?

It is a dozy sort of a day. In the morning we spot a yacht behind us, heading south, the only vessel we shall see all day. We also try to push a length of wire down the boom in an attempt to thread the outhaul back through it, but fail. And thanks to a turbulent sea I get a bit queasy preparing lunch. We are still enjoying Anthony Trollope's *Framley Parsonage* but rapidly reaching the end.

In the late afternoon we see a couple of petrels. With other species you see large numbers of birds flocking together but with petrels and shearwaters there rarely seems to be more than two. I set about cooking dinner and get queasy again, but David takes over in between times and we both enjoy the meal up on deck when it arrives.

We have changed our watch times so that David's final one coincides with our current weather forecaster. After reaching the BVI our SSB radio had trouble picking up Herb's broadcasts and we began using a local forecaster who has been very good. His name is David Jones and he broadcasts from Tortola every morning. Accordingly, I am now in bed from 6.30 to 9.30pm. It's a bit like being a small child again, going to bed in daylight on long summer evenings.

An hour into my first watch a tawny moon rises east-south-east. Initially it makes me jump. I think it's a cruise ship coming up fast again, it's so big so suddenly and sort of squarish, but that's because of the way it is tangled in low cloud. But quite suddenly it is round and solid and glowing like a moon should be and the boat and the whole night take on a different atmosphere; light and bright and even a flapping genoa and a faffing wind don't seem so trying any more. The wind, as always, is either a famine or a feast. After nights of anchor watches in up to 40 knots we now have barely enough to fill a sail.

With the morning light the horizon becomes visible. We have Puerto Rico and the Dominican Republic to our left, while stretching away on our right is the Sargasso Sea. This is a sea without shores, a region of the North Atlantic surrounded by ocean currents. Four of them to be precise and between them they create something called a gyre, a giant circling oceanic surface current. This one is called the North Atlantic Subtropical Gyre although 'Sargasso Sea', the name given to it by those 15th century Portuguese explorers, has a much nicer ring to it. It is 2,000 miles long and 700 wide, deep blue and so clear that visibility can be as deep as 61 metres.

Sometime after 5am a freighter passes astern of us. Like yesterday's solitary yacht, it is the only vessel we shall see all day. In fact, considering that this area is famous for its exceptionally busy shipping lanes it is surprising how few vessels come within sight.

According to BBC World Service this morning, the start of the British Grand Prix has been delayed for an hour because of fog.

According to the calendar, today is not only Easter Sunday but the anniversary of Shakespeare's birth and death and St George's Day as well.

In truth, nobody knows the date of Will's birth, only his baptism – 26th April 1564. Doubtless some antique PR person thought it would give added lustre to have the birth and death of England's national poet and playwright and the country's patron saint's day all occur together. By such strokes of the pen is history made.

But it makes me wonder how many of us actually celebrate the feast day of our patron saint. Apart from waving his flag about at sports events or demonstrations, do many of my countrymen ever give a thought to St George? I know I don't. And I don't think I ever knew that 23rd April was even his day before. So I look him up: 23rd April is the 'traditionally accepted' date of his death in AD303, although record keeping must have been even more hit and miss in the 4th century than in Shakespeare's time. And depending on whether it is the ancient Julian calendar that was being quoted, or the present-day Gregorian one, 23rd April would be have been 6th May anyway.

As more time passes, the less 'history' and 'culture' and the petty one-upmanship of 'nationality' have any relevance. Surely it's the fundamental truths of a Shakespeare play or the world's great religions that matter. Not the myths and manipulations of human gullibility. I mean, why *is* England represented by someone who 'according to tradition' (which means there is no evidence) was a Roman soldier in the Guard of the Emperor Diocletian and who *may* have died in 303 (possibly as young as 22) and who was canonised two hundred years later for acts 'known only to God'?

I think the biggest stumbling block for me has always been the dragon. I mean, is there something peculiarly English about having a patron saint whose origins and relevance are so obscure and whose only 'known' act is so improbable that most of us ignore him? A long sea passage provides an environment for this kind of thinking.

David decides that it would be useful to have the main out again but, despite trying several more times, we are still unable to thread the outhaul past the obstructions inside the boom. So he decides to jury rig a system instead. He rummages in his toolbox, finds some old pulleys and shackles and is quite pleased when he has the sail working. Sadly the wind changes direction shortly afterwards so we have to take it in again and resume sailing on the genoa alone.

We see some flying fish and a shearwater and around 2pm we get a glimpse of a tiny black bird with a forked tail to starboard. An hour later

I look up from the galley sink and see it perched on the rail outside the window. It has the grumpy little chestnut face of a barn swallow and a toe missing from its left foot. It appears anxious, making a couple of brief flights in different directions but returning each time to the same spot on the rail.

I put out a piece of pear for it, on the principle that it will at least provide moisture if the bird is dehydrated after a long flight. It stretches its wings a lot and does a fair bit of feather plumping, but mainly it just stands staring towards land. It seems very young, an impression created by the little bits of white fluff poking through the black feathers on its back. Happily, it becomes more relaxed as time passes and at 4.30 takes off in the direction of the Dominican Republic less than two miles away.

It is very dark when I begin the 9.30pm watch. The moon is not due for another two hours and there is a lot of phosphorous on the sea. Its eerie sparkle in the otherwise total blackness is vaguely unnerving tonight. At least we are under sail and despite a noisy sea it is nice to have the genoa up and no engine and be just *sailing*. And we shall purely sail for the next four days, only needing to run an engine to charge up the batteries.

Yesterday I noticed vaguely from the chart that our course was taking us across the Puerto Rico Trench. Tonight I read that this trench, which forms the boundary between the Caribbean Sea and the Atlantic Ocean is the result of moving tectonic plates. It has a maximum depth of over five miles and is the deepest part of the Atlantic. It may be irrational but I'm rather glad I wasn't aware of that yesterday when we were sailing over the top of it.

52

Deteriorating Conditions

Easter Monday. We finish *Framley Parsonage* and begin Homer's *Iliad*. Not too different really. Autocratic power thwarted by the power of love. One set in a 19th century English village, the other at the siege of Troy some time before the 8th century BC. Although there is a nice contrast in that when Trollope's impoverished young heroine is separated from the love of her life by his snobbish mother she takes it like a man. The warrior Achilles, on the other hand, deprived of the ornament of his life by King Agamemnon, bursts into tears. In 1966 I read Homer's *Odyssey* to David as we drove across hundreds of miles of Australian outback in a Triumph Herald convertible without a radio. I thought it time I read him the prequel.

There are lots of flying fish about today and it is much cooler now that we are 300 miles further north. The nights are heavy with dew, however, and the atmosphere during the day is clammy. The wheelhouse roof lining is slimy with salt. *Voyager*'s interior feels damp. And for the first time ever during a passage there is condensation on the inside of the windows. Even my hair feels as if it's going mouldy.

The only traffic we have seen all day is a cargo ship at midday and a small boat at 9pm. Once past midnight we are bathed in moonlight.

Today is Tuesday and our fifth day at sea. At 4.20am a white light appears in the south-east off our starboard quarter travelling only slightly faster than we are. After roughly an hour I can identify three vertical white lights signifying that this vessel and whatever it is towing have a combined length of more than 200 metres. Although I can see nothing behind the boat and no other light.

With the arrival of dawn, I can just make out that the vessel is a tug and that behind it is a grey unlit mass the size of a small island. Half an hour later, both are overtaking us, the one a vast distance behind the other.

While I am still gazing after it David enters the cockpit ready to take over the watch and I tell him we've just been overtaken by an island being towed by a tug. He takes a look and says maybe a rich American wanted an island of his own but doesn't like travelling. And, since the Bahamian government has hundreds of them cluttering up the place, it has decided to sell him a small one and this is it being relocated closer to the man's home. When I look at him sideways he shrugs and wanders off to put the kettle on for breakfast. I suppose it's his equivalent of my ruminations on St George. It's the isolation that does it.

In reality, we have just had our first glimpse of cargo shipment American-style. It is the result of one of those government initiatives intended to support an industry but which backfires to the detriment of those it was intended to protect.

The Merchant Marine Act of 1920 is a US federal statute regulating maritime commerce. Section 27 of it, also known as the Jones Act, deals with coastal shipping and requires all cargo transported in US waters and between US ports to be carried on US-built and US-flagged ships owned and crewed by US citizens.

The object was to protect the jobs and safety of US workers and merchant seamen but resulted in US cargo ships becoming ruinously expensive. Tugs and barges were not included in the Jones Act, allowing shipping companies to avoid the cost of cargo ships and at the same time use smaller crews.

Over time we shall discover that they can also be something of a hazard. To begin with, they use an incredibly long towline between the tug and the barge making the distance between the two enormous. The other problem is that the barge is poorly lit. Although my first sighting tonight involved a barge with no light on it at all, the most we will ever see is a very small one on the stern which is barely detectable from any other angle than directly behind the barge, and making it invisible in poor conditions. And we will subsequently hear of a yacht which unwittingly sailed between a tug and its tow in the dark with fatal consequences.

The sea's motion has been very uncomfortable for several days now, with waves coming from two directions. I feel particularly queasy on the 9.30pm to 1am watch. This is the second time in a few days and most unusual for me. In fact, I so rarely get seasick now that I've forgotten to have my favourite home remedy on board this trip – ginger. Ginger biscuits, ginger cake, anything with real ginger in it. It works better than any patent remedy for me.

A tropicbird flies very close during my final watch on Wednesday morning. I only know it is a tropicbird because afterwards I go and look it up as

I have never seen one before. It is that blistering white peculiar to seabirds, with black markings on its wings and extremely long tail feathers so that in flight they look like streamers trailing out behind.

Four hours later David has two of them begging off the back of the boat and squawking loudly but nothing we have to offer satisfies them and after half an hour they fly away in disgust. I am sleeping at the time. I feel very tired and ache all over. Whether it is the damp, the sudden drop in temperature, the uneasy motion of the boat, the broken sleep, or even the approach of the thunder and lightning promised in today's forecast, I cannot say.

While I am horizontal David collects some sargassum for me to look at when I get up. It is from that genus of seaweed after which the Sargasso Sea is named, since it is home to large amounts of it. Most familiar is the species that forms into vast free-floating weed beds, hated by coastal humans – especially in the Florida Keys – but providing an environment for some marine life not found anywhere else.

In the afternoon at about 3pm we leave the tropics behind when we re-cross the official northern boundary of the Tropic of Cancer.

The sun sets at 7pm. The wind is gentle and from the south but nevertheless we make reasonable progress. There is a clear sky with just the odd bit of cloud about and after a while a few stars become visible. Two hours later the forecast lightning arrives on our starboard horizon, out in the Sargasso Sea. Not the threatened thunder, just two kinds of lightning: heat and forked.

Meanwhile, *Voyager* rolls and shudders most uncomfortably in a very confused sea that is making everything on board rattle, bang and clatter; even things which have never clattered or banged before, like the door to the heads or the saloon table. I go around tying things open, or shut, and wedging things with towels, anything to reduce the awful racket we have on board.

Such innocuous words really, *the forecast lightning arrives*, and indeed it does begin pretty quietly. Yet it is the prelude to a night that will remain with me forever. For now, however, we drift on, unaware that we are being carried slowly but remorselessly into a blazing nightmare.

53

A Night to Remember

The wind increases a little during the night and the sky becomes increasingly cloudy so that when the moon rises at 2.20 on Thursday morning it is mostly obscured. By 4am, as well as lightning to starboard, it is also ahead of us and on our port side. David becomes convinced that a rainstorm is imminent so he battens down and lays out our wet weather gear in the saloon ready for us to put on quickly when the need arises.

The night becomes pitch black from heavy cloud cover and for about half an hour a bird flies round and round *Voyager*, close and screeching, although it is too dark even at such close range to see what kind it is. Whether wanting to land and afraid to we don't know but it sounds frantic. We stay as still as possible and hope that it will find a suitable place for itself on board.

At around 4.30 the wind dies away. We take in the genoa and turn on an engine. While we have no desire to rush towards the electrical storm up ahead, just wallowing in this confused sea is untenable and a little forward motion eases it.

At the same time David turns off all the non-essential electrics, because if they are switched on when a boat is struck by lightning they will burn out. If they are switched off, they stand a chance of surviving. He also puts our handheld GPS and VHF in a metal box in the oven. It is the same scientific principle as the Faraday Cage, a metal shield named after its inventor and designed to protect electrical equipment from lightning strikes. It will mean that if our main GPS, which is wired into the boat, burns out during a strike, and if we are still in a condition to continue afterwards, we shall have some form of navigation. This will be essential given the treacherous nature of these waters because what the lightning fails to destroy, the reefs and shoals off the Bahamas undoubtedly will.

During this time the lightning flashes have been getting stronger, brighter and more frequent, lighting up the sea intermittently like heavy-duty spotlights being randomly switched on and off. Then suddenly, a few miles directly ahead of us, the horizon erupts in the most stupendous explosions of gold and silver interspersed with bursts of red. There is a long line of them stretching for miles, like some monumental firework display featuring what I can only call fireballs.

For a time these massive fireballs, though expanding outwards and upwards as they erupt, nevertheless remain where they explode. After a while, however, more of these fireballs begin to erupt at right angles to the left-hand end of the original line and roll across the surface of the sea as if fired from some monstrous cannon. Within moments they are travelling continuously down our port side, perhaps a couple of miles away, and at tremendous speed, blazing and fuming, before disappearing over the horizon behind us.

Worse still is what now begins to happen at the right-hand end of the original line of explosions as another line forms at right-angles, although this time it is not fireballs. What now comes hurtling down *Voyager*'s starboard side are great arcs of zigzag lightning, a mile or two away and maybe two hundred feet high. I never knew lightning like this existed. My whole experience has been limited to heat lightning flashing in the sky and forked lightning snaking down from the clouds. These new varieties appear unconnected with the sky altogether. On the contrary, they seem wedded to the sea and their path is horizontal.

Like the fireballs rolling past on our left, this new line appears to take its energy from the blazing horizon in front of us. It rises up into a great jagged arc of red and gold before hitting the sea and immediately arcing upwards again. And again and again and again as it too careers past us towards the horizon behind us and out of sight. The speed of it is stupefying. So is the fact that we are now enclosed on three sides by what is effectively a huge blind alley of electricity. And as if this weren't enough, as we stand in our cockpit staring out at it all, it gradually begins to dawn on us that this blind alley we are in is slowly getting narrower and its blind end closer.

The more it closes in on us, the more horrifying it becomes because I've known from an early age what happens when lightning strikes you. As a child I walked my dog through the local park and across the municipal golf course but was repeatedly reminded never to shelter under trees during a thunderstorm after a golfer ignored all the warnings.

The extra height offered by something like a tree provides a quicker route to the ground and the lightning bolt travels down the tree's sap, exploding the bark as it goes. But lightning can jump and human tissue offers an even faster route so that anyone under the tree – especially if he happens to be clutching conductive material such as a steel golf club – is in mortal danger.

Cloud-to-ground lightning bolts contain an extraordinary power. The man, found later lying under a tree, looked as if he was asleep and apparently unmarked. But internally the damage was catastrophic, as the lightning burned its way straight down through his body, out through the steel studs of his golfing shoes and into the wet grass; water, like steel, being another highly conductive material. And that was just your everyday forked lightning. What these fireballs, or these great jagged, red and gold arcs can do, is unimaginable.

There is another dimension to our situation, something I have been trying very hard not to think about. It is that, several days ago, we entered a particularly notorious sea area. To be specific, we are currently in the Bermuda Triangle, a place made famous by stories of missing ships and lost aircraft. Looking around me I think I can guess what might have happened to some of them.

But fear is like the athlete's pain barrier: sooner or later you pass through it and simply keep going. You become practical. I am, I realise, keeping my balance on this turbulent sea by holding on to a winch. I look down at my hand and wonder if, with so much electricity about, 'earthing' myself to a great chunk of steel is really a good idea. I let go of the winch and brace myself against the coaming instead.

Fibreglass is presumably a bad conductor of electrical current. As are the rubber soles of our deck shoes. Although for the moment I can't quite see how these are going to be enough to prevent us from being fried. We could turn the boat around and try to outrun it, but given its speed over such immense distances – roughly fifteen or twenty miles in only minutes – outrunning it isn't an option.

All we can really do is turn everything electrical off as we approach the end of our blind alley and hope that when we get there it isn't the solid wall of lightning that it currently appears to be. And not forgetting to keep as far away as possible from the mast, of course, because like the golfer's tree it is the tallest part of the boat and likely to be the first thing to be struck, along with anyone standing close to it. And our mast is aluminium, a much better conductor than wood. But at least it isn't raining.

As time passes, and with nothing to do but stare ahead in a sort of mute dread, I find myself wondering if this is what it must have felt like for a young midshipman sailing slowly into his first sea battle, because you could almost mistake the smoking red, gold and silver explosions up ahead for cannon fire and burning ships.

It is difficult to estimate distance at sea at the best of times and at night even more so. But the great, blazing archways off our starboard beam are getting close enough to be of serious concern. However, we have not got as far as anything remotely resembling a strategy by the time they, and the fireballs to our left, begin to show signs of losing some of their energy. They are not rolling down our sides with quite the same frequency or quite as much speed as before.

And then the wind comes up very quickly from behind our stern. David unfurls the genoa and turns off the engine. The rise of the wind is followed almost immediately by torrential rain. By the time I return to the cockpit in my wet weather gear two things have happened: the lightning has vanished and the wind speed indicator is registering 39 knots. Either we are into a Force 8 gale or a very nasty squall.

With the genoa well-reefed, we wait for it to pass over us. It takes maybe three-quarters of an hour but at least the sea is less bumpy, with the force of the rain flattening the ocean and such a strong wind coming from behind. Then the rain stops and the wind drops; from gale-force to a few knots right on the nose. So we furl the genoa, run an engine again and David goes to bed.

We roll an awful lot. A whole new set of things rattle and creak: the wheelhouse roof, the boom, the crockery in the galley cupboards, the chart table and somewhere beyond the galley window somebody is playing a bugle, badly. I go around wedging things again and put up the stay sail, which helps a bit, until at 7.30 the sun finally struggles through the cloud, the world suddenly seems very bright and you realise with a shock that you are about to live through another day which, for a little while in the night, you hadn't thought you were going to see.

54

Normal Service is Resumed

Everything feels so much better now that all that electricity has expended itself. The atmosphere is lighter and fresher. I don't feel tired and achy anymore and David says he feels livelier too. All that clinging dampness has gone from the boat as well. Everything is dry again and even our wet weather gear is airing nicely out in the cockpit.

It is interesting how quickly you go back to normality once danger is over, to one of you resuming the watch and keeping everything going while the other gets some rest so as to be fit to take over at the proper time. There is no high-fiving and whooping like in the movies, just a peaceful tiredness and doing quietly whatever needs to be done. It is something David had noticed in *War and Peace*. Tolstoy describes soldiers after a battle sitting, smoking and talking quietly together.

When he gets up David listens to the morning weather forecast and then goes off to consult the gauge on our fuel tank. We are now down to 140 litres of diesel and must continue under sail alone wherever possible. Because of the wind direction, however, we shall need to beat, so over the next few hours we tack three times to try and find the best course to make progress in the right direction.

On one of them we end up in the same place we started. On another, *Voyager* takes so long to turn through the wind that the automatic steering (which we have forgotten to turn off) gives the most wonderful impersonation of an opera singer – one long drawn-out high note, then two enormous gulps of air and back into the melody again.

When the wind veers to the north we start to make progress in the right direction but very slowly because of the confused sea, although we have no idea why the sea should be so turbulent. Later the wind veers even further, to the north-east, and we begin to pick up speed.

Mid-afternoon two tropicbirds circle us, and a shearwater settles hopefully on the water as if ready for its tea. Then two barn swallows fly very close down our port side, try briefly to land on the foredeck rail, decide against it and fly on. Around 7.30 there is a big red sunset and shortly afterwards a southbound container ship. By 8pm we are off the San Salvador lighthouse. During the evening two brightly-lit cruise ships pass on our starboard side, probably heading for Miami.

It is a week today since we set out from the BVI. As we change over the watch in the pre-dawn this morning David estimates that we should reach Fort Lauderdale on Monday afternoon, three days from now. We can hardly wait. There is too little wind again and the waves hitting our port beam are very noisy. *Everything* is noisy. Out of doors is no better than inside. The genoa flaps, the sheet runners rattle and the shackles clatter. Our torch batteries are dead again and the new ones we bought at Road Town, especially for this journey, turn out to be duds. Our rechargeable ones barely last the night.

Dawn comes at 5.45 and sunrise at 6.25, a glorious crimson blaze that turns the sky red before transforming itself into pure gold – and visible from its first moment because for once we have a cloud-free horizon. At 7.50 I spot a cargo boat, probably out of Cuba via the San Salvador Channel. I nearly miss it, staring as I am through the binoculars at what turns out to be a plastic bottle.

We are conserving fuel but our progress is slow, with a noon-to-noon run of only 70 miles. In terms of ennui we begin to empathise with the cast of *The Iliad* languishing in their interminable siege. Although we are seeing more traffic today. In the afternoon we spot a southbound freighter on our starboard side which is going so fast that twelve minutes later it is level with us, proving yet again the virtue of ten-minute checks.

On Saturday morning the sun, like a celestial Salome, rises behind veils of cloud, only becoming fully visible three-quarters of an hour later. And a tropicbird pays us a visit. We get no weather forecast today as David Jones has taken the weekend off. I can't say I blame him after yesterday morning when some ill-mannered oaf kept yelling, 'Is Jones *doing* a weather forecast?' over and over again just because the man was a few minutes late coming on air. Mr Jones very generously gives his time free of charge to provide an essential daily service for which most of us are extremely grateful.

By 9am we are experiencing a number of problems. Firstly, while the autopilot (which contains its own compass) and the cockpit compass give the same reading, both of them disagree with the GPS. Secondly, we are being pushed against our will towards the Bahamian island of Eleuthera and its dangerous reefs. Thirdly, our progress is still pitifully slow.

We can keep ourselves off the reefs by altering course by 30°, which means we are crabbing at an odd angle to our destination but have no idea why we need to do this. There is nothing to explain it on the North Atlantic chart we are using so David gets out our Bahamian ones and finds a notation saying that, depending on the state of the tides, water rushes in or out of the Bahamian archipelago through the narrow gaps between the islands at a rate of up to 3 knots. We have obviously chosen a course too close to land and should have headed further out to sea. Our crab-like course across and partially against this current also explains, in part, our very slow progress.

Instead, we had expected to have a current behind us pushing us up the coast. *World Cruising Routes*, the *Atlantic Crossing Guide* and *Reeds Nautical Almanac* all describe it as the Antilles Current and as going north (that is to say, in our favour). However, on a later re-reading of the *Atlantic Crossing Guide*, David finds a reference saying that the Antilles Current is 'unpredictable' – and it certainly is.

David now turns his attention to the discrepancy between the GPS and the compasses. He gets out the handheld GPS to find out if that gives a reading consistent with our main GPS or with the automatic steering and manual compass. He puts the handheld GPS up on the coach house roof to give it a better chance of locking onto satellites quickly, but when it does finally produce a reading it insists we are in the Pacific. David looks tense and starts consulting manuals. He doesn't like this sort of thing at all.

And on top of everything else, we are still in the sea area popularly known as the Bermuda Triangle. Its three points touch the coasts of Bermuda, Miami and Puerto Rico with most of the incidents for which it is famous occurring along its southern boundary, where we currently are.

55

The Bermuda Triangle

From 1950 onwards popular writers have been attributing shipping and aircraft losses in this area to a variety of exotic causes but the more memorable have involved UFOs, alien abduction, the lost city of Atlantis and a giant squid. And it was in 1952 that one of these writers first conceived the triangular boundary which subsequent authors have largely used. The name was invented by a man called Vincent Gaddis in an article entitled *The Deadly Bermuda Triangle* which he published in a fiction magazine in 1964 and expanded the following year into a book. The area itself is not recognised by cartographers and the name does not appear on official charts.

At the heart of the triangle's notoriety is the disappearance in December 1945 of Flight 19, five US Navy TBM Avenger bombers on a training mission. The Mariner aircraft sent to find them also disappeared along with its 13-man crew, although it is possible that it simply blew up, as Mariners had a tendency to do. There have been many books written about the triangle's mysterious influence ever since, and in Steven Spielberg's 1977 film *Close Encounters of the Third Kind* the missing Flight 19 aircrews are portrayed as returning alien abductees.

No trace of these lost aircrews or their planes has ever been found, leaving writers free to offer any theory they choose as to their disappearance without fear of contradiction. Not so a considerable list of other aircraft and shipping claimed by triangle authors to have disappeared in mysterious circumstances. In fact, painstaking research of records and witnesses has established that some of the incidents ascribed to the area have been misrepresented, some occurred elsewhere, some never happened at all and some craft reported missing turned up later but unlike their disappearance their safe arrival was not reported.

This is also an area of many natural hazards which those with an interest in the supernatural fail to mention. But most compelling of all is the undeniable fact that given the number of craft using this very busy seaway and airspace the number of losses is not disproportionate. Especially when you consider that a lot of the traffic consists of amateur crews aboard yachts and small private planes. Or put another way, people not unlike us. In fact, there is more than enough out here to account for the statistics without ever touching on the giant squid.

Before the triangle authors bestowed its present name and boundaries on it, the seaway now known as the Bermuda Triangle was simply part of a much larger area of the western North Atlantic known popularly as the Devil's Triangle and one of the few places on earth where a compass points to true north instead of magnetic north. Another lies off the coast of Japan and is known locally as the Devil's Sea. Theorists say that the variation between true and magnetic north causes compasses to malfunction and navigators to go off course. Even Christopher Columbus noted in his log that he was having trouble with his compass in this area.

I once read an article by an author on how she got into the appropriate mood to write her highly successful romantic novels. There was her room's decor, in fondant pinks and greens, the satin cushions and the subtle lighting. And if memory serves, there may have been a mention of Turkish Delight. I can't help wondering where those writing about alien abduction and giant squid in the Bermuda Triangle find their inspiration.

At least writers within the romantic genre are likely to have experienced romantic love at first hand, and possibly unrequited love and the pain of separation or rejection, not to mention the salty passion of the sexual kind. But what about the triangle authors? What's the nearest they get to the essence of the salty experience they write about? Because to get the measure of this place you really need to be here.

For instance, I don't even want to *think* about the voltages involved in last night's pyrotechnics or what they could do to a vessel and its crew. And the Puerto Rico Trench we crossed the other day is not the only one of its kind around here, merely the deepest. There are many others, and their enormous depths mean that nothing sinking to the bottom of them will ever be found.

Nor are electrical storms, trenches five miles deep and magnetic anomalies sending your compass haywire the only environmental forces at work. There are waterspouts, another name for tornadoes at sea whose funnel-shaped wind sucks a column of seawater upward into cumulonimbus cloud and which are quite capable of destroying ships or aircraft. We encountered two of them in the Mediterranean and never want to see another.

There is also that giant circular surface current known as the North Atlantic Subtropical Gyre, and currents rushing between the Bahamian islands. Plus, there is a lot of seismic activity, recorded by scientists, resulting in undersea earthquakes and freak waves nearly a hundred feet high. In short, there is more than enough here to not only destroy vessels and aircraft but to swallow up or sweep away the evidence.

For the 24 hours to noon today we achieve only 68.4 miles. At one stage a container ship passes at what seems unusual slowness until we discover that we are actually standing still. So we take in the sail and put on the port engine. Because we have two engines, David has always kept a record in the log of which one has been running and for how long so that engine use is divided equally between the two.

While making a note about the port engine in the log down at the chart table he notices that the manual log, the one that measures our speed and is driven by that pesky little paddlewheel in the starboard hull, has jammed again. So we put on the starboard engine as well, to do a reverse thrust to clear it. Initially the starboard engine refuses to go into reverse. Then it keeps stalling and sending us in circles. It is possible that sargassum is caught underneath the boat and may be another clue to our slow speed. But doubtless this all keeps the crew of the container ship entertained. The starboard engine finally engages, however, the log clears and off we go again.

At 6pm there is a flurry of container ships. Half an hour later a family of common dolphins appears, our first sighting of this species since Tenerife where they brought two calves to swim between our hulls. These are very fast but sadly they don't stay long, although any visit from them, however short, is always welcome. At sea, captivating wildlife has a way of popping into view at unexpected moments. As earlier in the day, when dragging a backing genoa across to the opposite side of the mast, with all the attendant flurry, rattle and crash, a large and luminous dragonfly appeared, hovered over the port winch, circled it a few times and then went on its way.

With no weather forecast to get David up at his usual time tomorrow morning (Mr Jones being away) I am allowed to stay up (in my night attire and with teeth brushed) until 7.30 so I can watch the sun set. It is *stunning*. Huge and red. At first a solid, lazy red, then like a glass globe topped up with liquid gold, darkest red at the bottom and shading to golden red at the top. After I've gone to bed David records another electrical storm in the log, but this one is behind us, much further away and no threat to us.

56

Bird on a Wire

I am out in the cockpit just after 2am on Sunday morning as we skirt the northern reefs of Eleuthera. Once we are clear of them, we shall enter the Northwest Providence Channel which will take us to the Straits of Florida and Fort Lauderdale.

There is still an hour of my watch left but I go and wake David anyway. For some time we have had another electrical storm up ahead and on our starboard side. Huge silver blasts of heat lightning have been exploding in the sky ahead of us. To our right they are red and gold, like effusions from some monstrous furnaces whose doors are intermittently opened and closed.

Unfortunately, that *other* form of lightning has just erupted, the sort with which we so recently became acquainted and hoped never to see again, and its great zigzagging arcs have begun leaping across the surface of the sea at enormous speed. David stays with me until we clear the reefs and then we alter course to port by 20° to take us across the North*east* Providence Channel and into the North*west* which fortunately also takes us away from the electrical storm, although it continues unabated until 4am.

Around 6am the *Norway* (formerly the SS *France* and last seen anchored off Philipsburg, Sint Maarten) passes southbound down our starboard side and quite close but with very little wash.

We are motoring all the time now. Since yesterday lunchtime the wind has been next to nothing and at one stage we were becalmed. An advantage of motoring, though, is that we have sufficient juice to run the radar as we are now in amongst heavy commercial traffic.

By mid-morning the wind has picked up and we are able to turn off the engine and sail, thereby conserving fuel as much as possible as there are only around 100 litres left. We tack and tack and make virtually no progress whatsoever and at midday we put an engine back on again until an hour later when a strong north wind arrives and we can resume sailing.

It is very bumpy, with large waves pounding our beam, but at least we are making progress. For the first time in three-and-a-half days we record over 5 knots where before it had been mostly between 1 and 3. While we are in the shelter of Great Abaco Island we get some protection from the heavy sea, but once the island is behind us we are back into the turbulence again. It is a really uncomfortable night and we both get irritable. We decide, after we've finished shouting at each other, that we will sacrifice the price of a costly Bahamian cruising permit and an expensive marina fee in exchange for a night's rest and go to Freeport on Grand Bahama Island tomorrow with an estimated arrival time of around 1pm.

During the night there is the smell of fires on land to starboard and then an unwholesome smell that defies identification. The bumpiness continues until around 3am. After that it gets much quieter. Around 5am a sliver of russet moon rises but then cloud obscures most of it, leaving only the two tips of the crescent and the rim, like celestial headphones.

I'm aware that David has been giving me extra sleeping time during watches lately but I've been so tired I still could barely wait to become horizontal again. Once the sea calms, however, my energy revives somewhat and as David is looking so weary I give him an extra hour instead. At 6am he wakes naturally, which is what I had wanted him to do because that way you always feel so much more refreshed than if you are woken before your time. Then we discuss our situation.

With an extra hour of sleep and a less violent sea we both feel better. So we make a 30° change of course and head for Fort Lauderdale. This is not only our preferred destination but will also put the sea and the wind directly behind us which, as David says, 'is the best of all possible worlds.' Having worked his way through his first and second choice of the books on board he is currently immersed in Voltaire's *Candide*. It is amazing what the lack of TV and radio over time can do, although it hasn't yet driven me to study navigation.

David tunes into our SSB radio for Monday morning's weather forecast. Before giving it David Jones reports that a 40-foot British catamaran called *Albatross* with three people on board, north of Cuba and heading for Florida, has lost most of her rigging and is making her way north with difficulty. Her skipper has asked for someone to notify the US Coast Guard so that they will be aware of the situation, although he does not want help yet. *Albatross* had spoken to *Amadeus* who had relayed the message to *Lady B* who then speaks to David Jones who telephones the Coast Guard.

The latter has a vessel in the area and will make contact with *Albatross* and establish a regular radio schedule on a designated channel until the stricken yacht is safe. All of this precedes the weather forecast and the relays take rather a lot of time. Presumably *Albatross* and *Amadeus* are like us and have only VHF which transmits over relatively short distances and this requires the relaying back and forth to *Lady B* who presumably has an SSB transmitter and is able to talk direct to Mr Jones.

So while David waits below for the forecast I stagger up on deck – despite the improvement there are still occasional rollers and 20-knot wind gusts tossing *Voyager* about – and notice a bird the size of a pigeon standing unsteadily on our starboard crosstree. I call David to come out and have a look, and he throws out an arm to starboard and calls to it, 'Land's over there,' before returning below to the SSB. The bird looks wistfully in the direction he had pointed but remains where it is, although it is clearly finding its perch rather difficult. After about an hour it flies round the boat looking for somewhere more comfortable. It seems to fancy the cockpit but doesn't dare approach it with us in situ, so it settles on the starboard rail near the bow.

We now have a chance to see it more clearly. With its soft beige feathers, gentle eye and black half-ring around the back of its neck it is a collared dove. The poor thing gets more and more tired balancing on a wire in an erratic wind. Around 1.30 its lower body sinks onto its feet, its head droops onto its chest and its eye-blinks get slower until its black eyes remain covered by its pale eyelids for longer and longer periods. It is trying to sleep without falling off its perch.

I want desperately to go and grab it and put it somewhere it can rest in safety, but dare not. Better for it to survive in discomfort than be driven out to sea and perish from exhaustion before it can reach land. Occasionally it will change its position, trying to get more comfortable because its legs ache from having to hold on sideways into the wind, but it soon has to turn back again because in its new position the wind keeps raising its tail and throwing it off balance.

Its discomfort makes me feel guilty because for us it is just the opposite. Downwind sailing is smooth and rhythmic and the opposite from yesterday's bone-jarring, nerve-jangling, boat-rattling passage. And it is so exhilarating you want it to go on forever. Our only concern is what will happen to our small guest if we find it necessary to gybe.

We have just the one sail up and not much to do except keep the wind slightly off our stern. We even have a Happy Hour before lunch. What a difference a day makes. Yesterday I could have walked off the boat forever. Today is bliss, despite huge container ships passing either side of us. And there is a time delay involved here. A ship passes and you forget about it. Then 15 minutes later its wash hits you and your happy hour wine glass topples over. And sometimes so do you.

Since entering the Northwest Providence Channel we have kept to its north side, thereby avoiding commercial traffic, and making it less fraught, especially at night. At 3.20pm we do have to gybe. I watch anxiously but the dove simply ducks as the genoa passes over its head. I wonder how much longer it can hang on. We are still 60 miles from Fort Lauderdale.

The news on World Service today features May Day anarchy in London – an anti-capitalism/anti-globalisation demonstration. And somebody has trashed a McDonalds. I wish I could feed our passenger.

The wind starts to get lighter and by 8pm David decides it isn't worth messing about with the genoa any longer and hauls it in; being careful not to disturb the bird, of course. Then he starts the engine and puts on *Voyager*'s steaming lights. Over time the dove has become much chirpier and twenty minutes later it is gone. To where, we are not sure. In a direct line between us and Great Isaac Lighthouse is a brightly-lit cruise ship going in the opposite direction. Whether the dove has headed for the cruise ship and a return from whence it came, or the lighthouse – which is an ideal staging point for a land bird blown out to sea to reach land again – we cannot know. We simply wish it a safe harbour.

We shall now motor for the rest of the night as we have enough fuel to get us where we are going. It will also produce enough battery power for the radar to identify the increasing amount of shipping on the approach to Fort Lauderdale through the darkness. It has surprised us, in such a busy seaway, how few other vessels we have actually seen, averaging barely more than one a day until we joined the container ships on the approach to Florida.

To get from the Northwest Providence Channel to Fort Lauderdale is virtually a straight line going west. Unfortunately, in between them is the Gulf Stream, a powerful river within an ocean, travelling north at around 2.5 knots, although some reports say it can get as high as five. In this area it is 45 miles wide and its remorseless current means that to sail west you have to steer to the southwest and crab across the Straits of Florida to avoid being swept north.

It is very bumpy, pitch black and our progress is very slow. At one stage we are doing only 1.8 knots. But there is an advantage to being kept out here at sea, where it is safer, instead of approaching an unknown and busy commercial port in the dark. In fact, the night is so dark that when a small white light appears within feet of our stern we can see nothing but the light itself and before we have time to react, it goes out again. Heaven knows who it is. Someone very low in the water, judging by the height of the lamp, and if there is an engine we do not hear it above our own. Silent and furtive, whoever it is simply melts back into the darkness and the violence of the Gulf Stream.

These final hours, as we approach the south-eastern coast of America, seem to take a very long time to pass, for despite not being in a hurry to reach anywhere until daylight we *are* tired. It has been a long, slow passage – ten days in all – and a turbulent one. And we have both been without sleep for many hours now. At the same time there is a sense of excitement as we stand together in the cockpit in the darkness, gazing out at the distant lights of the Florida coastline. They represent a whole new and very different sailing experience about to open up before us.

Sailing offers you a different way of seeing a country and you do not have to visit many or for very long before preconceptions and stereotypes fall away. At the same time you acquire an entirely new perspective on your own.

Perhaps, of all the countries in the world, we all think we know America intimately because we all receive so much of its film and television. To spend a whole summer and autumn in the reality is an opportunity not to be missed because, as Marcel Proust observed,

> 'The real voyage of discovery consists not in seeking new landscapes, but in having new eyes.'

Glossary for Non-Sailors

Anchor winch – raises the anchor.

Antifouling – paint put on the hull below the waterline to deter marine growth and shellfish which reduce the speed of the boat.

Autopilot – device to hold the boat on a set course automatically.

Beat – when sailing with the wind coming from in front of you rather than from behind or to the side.

Blue water cruising – long distance ocean sailing.

Boom – a hinged pole attached to the mast which holds the bottom of the mainsail and allows it to be set in various positions to catch the wind.

Bunkering – refuelling ships with coal.

Carpe diem (quam minimum credula postero) – Seize the day (and think as little as possible about tomorrow). Roman poet, Horace.

Clew – the lower corner of a sail through which an outhaul is tied.

Coaming – raised edge on deck which helps prevent water entering the cockpit.

Courtesy flag – acknowledges that you are in someone else's country and recognise its jurisdiction.

Crosstree – small horizontal spars, or spreaders, enabling the shrouds to better support the mast.

Currency exchange rate – during the period of this book £1sterling was roughly equal to US$1.50, and US$1 to EC$2.

Davits – two small hoists to lift and hold a dinghy, usually at a boat's stern.

Dead reckoning – the process of plotting a course or position from a known point using charts and tide tables.

Drift net – a fishing net at least a mile long, with one edge held at the surface by floats and the other edge floating free. Fish are caught by their gills. Also trapped by them are dolphins, whales, turtles, diving seabirds and yachts.

El Niño – a warming of the Pacific Ocean's surface and a change in air pressure which has a negative impact on weather patterns worldwide.

Gash bag – all refuse (gash) on board is bagged and taken ashore for appropriate disposal.

Gelcoat – the hard shiny outer layer covering the fibreglass from which our boat is built.

Gallows – a frame on the stern which on *Voyager* supports the wind generator and a variety of aerials.

Genoa – the large sail in front of our mast.

Gybe – when the boom swings rapidly from one side of the boat to the other.

Hard – abbreviation for *hard standing*, when a boat is lifted out of the water to allow work to be done on its hull.

Heeling – when the force of the wind on its sails inclines a boat from the vertical.

Heave-to – to stop a vessel's forward motion by keeping its bow into the wind.

Hobie Cats – a two-hulled sailing dinghy.

Jury rig – a repair, either temporary or emergency, using improvised materials.

Knot – one knot equals a nautical mile covered in one hour and is roughly equivalent to 1.15mph.

Lazy line – when a boat is berthed bows-on, it is held off a quay or pontoon by a lazy line, a mooring rope which is fixed to the seabed at one end and tied to the boat's stern cleat at the other.

Lines – ropes. See also Mooring and Shore.

Log – (1) a speedometer;
(2) a written record which in our case includes weather, location, direction, events.

Main sail – the large sail behind the mast.

Monohull – a conventional yacht has a single (mono) hull, unlike *Voyager* which has two, or a trimaran, which has three.

Mooring lines – ropes used to tie a boat to the shore.

Nautical mile – see Knot, above.

Navtex – receiver for international weather forecasts in English, either on a screen or as a print out.

Outhaul – a rope tied to a sail and hauled on to pull the sail out.

Painter – a rope attached to a dinghy's bow to tie it up.

Port – left-hand side of a vessel looking forward.

Pulpit – a hand rail round the deck at the bow.

Pushpit – a hand rail round the deck at the stern.

Q flag – a small yellow flag denoting that your vessel is free of disease and requesting licence (free pratique) to enter a foreign port.

Red ensign – the official flag for British Merchant Navy ships and British leisure boats, it has a red ground with the Union Flag in the top left-hand corner.

Reefing – reducing the size of a sail to prevent excessive pressure on the mast from high winds and also to slow the boat down.

RIB – rigid inflatable boat; a high-speed rubber dinghy with a rigid, glass fibre bottom.

Self-furling gear – a way of rolling up a sail without leaving the security of the cockpit.

Shore line – see Mooring lines, above.

Shrouds – multi-strand, stainless-steel wires which hold the mast in place.

Snubbing line – a rope from a cleat to a link on the anchor chain to take the strain off the anchor winch in bad weather.

Spring – while a mooring line ties a boat to a pontoon fore and aft, a spring is added to prevent the boat from surging back and forth.

Squall – sudden increase in windspeed, often accompanied by brief but heavy precipitation.

SSB radio – marine equivalent of ham radio.

Starboard – right-hand side of a vessel looking forward.

Stay sail – small sail between the genoa and the mast.

Tender – a small boat used for ferrying people and goods between a larger boat and the shore.

Toe rail – a small rail, flush with the edge of the deck, for a yachtsman to brace his foot against when the boat is heeling.

Topping lift – a line from the top of the mast to the end of the boom which keeps the boom in place when the sail is furled.

Topsides – the sides of the hull above the waterline.

Winch – used to put tension on sails.